M000159161

Published by:
Smart Media Africa
info@smartmoneyafrica.org
www.smartmoneyafrica.org
Instagram: @smartmoneyarese
Twitter:@smartmoneyarese
Facebook: www.facebook.com/smartmoneywitharese

Package of Edition
ISBN 978-169-568-511-6

Cover Illustration: Peniel Enchill
Design: Yetunde Shorters
Photography: Adebayo Wasiu Jolaoso

I

THE SMART MONEY TRIBE

An African Woman's Guide to Making Bank

ARESE UGWU

For my daughter Zikora,
I pray my life is proof that anything is possible.

TABLE OF CONTENTS

Prologue

Zuri

"The award for the most commercially successful private equity deal of the year goes to Mr Tsola Preware, CEO of Zuma Capital!" The audience burst into applause.

Zuri couldn't stop smiling as Tsola kissed her on her cheek then strode on stage with his signature confident swagger to receive his award from the publisher of BusinessDay newspaper, Frank Aigbogun.

They were at the paper's annual CEO Forum gala, the most prestigious business event of the year. Every professional in town wanted to snag an invitation, every CEO wanted a table, and better still, everyone who was anyone wanted to bag an award. Just being on the nominees' list alone gave them bragging rights for years to come.

Tsola being nominated was no surprise; he was Nigeria's private equity golden boy and the youngest nominee on the list. He'd had some of the most lucrative deals under his belt all before he turned forty, and this year he had worked on a highly publicised telecoms deal that had broken records in terms of its size and its impact on the business environment for SMEs.

"Thank you for this prestigious award. It was an honour to be nominated alongside so many great CEOs. Doing business in Nigeria is certainly different from what we learnt in business school," Tsola joked.

The crowd laughed in agreement.

His voice took on a more serious tone. "However, it's a privilege to be able to identify the problems in our country and work to solve them. It has been quite a journey to overcome the many obstacles that are inherent to doing business in Nigeria and it would have been impossible to do this without my team at Zuma Capital who worked tirelessly to get us all to this point."

The Zuma team applauded loudly from their table, standing up to cheer.

He held out the award and looked directly at where Zuri sat along with her besties Tami, Ladun, Lara and Adesuwa and continued, "I could also never have accomplished this in peace—" he paused and grinned, "without the support of my beautiful girlfriend, Zuri. We did it, baby! All the late nights and early mornings paid off! Thank you for understanding!"

He lifted his award triumphantly as he left the stage to another round of applause. Zuri couldn't help feeling shy. Only he would have the nerve to acknowledge his girlfriend so publicly in such a formal setting; most Nigerian men would have reserved such public declarations for their wives. She tried to avoid the teasing stares of her friends who were all there to support Tsola because she knew she would burst into laughter and she was trying to keep calm as Tsola walked up to the table. She stood up and smoothed her red Fablane by Derin dress, hugging Tsola before he sat down.

Her phone beeped. It was a text from Olumide Sanni, an ex-boyfriend who had popped up recently and wouldn't stop sending unwelcome, overly familiar messages asking her to dinner.

You always looked so sexy in a backless dress. Can't stop thinking about you, the text read.

He is clearly in the room, she thought, slightly panicked, as she glanced around the banquet hall. She knew his father's company was being honoured tonight as well. As she reread the text, her heart jumped—just a tiny bit—and she couldn't help a small smile. She was flattered, but it was inappropriate.

Zuri put her phone away. The last thing she needed was for Tsola to see her smiling over a cheeky text. He would freak out because they had just gotten back on an even keel after this deal closed, and she wasn't sure their relationship could survive another fight.

She couldn't help it, but it upset her that he was so extreme when it came to his work schedule. When he was in work mode, she hardly saw him—no calls, no texts, no visits to see how she was doing. When she complained about wanting to spend more time together, his response would always be a fait accompli: 'You can either deal with a broke man or a busy man.'

****

Tsola

Tsola walked through the tables trying to get back to his seat, stopping to greet several businessmen who stood up to congratulate him but his eyes remained glued to Zuri the entire time.

She looks magnificent in that red dress.

The backless dress hugged every curve on her body, ending just above the curve of her bum. He felt that the dress was a touch too sexy for this event, but he had learnt in the almost two years of dating Zuri he should keep those thoughts to himself.

If he was honest, there was nothing wrong with the dress, but he always had mixed feelings when they went anywhere together. He loved that when he walked into a room with her on his arm men couldn't keep their eyes off her, but at the same time, he hated it because she was his and he disliked the idea of any other man coveting her. Zuri was the only woman in his entire dating history that made him feel this way.

She drove him absolutely crazy, and it wasn't even about how she looked. She was brilliant, stubborn, and strong-willed, listened to him but still insisted on doing things her way. He loved that she was such a go-getter with work and had become a fast-rising star at the real estate development company where she worked. There was a fire about her that was contagious, and he had known for a while that he wanted to marry her. He couldn't explain it, but Zuri was his ideal partner. She just made his life better. She made him want to be better, to do more, to want more.

"You are a joker. You know that, right?" Zuri whispered in his ear as she hugged him.

"Only you would accept an award and mention your girlfriend. 'Baby, we did it!' *abi*?" She laughed. "You know you are in Nigeria, right? This is not the Oscars, babe. I'm sure a lot of these old fuddy-duddies baulked when you said girlfriend instead of wife."

"But you are going to be my wife," he smirked.

"Talk true," Zuri said sarcastically, in pidgin English, sounding like a real Bini girl. It made her smile every time he made these declarations. *However,* as much as she loved Tsola, their recent spate of arguments made her question if they were compatible for marriage.

She wanted to say *time will tell,* but instead she said softly, "I'm so proud of you, babe."

****

Tami

As the waiter came to top up their drinks, Tami couldn't help smiling as she observed Zuri and Tsola, simply because she loved the way they were together. They were definitely "couple goals" tonight! Tsola was looking good and giving her 'African James Bond' vibes in his Mai Atafo tuxedo. At his age, he had accomplished more than half the men in this room, and that was saying a lot—these were men responsible for at least half of Nigeria's GDP.

More than anything else though, she appreciated the way he was with Zuri, having watched her friend blossom while the two dated. She could tell he wanted to see her win, but the cynic in Tami was waiting for the other shoe to drop.

Because, some guys end up being Yoruba demons, but God forbid, sha, Tami thought.

She had to admit that even though Zuri was not wearing an Irawo by Tami outfit, she looked gorgeous in a dress whose cut and style did many, many *flattering* things for her figure. She had planned to dress all her girls for this event tonight, but her staff were overwhelmed, so she had to focus on Lara, Ladun, and Adesuwa. They were each going through different strains of drama at the moment and had little time to think about what to wear. She had put Lara in a cobalt blue floor-length dress with sheer sleeves and a diamante neckline. She looked stunning. Adesuwa was conservative-but-chic in a pink double-breasted suit, and Ladun was wearing a black two-piece that accentuated all her curves.

Her girls looked good and represented Irawo brilliantly, and she couldn't help the tingle of pride she felt about the strides her fashion brand had made in the last year—it hadn't quite become a household name, but it was semi-popular on Instagram.

The fly in the ointment was that even with the increased recognition for Irawo, she often had to admit to herself that she still struggled with the entrepreneurship thing. It felt like no matter how much effort she put in, she was fighting weekly fires to stay in business. The work she put in never seemed to match the money in her bank account.

****

Ladun

Ladun toyed with the braised beef on her plate as she observed Tsola accepting his award. She was so proud of him and all his hard work. Out of the corner of her eye, she observed an exchange between Bode and Chief Coker, Chairman of Carbon Industries and her stomach churned in anger and disgust.

She couldn't stand the short, potbellied man and more importantly, she couldn't believe Bode was being so nice to the old snake who was supposed to have been one of her father-in-law's closest friends. He'd been at every Ashoni family function at home and abroad, and the two had made many money-spinning deals together over the last thirty years. He had been in Chief's (or Baba as her father-in-law was fondly called) inner circle.

When Chief passed away, and the financial scandal broke, Chief Coker had been nowhere to be found. He'd come to the house once to commiserate with Bode's mum, attended the funeral, but that had been it. He'd offered no financial assistance or asked how they were faring. Instead, they'd heard recently that he was in bed with one of the banks to cherry-pick some of the assets the family was planning to sell to cover the debt Baba had left behind.

Snake.

This public display of bonhomie with Bode was playing to an audience, and she didn't even bother to get up when he came to their table. She had mumbled her hello and faced her front. It was all she could do to stop herself from eyeing him or hurling insults at the old goat.

She had been reluctant to come to this event because she knew that this was the playground for a lot of Baba Ashoni's so-called friends and business associates. There would be fake smiles and pleasantries followed by whispers, pointing, and staring. She just wasn't in the mood, but she had to be there for Zuri and Tsola.

"Swallow your food well, oh, before you choke," Bode looked amused at her almost hostile expression as he sat down.

"I don't know how you do it, *sha*. After everything we heard last week about this old fool's plans, you are still smiling with him and being polite. He must think you are stupid and you don't know what he's up to," Ladun fumed.

Bode shrugged. "I'm no one's fool, babe. There's no point confronting him or being rude. The lawyers are working to block him, so I'm certain he won't succeed. Men like Chief Coker want you to come and grovel before them to beg for favours, and I wasn't raised like that. My father left us with a tough situation, but we Ashonis are fighters, we will get out of this no matter how long it takes. Besides, you know what I learnt from my father's mistakes?"

"What?" Ladun asked.

"When it comes to friendships, business or personal, take quality over quantity," Bode declared with a smile.

"You see, my father did business and served on executive councils with many of the men in this room, but in times of trouble, they were nowhere to be found. He donated to their charities, funded their children's weddings, gave many of them opportunities, but what did they ever give back? I don't want to invest in one-sided relationships and wake up at seventy to learn I have no real friends. This experience has taught me to be circumspect about the people in my inner circle." He took a sip of his drink.

Ladun smiled as she held his hand. "You are right."

Through all the chaos, he had been a warrior—for her, their children, for his mother. Their financial situation had changed dramatically in the last year and a half, but instead of sinking in rough, murky waters, Bode was doing his best to keep them all afloat.

She was proud of him but admitted to herself that in her quiet moments, she was scared. She had fears about their financial situation that she couldn't voice to Bode or even her girls and to be honest she wasn't sure how much longer she could manage. They were still a long way from where they had once been, and it was a bitter pill to swallow. Her life had gone from fabulous housewife to struggling employee in less time than it took a Porsche to get from zero to sixty.

She had taken an advertising job she hated so their combined incomes could make ends meet, but the reality was that they were barely keeping their heads above water and she wasn't sure how much more she could take.

She took a gulp of wine from her glass.

****

Adesuwa

Frank Aigbogun reached forward and shook Adesuwa's hand. "We loved your last article about entertainment law and the Nigerian music industry," he told her. "It was very insightful. Well done."

"Thank you, sir." Adesuwa tried not to look too pleased with herself but gave herself a mental high five. She'd spent the better part of a week working on it, researching and fact-checking despite her heavy workload. She had really enjoyed partnering with them in the last few months to create content that appealed to their growing millennial audience. The partnership was great for her personal brand and had attracted some very lucrative opportunities.

Adesuwa wrapped up her conversation and walked to the back of the room to wait for the last award recipient to finish delivering her acceptance speech. Finding her way back to her table now would be distracting as the room had quieted down.

She was scrolling mindlessly through her Instagram feed when her eye caught a post by Gbenga, one of Soji's friends. Shock pulsed through her, followed by an overwhelming wave of sadness. It was a shot of a group of guys over drinks, and she spotted Soji's profile next to a light-skinned girl in a midriff-baring, skimpy outfit standing on the edge of the table. There was nothing to suggest that the girl was with Soji or that they were doing anything inappropriate, but Adesuwa knew better.

As she walked through the room, she wiped the lone tear that found its way down her cheek. She knew she had to get it together before she got to her seat because it would be difficult to explain to her friends why she was crying.

She had been separated from her husband for over a year and had even started divorce proceedings, but a few months ago, Soji came back hat in hand to beg her to work things out, especially for their son's—Soji Junior or SJ—sake.

At first, she was reluctant to even listen because she didn't know how she could ever trust him again, but two months ago she let him back into the house on a trial basis—something she hadn't found the courage to tell her friends yet. She knew they would be furious after the whole debacle with Soji running off with that Chinasa girl, along with all the money in their joint account. They would never understand her even considering taking Soji back, and they were probably right.

Adesuwa suspected that he had only come back when the money had run out, and his business endeavours weren't generating enough income to sustain his lifestyle. She didn't trust him. How could she? This was a man that had thrown away the life they had built together over the last fifteen years for a piece of ass. They had started dating when she was nineteen but had not exchanged vows until she was thirty.

If she was honest with herself, throughout their relationship, he had always cheated. It was his failing. Although she had had her fair share of confrontations with other women, she'd always convinced herself that she was his number one, his rock and that he would never leave her. When he'd left her for Chinasa, she'd been blindsided, devastated, and left feeling unproductive for months as she fought to get over the humiliation.

Then out of the blue, he'd shown up with his family in tow, begging. Adesuwa had felt a strong urge to forgive him because even after a year separated, she still couldn't stand the thought of being labelled a divorcée. It made her feel like she had failed, and it gave her so much anxiety around being a single mother. During their separation, there were many nights when the fear of raising SJ on her own kept her up. In reality, even when Soji was there, she was still the primary parent, but it was easier to have a father figure in the household than none at all.

Her parents had also put her under severe pressure. There had been incessant phone calls from her mother daily, saying, 'Don't throw away your marriage because of a small girl', 'At least he is begging', 'He has seen the error of his ways', 'Adesuwa, you are a strong woman. You have to persevere', and worst of all, 'Think of your son. *Abi* you want SJ to grow up without a father because you are being stubborn?'

Her mother often said the mark of a strong wife was her ability to endure, but Adesuwa wondered why the strength of African women was measured by the amount of pain and struggle they could tolerate. Was it truly wisdom to suffer constant humiliation? Or was it actually a weakness? Was it the fear of letting go because of the many years she had invested in the relationship? Or the fear of being ostracised by society for failing at marriage? Was marriage supposed to be endured or enjoyed?

Anyway, she couldn't allow herself to be paranoid right now over a picture; she had given him a chance, decided to make her marriage work. She had to stick to it.

"I'm happy with my decision. My family is intact. I'm happy. I. Am. HAPPY." Adesuwa repeated it like a mantra under her breath, trying to make herself believe.

****

Lara

They had reached the networking portion of the event. Awards had been collected, guests had eaten, but the champagne was still flowing. It was time to mingle and connect with the crème de la crème of the Nigerian business community.

Zuri and Lara were deep in conversation with a real estate mogul, a woman who was, to put it simply, incredible. She was beautiful and accomplished, but most importantly, she brought such positive energy to every room she walked into. It wasn't because her life was perfect—she had overcome a lot of obstacles and was a breast cancer survivor. Zuri and Lara were in awe of her.

I hope my mum has this attitude to life when she beats this thing, Lara thought.

It had been a tough couple of months with her mum being diagnosed with breast cancer, and things were not looking good. The last three months of her life had been consumed with hospital visits, doctors' appointments, and second opinions on treatment plans.

It was all so exhausting.

At first, she'd felt guilty about taking the night off to celebrate with Tsola and Zuri, she had gone back and forth, but in the end, she had decided to come because she knew it was important to Zuri. More than that though, she needed a bit of a break. She felt guilty just thinking about it.

Her phone rang, making her heart skip a beat. It was Aunty Ifeoma, her mother's younger sister who had taken tonight's shift to watch her mum at the hospital. She glanced at her watch. It was almost one in the morning. Her aunt wouldn't usually call at this hour. Lara's heart dropped to her stomach.

This couldn't be good. Something was terribly wrong.

CHAPTER 1   BROKE. AGAIN.

Lara

"I think she should be buried in her wedding dress!"

Lara raised her head to see who had made the ridiculous suggestion. Of course. Aunty Nkechi.

"You think she should be buried in her wedding dress," Lara repeated, her sarcastic tone obviously lost on her Igbo relative.

"Yes! What is wrong with that?! Our mother was buried in her wedding dress, and it was a very elegant affair," Aunty Nkechi said matter-of-factly, her nose pointed in the air.

Of her mother's three siblings, Aunty Nkechi was the eldest of the three, always the loudest in the room, and definitely the most difficult.

Lara could also never understand why her aunty insisted on speaking in a grating, obviously fake American accent that was layered over the thick Igbo pronunciation she had clearly been raised with. To the best of her knowledge, there was no valid explanation for the awful intonation because her Aunt hadn't left the shores of Nigeria until she had been in her fifties and went to Texas to do *omugwo* for her son's wife.

The last few months of planning her mother's funeral made her life seem like something out of a low-grade Nollywood movie. Her mother's only brother had come in from Anambra state the night before and insisted they had an "emergency" meeting at her house. A meeting that had lasted four hours already.

"The elders are not happy with you at all, Lara!" Uncle Festus said sternly. "They want the burial to take place in Ogbunike in our father's compound. It is tradition. You have to do things the right way! Burying her in Lagos should not even be an option."

"Uncle Festus, I'm sorry you came all this way to discuss something that had already been decided weeks ago," Lara said calmly, trying not to let the anger she felt show. It would come across as disrespectful.

"Is it me you are talking to like that? You are boldly telling me you decided about my own sister without my consent or the consent of the elders for that matter?" Uncle Festus slapped his hands and shook his head in disbelief. "You young people of nowadays, you think you know everything!"

"I apologise, Uncle." Lara looked at the man who, apart from the rare village holiday, she'd had very little contact with over the years. He seemed genuinely offended that he didn't have a say in the funeral arrangements of a woman he had barely spoken to in years unless to request financial assistance.

At this point, Uncle Festus was gesticulating wildly as he strolled around her living room, dishing out instructions on traditions—traditions that, for all intents and purposes, were alien to her.

"Festus, please don't come here and cause confusion! We already settled this matter last month and decided that Adanna should be buried in Lagos," Aunty Nkechi interjected, standing up to deliver her own lecture.

"After all, that is what Adanna would have wanted—a classy Lagos funeral. I mean, how many times did she even go to the village? Lagos is what she had become accustomed to in the last twenty-five years. It is where her friends are, it is where her church is, and I'm sure she would want to be buried close to her children. Besides, we have almost settled on a casket and Lara has already made a deposit on a plot of land in Ikoyi cemetery, even though I think Adanna would have preferred to be buried in Vaults and Gardens." Aunty Nkechi ended her mini tirade with a disgruntled huff.

Lara looked at the duo, now at each other's throats. To a passer-by, these were two people who loved their late sister profoundly and were very passionate about her final resting place because they each believed that they knew what she would have wanted. Interestingly, Aunty Ifeoma, the youngest of the remaining three siblings, had been sitting quietly on the sofa in the corner and had barely volunteered an opinion since this tedious meeting had started. It was a touch ironic because of the three, she had been the closest to Lara's mum. She tended to reserve her opinions until after the meetings, when she would then offer Lara gentle counsel.

For instance the week before, Aunty Nkechi had announced that she had picked the *aso ebi* the family was going to wear and informed Lara that it would cost guests one hundred and fifty thousand naira each, but Lara had to put a deposit down of six hundred thousand naira before the supplier could set it aside. It had taken everything in her not to scream, and luckily Aunty Ifeoma had been there to diffuse the situation.

"You shouldn't have spoken to Nkechi like that. She means well... she just has a different approach," Aunty Ifeoma told her diplomatically after Lara had snapped at her older aunt. "Make your point, Lara, but don't be rude. Your mother would never have approved of that."

In the last couple of months, Lara had learnt that when it came to death, everyone had their own agenda. Aside from Aunty Ifeoma, nobody cared what she wanted or had even bothered to ask how the funeral was going to be funded.

As she looked around her dimly lit living room and watched the shouting match in front of her, frustration began to set in.

"When should I expect your financial contributions to the funeral?" Lara asked suddenly.

"How do you mean?" Uncle Festus responded, his Igbo accent thicker than ever.

"She means how much are you contributing, Festus, and when should she expect the money," Aunty Ifeoma interjected, speaking for the first time since the meeting began.

"Nkechi, ngwanu. What about you?" Aunty Ifeoma challenged her older sister.

There was silence in the room, and Lara couldn't help but smile. Aunty Ifeoma was the quiet one but when she decided to speak, she went for the jugular.

"The girl is asking a valid question," Aunty Ifeoma continued. "Nkechi, for months I have heard you volunteer unsolicited opinions and suggesting expensive options as though Lara has an unlimited bank account or a tree in the back yard where she plucks money."

"I will not be insulted, Ifeoma," Aunty Nkechi stood up from the cream leather sofa she had been sitting on all night, marching to the centre of the room and stabbing her index finger in Ifeoma's face. "You have obviously forgotten that we are not mates," she screamed. "How dare you!"

"Nkechi. Nobody is insulting you," Aunty Ifeoma responded calmly. "This is not about mate or no mate. It is just a simple question, my sister. How much are you contributing to the funeral costs? Or is Nedu sending dollars from

Texas?" Her tone had turned mischievous.

"Please leave my son out of this!" Aunty Nkechi shouted. "Is it his mother they are burying?" She tried to deflect.

"Ah, but it is your sister that is being buried, *now,* Nkechi. It's your sister!" Aunty Ifeoma repeated firmly. "After all, when you were saying, 'Only the best coffin for Adanna,'" she mimicked Aunty Nkechi's facial expressions and awful accent to perfection. "Who did you think was going to pay for it?"

"You that is talking, Ifeoma. How much are you contributing?" Uncle Festus demanded pompously.

Lara watched the exchange in bemusement. All three were all in their fifties, but here and now, they were no different from her and her siblings.

"For your information, I've given Lara two hundred and fifty thousand so far, and I know that my contribution will do nothing to dent the mounting costs of this funeral. Even so, I have no opinions on where my dear sister should be buried," she said, looking pointedly at Uncle Festus. "Or, how extravagantly she should be buried," she added as she turned to face Nkechi.

"What exactly are you playing at, Ifeoma?" Aunty Nkechi spat through her pursed lips as she clapped both hands in an exaggerated manner.

Aunty Ifeoma stared at her.

"So, you mean you went behind my back to give Lara money for our sister's funeral? *Ehn,* Ifeoma? Are you trying to make us look bad?"

"Make you look bad?" Aunty Ifeoma laughed. "How can doing my bit to help out my niece with the little I have constitute making you look bad? It's called being a decent human being! You should try it sometime. We both know Adanna would roll in her grave if she knew the undue pressure you were putting on her children to spend money they don't have, especially in their time of grief."

"What do you mean, 'Money they don't have,'" Uncle Festus harrumphed from his self-appointed throne, speaking for the first time since the money exchange began. "Look at this big house Lara lives in! Lekki Phase One, one of the most expensive parts of Lagos. How can you say she doesn't have money? She works in oil and gas, for crying out loud. *Abi*, Lara? Who are you fooling? Is it me that is just managing to pay my bills in Enugu that should foot the bill for *your* mother's funeral?"

Lara winced but remained silent.

"*Ehn*! Festus, so we can't expect you to contribute money, but we can expect you to come to Lagos and dictate how Adanna should be buried?" Aunty Ifeoma asked.

"So, because I'm not rich, Ifeoma, I cannot educate my niece on what tradition expects from us?"

"Uncle, I don't know if you've been reading the papers, but the oil and gas company I work for has been having issues with the regulator, and we are in trouble. I have not been paid a salary for four months, and, between mum's cancer treatment and the mounting costs of the funeral, I am broke."

Her uncle arranged his face in some semblance of sympathy. "Sorry to hear that, Lara," he said solemnly. "It is well! But I'm sure you have savings. You've been working for a long time, my dear, and I'm sure you've made a lot of money over the years. There must be money you have saved somewhere that you can use to give your mother a befitting burial."

"Exactly!" Aunty Nkechi chimed in.

Aunty Ifeoma rolled her eyes.

"Ifeoma, what? We are just advising her!" Aunty Nkechi responded. "Is it a crime?"

"Yes, I have savings, Uncle," Lara explained. "I have been living on those savings in the last few months. I have had to liquidate several investments just to meet up with the costs of mum's specialised treatments and funeral arrangements. In fact, I'm not quite sure if I still have a job because the company's remaining assets are on lien and we've barely been operational this month because of the liquidity issues."

Aunty Ifeoma hissed in derision at her brother and sister. "This is ridiculous. You people are stressing this girl." She picked up her bag and walked out of the room, leaving Uncle Festus and Aunty Nkechi to continue arguing.

As Lara watched, she understood that all of the drama was just a deflection from the real issue—they did not want to contribute financially to this funeral they had so many opinions about.

****

Zuri

As she walked down the hall towards the conference room, Zuri could feel the toll her trip had taken on her body, but she also felt strangely energised. She was about five minutes late for the meeting, but she'd had to stop and freshen up in the bathroom because she looked a hot mess. She had changed into a grey, no-fuss, pinafore-style shift dress with a white shirt that was slightly rumpled but presentable.

"Sorry I'm late," Zuri apologised as she walked into the conference room. As she took her seat, Mr Tunde stood up and started a slow, dramatic clap, and the rest of the room joined in.

She had just returned from a weeklong trip that took her to two countries on two continents, trying to secure financing for a new middle-income housing development she was spearheading for Richmond. She had been living out of her suitcase and running from one meeting to the other, but she couldn't complain because two years ago, this was the life she prayed for: work she enjoyed, international travel, and feeling like a valuable member of a thriving organisation.

"Welcome back, superstar," Mr Tunde said. "This young lady has spent the last six months trying to secure financing for our latest development and yesterday she succeeded in closing a deal that will bring five million dollars in funding for the project. To be honest, I had my doubts during the process, but our girl pulled it off."

Months before, Zuri had been looking into how Richmond could help solve the problem of affordable housing, and she had become fascinated with the middle-class neighbourhood called Yaba, which was situated in the heart of Lagos between the mainland and Victoria Island. With the work the Lagos state government was doing in the area, it was much cleaner and safer, and ripe for this kind of development.

Zuri had suggested to Mr Tunde that Yaba would be an ideal location for a gated community with affordable housing that catered to young workers, students, and the growing tech community in the area. The partners had been sceptical due to the enormous capital outlay that would be required as well as the fact that they would prefer to cater to a customer base with a more substantial purchasing power.

However, Zuri had presented a business plan to the board that laid out cheaper financing options, partnering with a construction company that specialised in affordable housing and utilising a new tech platform that allowed tenants to pay monthly rent instead of yearly. Richmond would take the burden of risk from the landlord by paying the rent up front, then dealing directly with the tenants for rent every month. It also allowed for retail investors in the diaspora to purchase property in Nigeria on a controlled platform. The board had loved it, but its execution was contingent on Zuri securing the funding.

In the last few months, Tsola had made introductions with several financial institutions in South Africa, Dubai, Switzerland, and London to help her secure cheaper financing for the proposed development. She had finally settled on a private equity firm that had a strong base in South Africa with its head office in London and finalising the agreement had entailed meeting with partners on both continents.

Zuri gracefully acknowledged the praise. "It was a group effort, sir. I couldn't have pulled it off without you and the team," she said as she looked around the room and acknowledged the other members of her team who had worked tirelessly with her to make this happen.

"You've definitely earned your promotion to Vice President of Business Development with this win," Mr Tunde concluded.

He switched gears and said, "Well Zuri let's catch you up. We have some good and bad news on this site as well, but all in all, it's progress. Actually, I'll let Obinna tell you."

"Well! We've found an ideal location for the development that seems to be within the budget," Obinna said.

"Okay! That's good news," Zuri said. "How many square meters?"

"Sixteen thousand," Obinna responded. "It'll be adequate space to develop two hundred and fifty units of maisonettes, duplexes, and two- and three-bedroom flats as discussed."

"Nice!" Zuri said. "So, what's the bad news?" She asked as searched the faces of her colleagues for answers.

"The thing is we've been speaking to the agent for a few weeks now about the structure of the joint venture we are proposing," Obinna looked worried. "Yesterday, he finally came back with the terms from the family, and they were not great."

"How so?" Zuri asked.

"Basically, the baba and his extended family look like they are going to be an issue," Teju, one of the project managers chipped in.

"Please explain," Zuri said. "Did you tell him we were giving them twenty-five units valued at five hundred million in exchange for letting us build on the land?"

"We did," Obinna said. "But the agent insists that the family also wants a hundred million upfront and want to choose the construction company that develops the estate."

"Are they joking?" Zuri gasped. "That's outrageous."

"Yes, it is," Teju concurred. "I was just suggesting that we find someone that knows the family better so we can get a face-to-face and negotiate better terms."

"Do we know the name of the family that owns it?" Mr Tunde tapped his pen on the table as he asked the question.

"Yes, sir!" Obinna responded. "I've been doing some digging, and the land belongs to the Sannis."

"Ha! The baba is old," Teju said. "But I've heard his sons are the ones that control things now and they are a mess. Maybe we should look for an alternative?"

"Trust me, this is prime real estate," Obinna replied. "There's nothing like it in the area. The location and access to roads is quality. In my opinion, we should do our best to secure it."

Zuri was quiet.

Just great! She thought. *Of course, this would be happening to me just as I wrap up everything.*

Olumide was her ex and Baba Sanni's second son. It was one thing to field his cheeky messages and return his unsolicited gifts, but he continued to be a badly behaved, entitled rich kid who certainly thought the world revolved around him. He was certainly not someone she wanted to negotiate with.

This was going to be a nightmare.

The meeting wrapped up, and Zuri headed back to her office. As she tried to call Tsola again to update him on her progress for the second time that day, she was interrupted by Tejiri, her fun, fashionable, over-the-top colleague who loved to gossip.

"Madam Vice President, Business Development. Since this promotion, *e be like say you don break bank, oh!*" Tejiri exclaimed, turning up his brand of Warri pidgin to eleven. "*You dey busy!* Today Gucci, tomorrow Chanel. And all these hot outfits from African designers... *e be like say you and that zazaii.com don become best friends. I no sure say na the same office we dey work! I doubt am."*

"Tejiri, what are you on about?" Zuri giggled

"Beyoncé *no do pass like this,"* Tejiri laughed in delight. "Your fashion game is on another level. Show me the way, *now!"*

"You are a clown," Zuri said, laughing as she walked away.

She had avoided answering but had to admit that he was right. She had stepped it up a few notches since her promotion, with her personal shopper on her speed dial sending her regular Instagram posts of designer items. Banke had DMed her a picture of a Birkin bag on Instagram with the message: *My personal shopper can get this for you for twelve thousand dollars.* It was a steal! The Hermès bags were difficult to find, and this particular colour was rare, but Banke's personal shopper had an in with the stores for which she charged a healthy commission. She didn't feel bad; life is for the living, and at least she could afford it.

****

Ladun

As she came out of the elevator, greeting her colleagues as she strolled to her cubicle, Ladun couldn't help but think the second floor of the office smelled of instant coffee and disappointment. It had been eight months at this job, but she still dreaded coming in to work every morning. She hated the humdrum work she was doing in advertising sales but most of all, she hated the people and the politics. Ladun often wondered whether a career in advertising suited her personality. However, her family needed the paycheque.

After the death of her father-in-law and the series of financial debacles that followed, their lives had changed dramatically. Bode's father's death had exposed a black hole at the centre of all the wealth that came with the Ashoni family name. Legal battles had ensued between the family company and its creditors, as well as lawsuits between family members who couldn't agree who owned what. It was a nightmare!

To Ladun's embarrassment, it had become a huge financial mess that had been splashed across the front pages of the major newspapers, causing her to be shunned in certain social circles. Fortunately, she'd had zero time to dwell on her societal standing because she and Bode had soon realised that not only was there no real succession plan in place, their personal net worth was nearly non-existent. Everything he owned was somehow tied to his father's wealth; even Bode's house and cars were in the company's name.

The quarterly dividends Bode had been receiving from the family company largely covered their holidays and lifestyle expenses, but after the bank took over, the dividends were promptly stopped. With all their assets tied up, they were broke. The bank had repossessed their Banana Island home and auctioned it alongside other family-owned properties, to pay off Bode's father's debt. They downsized from living in a mansion in the most luxurious suburb in Lagos with a ten-man staff that was made up of one chef, two drivers, one housekeeper, two nannies, two security guards, one steward and one gardener to a two-bedroom apartment in an area after Chevron but before Ajah.

It isn't quite the hood, Ladun thought. There were lovely middle-class families that lived in the area, but it was undoubtedly a downgrade compared to the wealthy life she had taken for granted barely eighteen months ago. Now she had a girl, Sikira, who came three times a week to clean the house and help out with the kids. For the first time since she had married Bode, Ladun had to cook, tidy up, and look after the kids when she picked them up from crèche or their grandmother's in the evenings.

"Welcome, madam!" Mrs Ebhonu said sarcastically. She was Ladun's direct boss and was incredibly petty about arrival times at work. Start time was at eight every morning, but Mrs Ebhonu prided herself in the fact that she got in at seven without fail.

Ladun glanced at her watch. It was seven fifty, but there was no need to point it out to her boss that she was early, because it would only lead to an inane argument about punctuality. It didn't matter that the only reason Mrs Ebhonu was here at seven every day was that the woman lived in Egbeda and if she didn't leave home at the crack of dawn, she would get to the office at well after nine thanks to the horrors of Lagos traffic.

As she put her bag down and settled down in her cubicle, she marvelled at the fact that just six months ago, getting to work so early in the morning so effortlessly would have been almost impossible for her. She had been a housewife for the last ten years; the concept of waking up while it was still dark to get the children ready for school and still manage to get to work on time was foreign to her.

In her millionaire housewife life, she was only fully awake at half-past ten on most days, unless she had a flight to catch. So at first, the call time for work was a severe and painful struggle, but she got through it, pushing through until it became routine.

The problem was, eight months into the job, she hated every minute of it. She hated driving herself in traffic for two hours just to get to work. She hated the fact that she worked in a company that had secured big clients in its early days and cemented those relationships to the point that they didn't feel the need to innovate anymore. She hated the fact that the people she reported to seemed unexposed and uneducated, even though ironically, they had a million degrees attached to their names. The company was clearly out of touch with the times.

At first, she had tried her best to pitch her ideas to Mrs Ebhonu and other management staff, but after they shushed her for the hundredth time, it became clear that her opinions didn't matter and she focused on doing as she was told from eight in the morning till she closed at four—nothing more, nothing less. On the outside, she acted like it was just a paycheque and she couldn't be bothered, but on the inside, she felt hollow and a little depressed that she was irrelevant to the process. Her job wasn't revolutionary; her tasks were so mundane they could probably be done by anyone with a high school diploma and a brain.

Her phone beeped—a WhatsApp message from Zuri sent to their group.

Back in town. Join me for drinks after work with Tsola? Good news! Deal closed. Bad news. I may need to get back in touch with Olumide. Will fill you in later. xx

"Hi, Ladun! Do you have a minute?" Said an unfamiliar voice. As she turned around, she realised it was Belema, the boss's daughter.

OMG. What now? Ladun groused in her head.

Belema had joined the company two months ago, and Ladun had done her best to keep her distance because the uncharitable consensus in the office was that she was a spoiled rich kid that had become "baby boss" in her daddy's company. Some of the top management were up in arms because she had joined as a director for business development, and she was barely thirty years old.

In Ladun's opinion, the instant promotion had reeked of nepotism. However, when she had discussed it with Bode at home, he had a different view and thought that Belema's Yale degree, as well as experience working in a boutique advertising firm in New York, gave her qualifications for the position. She had every right to be a director in her father's company.

"Hello, Belema! Of course I do! How can I help?" She said with a smile she hoped seemed genuine.

"Actually, I need more than a second. I'm pulling a few people together to push a new project, and we are having a meeting in the conference room in ten minutes. I loved the idea you had for Youtopia Beauty's social media campaign last week, and that sort of fresh thinking would be valuable on this."

Ladun looked pleased at the unexpected compliment. Her entire time at the company, the biggest commendation she had ever received from anyone was for making a decent cup of coffee.

She must have instinctively looked at Mrs Ebhonu because at that moment Belema smiled and said, "It's okay. I gave all managers a heads up that I would be borrowing a few of their people to work on this project for the next couple of weeks, and if things go well, possibly the next couple of months."

As Ladun picked up her notebook and walked towards the conference room, she wondered what this new project was about. She had heard chatter around the office that Belema was a bit radical. The exact words were something along the lines of *'Hmmm! This oga pikin tink say she still dey Amerika. Someone should tell her this is Nigeria! That's not how we do things! All this one she dey talk na oyinbo.'*

****

Adesuwa

She bounced around the boxing ring on the tip of her toes, her body automatically responding to the count of her trainer.

"One! One, two, jab!" He bellowed. "One, two! One, two, right hook!"

Adesuwa couldn't help but feel like she was boxing away her problems. These days, her boxing class at Elitebox Fitness was the only thing that helped release stress and had become her daily morning routine from Mondays to Saturdays.

By the time the class had finished, she was dripping with sweat and her scalp beneath her natural hair—braided all the way to the back—was soaked. Multiple sets of HIIT, plus the lack of air-conditioning in the gym, compounded by the humidity caused everyone to sweat so profusely. At the end of every class, she swore she would never do it again, but she enjoyed the sweet pain, and it kept her coming back.

As she put her boxing gloves in her gym bag and proceeded to haul her body down the stairs to her car, there was a beep from her phone. Her arms felt heavy and non-existent at the same time and she was tempted to ignore the text, but she reached into the side pocket of her bag to see who it was.

Her head began to throb as she read the debit alert. *One million naira? For what, exactly?!*

"This better not be what I think it is," Adesuwa murmured to herself.

She hadn't made any large purchases this week, and she had been very careful with money in the last couple of months because between payments for her IVF and repayments to the bank for the loans she had taken out for Soji and his series of failed businesses a few years ago, she was just keeping her head above water. Her spirit told her that this could only be one thing, but she didn't want to jump to conclusions.

Maybe it was a mistake from the bank because this couldn't be what I suspect it is. It isn't possible Soji could be that stupid or insensitive, for that matter!

She ran all through all sorts of scenarios in her head.

Adesuwa opened the car and got in behind the wheel, placing her gym bag on the floor of the passenger's seat beside her and settled into her seat. She put both hands on the steering wheel before taking a deep breath, knowing she would have to be calm to deal with the events that were about to unfold.

What possible explanation could Soji have for withdrawing one million naira from their joint account without talking to her first?

"Money he had no part in earning!" she fumed.

She was so angry! Angry with her husband, and angry at herself for being foolish enough to trust him again after the stunt he had pulled almost two years ago when he emptied their joint account, left her penniless and ran off with that little twat, Chinasa!

They were headed for divorce until the slut he'd been shacking up with dumped him after he ran out of money, so he had come crawling back to her, claiming it was the devil. At first, she had been resistant to his pleas and constant begging because deep down in her heart, she knew he only came back because she was his financial crutch and he didn't love her, not in the real sense of the word. He needed her to maintain the lifestyle to which he had become accustomed and had lost access to when he left her.

She knew it would have been better to call it quits after his very public betrayal, but he started going to her parents' house every day to beg with his mother and other family members. Her father had initially been angry and didn't want her to go back to the marriage, her mother had told her to pray to God to heal her marriage, but like typical Nigerian parents, they eventually instructed her to forgive him. "You have a child," they'd told her. "It would be foolish to abandon your marriage now for another woman to come and enjoy the fruits of your labour."

At first, Adesuwa had resisted. She didn't know how she was going to resume a marriage that was so broken. A marriage with no trust. For the first few weeks after he moved back in, she felt like she was sharing her bed with the devil. They lived like strangers, like roommates sharing their individual responsibilities in the household but with no emotion. However, as months passed and Soji's good behaviour persisted, her walls began to fall. He would even wake up early to do school runs and pick Junior up from school in the afternoons, so she didn't have to leave work. He would leave little surprises on her pillow in the mornings like a single red rose with a note underneath that said:

I love you forever... Soji.

He was no longer hiding in the bathroom to take secret phone calls or staying out late saying he was in a meeting. He was home every single day at seven at night. He seemed to be making a deliberate effort to find a job and Adesuwa was happy. She felt as though the guy she had fallen in love with was back. She didn't mind that she still had all the financial responsibility just as long as he was faithful, and he showed that he loved her and was committed to their family. However, her happiness was short-lived. They had decided to try for a second child, which had spelt the beginning of the end as they began to deal with all the emotional and financial pressure that came with repeatedly failed IVF treatments.

Soji had reverted to being Soji—unavailable, unreliable and dedicated to his "baby boy" lifestyle. He was out almost every night: Hard Rock Café on Wednesdays, Cocoon on Thursdays, Club 57 on Fridays, the Boat Club on Saturday and Cocoon again on Sunday night. It was exhausting! She didn't know how one person could drink that much when they weren't making any money, but she was tired of complaining. She had decided to focus on her life to prevent herself from running mad from frustration, but this?

This is absolutely insane! Adesuwa thought as she looked at her phone and confirmed the debit alert for one million naira to Cocoon, Lagos.

"Who does this?!" Adesuwa screamed as she banged both palms on the steering wheel of the car in frustration. Everyone in the compound was staring at her like a madwoman. She took a few calming breaths, started the car and drove off.

As she drove past Eko Hotel, she fought the urge to call Lara or Zuri. She still hadn't admitted to either friend that Soji was back in the house. She'd kept waiting for the right time but the longer she put it off, the more awkward that conversation would have been and if she told them now, they would only blame her. They had repeatedly told her before the marriage crumbled to remove all of her money from the joint account so that Soji wouldn't have access to it. And at first, she had listened, but as Soji's good behaviour persisted, she foolishly began to trust him more. As time went on, she had felt guilty holding her money in her account.

She had convinced herself that, if she let go of the past and showed him she trusted him by resuming the use of their joint account, it would help to heal their marriage. She felt like a fool for allowing her parents to convince her that taking the ungrateful bastard back was the right thing to do, despite his repeated betrayals. 'Once bitten, twice shy' they said, but in her case, it was more like once bitten hundred times foolish! She forgave him for all of his transgressions, every single one. Her phone beeped again. As she stopped at the traffic lights on Ozumba Mbadiwe Road, she turned her phone over and read a message from Soji.

My babe, the text read, *I'm sure you are still in the gym but if you get a debit alert for 1 million don't be alarmed. I can explain. Let's talk tonight. I love you forever.*

At that moment she knew she was his enabler, that she had created this monster! This Yoruba demon! He would create this elaborate lie around why this was an emergency or a mistake or the devil, and she would forgive him. It was their way, but it hadn't always been.

She sent him a message. *Soji that money was a huge chunk of SJ's school fees.*

****

Tami

"Oh my God, Tami! I love it!" Amaka squealed with excitement as she stared at her reflection in the full-length mirror in her Eko Signature Hotel suite.

Tami struggled to maintain a professional demeanour and not sigh simultaneously in frustration and relief as she replied, "You are most welcome."

Well, that was a surprise! She thought.

Given all the tantrums Amaka had thrown in the last couple of weeks, Tami was convinced that no one living or dead could please this bride. She had changed her mind about the design of the dress at least five times. Then she had changed her mind about the fabric—first satin, then she wanted lace. *Then,* she'd come back wanting an entirely new colour.

As Amaka leaned in to hug her, Tami tried her best not to grimace and strangle the nightmare of a woman. She was mentally and physically exhausted from dealing with this tyrant bride who had made her life a living hell in the last few weeks and was ready to move on from the incessant phone calls to rant at two in the morning and the text messages full of insults and complaints about the dress. It was all too much.

I mean, how did one describe a bride calling in the wee hours of the morning to say I must be plotting against her with her enemies to sabotage her wedding, Tami thought. *All because her dress wouldn't zip up.*

Was it Tami's fault that she had obviously been stress eating and gained a few pounds? In the months they'd known each other, Amaka's weight had... fluctuated all over the place, but instead of coming to terms with that and asking Tami politely to alter the dress, she dealt with the situation like a person unhinged.

Kneeling to make some adjustments to the hem, she looked up to observe Amaka in the dress she had spent the last few weeks making. It was beautiful in all its hand-beaded glory. A stunning full-length, form-fitting, white lace dress that accentuated all her curves and had a detachable train. It was her second dress for her wedding reception party, the dress that was sure to dazzle the guests as she danced into the hall for the first time as Mrs Igbojekwe.

After taking several pictures and going over the final handover notes for the dress, Tami packed up her things and headed for the door, when one of the bridesmaids offered to walk her out.

"Thank you, Tami," Stella said as they walked to the elevator together. "You've been great. So patient! You are honestly a saint. I don't know how you dealt with that witch."

"Pardon me?" Tami said, taken aback in shock.

"She's my friend, but I have to be honest. Just because she's getting married doesn't mean she should treat everyone like slaves, her bridesmaids included," she said as she rolled her eyes.

"She wasn't that bad," Tami prevaricated.
"Wasn't that bad?" Stella hissed. "In some cultures, Amaka's bad attitude

could be described as witchcraft. If I were you, I would have refunded her money weeks ago and sacked her as a client."

"I think she was just under a lot of pressure," Tami replied diplomatically. She did not want to end up on some thinly veiled Instagram, Facebook, or Twitter post about back-biting designers.

"Storyyyy!" Stella responded. "I just hope she doesn't take this bad behaviour to her husband's house. It's funny how the badly-behaved ones are the ones getting married. Meanwhile, us well-behaved women can't find decent husbands."

"Hmmm," Tami answered non-committally as she smiled uncomfortably. It felt like the lift was taking forever to come. And this conversation? Was a road to eternal social damnation if she wasn't careful.

As much as she detested the behaviour of brides like Amaka, she hated toxic friends like Stella even more. There was some truth to what she was saying, but she could also smell jealousy. She really wanted to tell Stella that it wasn't by force to be friends with Amaka and she should either be loyal and shut up or stop being friends with her instead of all this fakery.

Saved by the bell, Tami thought as her phone rang.

"Excuse me, I have to take this," Tami smiled. "It's my atelier. I have a few missed calls from them, so I'll just take the stairs. Thanks so much for everything. Have fun at the wedding!" She pressed her phone to her ear and hurried towards the stairs.

"Hello, Basirat. What happened now?. You've called me like three times." She rushed down the stairs and listened in growing horror as an anxious Basirat dropped yet another piece of bad news.

"Ma, *na* the generator, oh," Basirat said. "E don stop working since afternoon. We call the generator man again, and he said he no fit fix am. Ma, he said we need to buy a new one."

"New one, *ke*?" Tami sighed, resigned. The number of times they had fixed that generator in the last couple of months had been an indication that it would soon pack up.

"Ma, we get plenty orders but the tailors no day work since because no light," Basirat whined. "What should we do, ma?"

This was the thing about running a business in Lagos, just when you thought you were getting out of one wahala, *another one would rear its ugly head. From difficult clients to generator packing up,* Tami thought. *What a day! What a life.*

"Okay, Basirat. I'm coming to the office now. Tell them to hold on."

Her car pulled up, and she jumped in, making a call to her accountant.

"Mr Bola, good afternoon."

Mr Bola's voice came through faintly on the other end of the phone. "Good afternoon, ma."

"Mr Bola, we need to buy a new generator," Tami told him.

"Ma, there's no money for that, oh," Mr Bola said. "I checked the balance in the account this morning, and I can tell you there isn't enough cash to buy a brand-new generator. The best we can afford right now is an 'I betta pass my neighbour', and that is not going to be useful given the number of machines that we have."

"You are funny, Mr Bola. What do you mean there's no money for that?"

Tami said patiently. "We've been working nonstop in the last couple of months, so how can there be no money?"

"Ma, the thing is we've spent a lot recently," Mr Bola said. "On the one hand, we just paid off your fabric supplier, salaries, and service charge. On the other hand, it is my understanding that a lot of the work you are doing at Irawo is for non-paying clients, celebrities and influencers, ma. Also, the clients that are due to pay have not made full payments, so we have a lot of cash outside, ma."

"Okay, thank you, Mr Bola. Let's have a meeting this week to review the books. I need to figure out what is really going on." A frustrated Tami wrapped up the details and ended the call.

In the last eighteen months, Tami had really stepped up her game. She had recognised that despite starting the business years earlier, she had treated it like a hobby, relying on her daddy's money to keep the lights on. Irawo had only become somewhat self-sufficient in the last year after she had buckled down and started taking the work seriously. She began to put all her years of going to parties and meeting celebrities and socialites to good use, getting them to wear her designs, so they could be photographed and featured in the style section of BellaNaija—and it had worked.

The more her designs featured on their website and Instagram page, the more popular Irawo became with Lagos "it" girls. In fact, she had grown her Instagram following to about three hundred thousand, experiencing a spike in follows and engagement after she started dressing brides. Business seemed to be booming! But even with the increased demand, something wasn't adding up. She was tired of feeling like a slave to her business and working long hours, with no substantial profits to justify the blood sweat and tears she had put into it.

She loved it all, so she felt terrible complaining, but it had become clear that her business as it stood now would be difficult to scale. Even on the good days with the sweetest brides and the most reasonable celebrity clients, she felt drained. As it was, her business couldn't run without her physical presence, and she knew in her heart that it wasn't sustainable. All the effort she was putting into her business simply did not match her bank account.

****

Lara

"You look well, Lara, considering the circumstances," Toju said as he ushered her into his office and closed the door behind them. "Please sit down."

"Thank you," she replied, wishing she could return the compliment. She had never seen Toju look so dishevelled and browbeaten in all the years she had worked for him. Instead of his usual well-tailored suit, he was wearing chinos and a wrinkled denim shirt that hung untucked. It didn't even look like he had shaved for the last few days.

"What's the plan to resolve this, *oga*?" Lara's voiced was filled with forced cheer as she walked to his desk and sat across from him.

"Look, Lara," Toju said solemnly. "I don't want to lie to you. You've been a loyal employee, and we've made some good money together, but I don't see a way out of this."

"I don't understand."
"I don't see a way out," Toju repeated. "The money we invested in OPL five-sixty-seven to secure constant crude streams for our trading business is gone! The company has completed its drilling programme. They made no discovery and revealed two dry holes."

Lara put her hands on her chest. "That can't be, right? Do they have another producing asset that they can pay us back from?" She asked desperately.

"No. That was the company's sole asset. But even if it wasn't, we can't do that because each asset is ring-fenced so they can't transfer the profits or losses."

Lara sat in shocked silence.

"So, what does this mean for us going forward?"

Toju sighed and leaned back in his chair, closing his eyes. "This is a cyclical business. We've taken too many losses, and on top of that I've just been notified that we've been blacklisted by the regulator because we've not been able to meet up with payments."

"And the banks?"

"I've had several meetings with bank MDs, and they've refused to extend our credit. They claim we are over-leveraged. Listen, I've done everything I can at this point, but the reality is we are illiquid, and I'm being forced to file for bankruptcy."

"This is unbelievable. What happens to our back pay?"

"Lara, we are illiquid," Toju said plainly even as remorse tinged his tone. "I'll see what I can salvage to pay the staff, but it doesn't look good. I called you in here out of respect for our working relationship over the years. I wanted you to hear it directly from me."

Lara stared at him, speechless.

"I'm sorry this is happening when you just lost your mum, but it couldn't be helped. We made some bad investments, and we've just been unlucky. I'm sorry."

"Toju, this couldn't be happening at a more impossible time," Lara said, a tear trickling down her cheek. "I've barely finished covering the cost of cancer treatments for my mum, funeral costs are mounting, not to talk of all my other financial obligations. My siblings' school fees, for God's sake! I've been living off my savings the last few months in hopes that things would sort themselves out. I've sold stocks, I've been trying and failing at selling the last piece of land I own enough to keep up with my mum's hospital bills and other expenses. I'm wiped out, and now you are saying I don't have a job?"

"I don't know what else to say, Lara," Toju said. "I'm sorry. I didn't mean for anything like this to happen."

At this point, she was on the brink of being hysterical, but as she looked at Toju, she knew he couldn't do anything to help her. She needed to contain her anger, and she needed a plan. She thanked him and left, heading back to her now old office.

She collapsed into her chair and tried to gather her thoughts, tears running down her face. She thought she had cried all the tears she had left when she lost her mum, but this situation was heavy.

What am I going to do now? Lara thought. *On top of everything else, looking for a job in this economy was a tall order. I haven't been in the job market for at least seven years, where do I even begin?*

Then, fear caught her throat as she thought through the ramifications of her meeting with Toju. She opened her banking app to look at the balance in her money market account, mentally calculating how much runway she had before things got dire. She ran through some rough calculations about how long her money would last before her expenses overran her income.

As she stared at the numbers in front of her, panic began to set in. How did I get here she thought? She had spent years working hard and making money. She had saved and invested, but it was clear that she hadn't saved and invested enough compared to her income. She had some real estate holdings, but it was a tight market, and they were difficult to offload. Even then, her lifestyle costs far exceeded her investments.

Her mind wandered to a time similar to this when her father died. She had been quite young, and his death had left Lara, her siblings, and mother in near poverty because he had not had his financial affairs in order.

The dramatic change in their lifestyle had been a wakeup call for her, even at that age. As a family, they had hit rock bottom, but the bitter experience of losing her dad and financial stability in the same blow had helped to build her resilience. As she'd gotten older, she'd been grateful to have gone through it at a young age because it became her driving force. She'd learned two hard lessons: never to depend on anyone but herself for financial stability and even if you worked hard, it was possible to lose it all at any point.

The experience had driven her to work harder than anyone in every situation. She had been a single-minded student in school and a top employee at work, always closing the biggest deals and get the biggest bonuses. She was very competitive, but she was mostly competing with her last achievement. The fear of "not having" or losing it all forced her to keep pushing and building.

She had naively thought the loss of her dad and the financial obstacles that had come with it would be the most difficult time she would ever have to face, but she was so wrong; this was worse because she was grown and she knew better.

As she stared at the numbers again, she tried to wrap her mind around the undeniable fact: she was broke.

SMART MONEY LESSON:
THE RICH ALSO CRY

At its core, the Smart Money mantra is not necessarily about being the wealthiest person in the room. It is about learning how to optimise your resources, mastering skill sets you can monetise, cutting expenses ruthlessly on the things you don't care about, and spending intentionally on your goals. It is a concept that encourages you to find strategies to help you cope in times of difficulty and leverage on what you have to get what you want, thereby systematically building the life you desire.

In the first book, many were uncomfortable with the fact that the characters (especially Lara) earned high incomes which were not relatable to the average African millennial. My theory, however, is that in Africa, we are in love with the rags-to-riches story. We want to hear about people who started out with nothing and then toiled to make phenomenal wealth—that story is inspiring and it is one that I hope will be repeated a million times more throughout the continent. One has to remember, though, the cautionary words that are the title of Ms Chimamanda Adichie's famous TED Talk: the danger of a single story.

I want to tell a different kind of story—the story of what happens when you move to the middle class and have the privilege of making financial choices, and what can happen when you don't have adequate strategies and the mindset to preserve it. The reality is that most people move from the lower-middle income bracket, where financial planning tends to focus solely on earning more as the solution to financial success, to the middle-middle or upper-middle income bracket. As people move up, many end up living from paycheque to paycheque because they lack the financial literacy tools to help them keep and grow their money.

We also have to acknowledge that life is in seasons and the "rich" also cry. It is possible to earn a high income, not be irresponsible with money and still find yourself broke. Like in Lara's case, life just happens. When a financial catastrophe occurs, most people tend to find themselves in one of the four categories below, each with their pros and cons.

'I Have Arrived' Syndrome

Sometimes earning more doesn't mean you have arrived. You have just received the invitation to the party. Let's say you get a promotion, a new job, sign a new contract, or a windfall hits your business. All of a sudden, you have access to more money, and your brain has shifted gears to 'I have arrived!' Nine times out of ten, you are just "pre-rich", but you've given yourself license to spend like a billionaire. Your consumption rises to meet your income, and you become a revolving door for your money. So even if you earn a million naira a month, because you have stepped up your spending to a million naira a month as well, what you have left is zero. So, if and when trouble arrives, your high income will not give enough of a cushion to escape being broke because your finances cannot absorb it.

Cash-rich and Asset-poor

If we were to assess a spectrum of assets according to liquidity, cash would be the most liquid and a small business would be the most illiquid. Treasury bills, stocks, bonds and real estate would fall somewhere in the middle.

Risk-averse people want to see their money in the bank because they don't want to hear stories about asset devaluation a.k.a. the money you invested can no longer buy what it could before. While you should have cash on hand for day-to-day living and in case of emergencies, having more cash than assets can put you in financial trouble because while cash is king, cash also loses value over time because liquid assets are more vulnerable to the negative impact of inflation. For example, you could buy more with one million naira in 2017 than you can buy in 2019 because with inflation at 11.25 per cent in April 2019, goods and services have become more expensive.

It is vital to find a balance by investing in assets that either appreciate faster than inflation over time or produce returns that are not entirely eroded by inflation. For example, if the one million naira was put in treasury bills with a return of 13 per cent or used to buy land that appreciated by 20 per cent since 2017. Having cash that reduces in value over time but not having assets that can protect your financial future can lead to setbacks.

Now there are people on one end of the spectrum that tend to be more cash-rich but asset poor because they would rather see their money in the bank and don't want to hear any stories about asset devaluation. The advantage of being cash-rich is that there's money on hand in case of emergencies. However, the disadvantage is that inflation erodes the value of cash over time because it is not being invested in instruments or assets that can hedge against inflation.

Asset-rich and Cash-poor

On the other hand, there are those who prefer to invest aggressively and put most of their money in assets for fear that cash on hand will lead to overspending or be eroded by inflation. However, while assessing a spectrum of assets, it is important to note that assets like real estate and small businesses are less liquid than stock or treasury bills, posing a potential problem if the need for short-term cash flow that was not adequately planned for arises.

Also, Africa is a continent of entrepreneurs, mainly because the high unemployment rate means that most people start businesses out of necessity to earn a living. Entrepreneurs are risk-takers and mostly bet on themselves. Many business owners tend to put the majority of the income they earn back into their businesses without really diversifying because they see their business as their biggest asset. You hear them say things like, 'Why should I invest in Dangote stock when I should be investing in my own business?', which is a fair point.

However, the result is that for most of the people in this category, at least 70 per cent of their personal net worth is tied to their businesses. Even entrepreneurs with businesses that have healthy balance sheets, which might look good on paper, but their personal bank accounts may not reflect this. The reality is, in Africa, small businesses are not as easy to sell as their counterparts in the west. So although on paper your business might have a decent valuation, if you need cash in a time of crisis, is it sellable or illiquid?

Inadequate Asset Protection

In building wealth, we need to also be thinking about asset protection. In Lara's case, health and life insurance for her mother could have helped to cushion some of the financial blows she suffered. Insurance is not an asset *per se* but acts as protection for the assets you do have.

EXERCISE:

Even when you have a positive net worth you should ask yourself these questions:

- How diversified is your portfolio?
- What types of assets are in the portfolio?
- How can their liquidity affect the different seasons in your financial life?

CHAPTER 2   FINANCIAL ABUSE
                          IS A THING

Zuri

Zuri walked past a sea of blue and red ankara, fascinated by the manic hustle for everything from food to party gifts. The spicy aroma of Jollof rice being cooked by firewood in a big metal pot wafted past, making her nostrils twitch involuntarily. She couldn't blame them; there was nothing sweeter than freshly made party Jollof.

As she found her way back to the friends' table, she watched Lara gracefully go through the motions of being a host—asking guests about their welfare and making sure that the edibles and drinks continued to flow. It was a miracle that the girl was still standing because as soon as her mother had been diagnosed with stage three breast cancer, things had escalated rather quickly. At first, the doctors had been cautiously optimistic that aggressive chemotherapy would work but after months of treatment, it became clear that Lara's mum wasn't going to survive.

It had been a hellish few months; Lara's four friends had watched her go from oncologist to oncologist seeking a second, third, even fourth opinion. She even went as far as sending her mother's test results and blood work to specialists in South Africa and London to see if there were alternative treatments, but her mother's age and the fact that it was a late-stage cancer were limiting factors. It had been tough to watch, but they all understood that Lara's mother was her best friend, and their friend would do anything in her power to keep her alive.

Still, as much as she admired Lara's strength through this ordeal, Zuri was worried about her dealing with both the death of her mother and the loss of her job simultaneously. It was a lot for one person to take.

Lara wouldn't admit it though and every time she was asked how she was faring, she would shrug and reply 'Okay'. Her friends knew better because she'd stopped eating and Zuri reckoned she had lost at least twenty pounds. Her usually skinny-thick frame was now reed-thin and borderline unhealthy. A few pounds were one thing because all five friends were constantly trying to lose weight or stay healthy, but the stress showed. The circles underneath her eyes were dark and more than obvious, and one could tell she hadn't slept in weeks. Her usually supple golden skin was now sallow and wan.

Zuri snapped out of her reverie to see Ladun and Bode approaching the table, Ladun with food in hand while Bode carried the drinks and glasses. Ladun set the plates down on the table, clearly having gone to town on the buffet. Bode's plate was piled with pounded yam, egusi, and snails, while hers was a mixture of Jollof and fried rice, plantain, coleslaw, and two rather juicy-looking pieces of fried meat.

She plonked herself next to Zuri. "Ah, ah? Why are you sitting here all by yourself?"

Bode smiled and waved his hello as he too sat and began to dig into his meal. Zuri smiled back. She often thought about how, despite how different these two were, they still functioned as one unit. It was inspiring to watch them go through their biggest financial setback after Bode's dad passed with such grace, grit, and determination. In the past year and a half, they had weathered turmoil that would have broken a less devoted couple, but they were a team and their marriage was stronger for it.

"Hmm! I don't know, oh," Zuri replied. "Last I checked, Adesuwa was distributing souvenirs to the guests and Tami and I were serving Lara's relatives' food and drinks. Then it all got a bit too hectic for me. So, I just came to sit down and sip my palm wine. I cannot come an' kill myself."

"My sister, tell me about it!" Ladun exclaimed. "I am not quite sure how Lara has dealt with those people's drama in the last couple of months. They are beyond dramatic! She is a saint. If it were me, I would have given them a piece of my mind a long time ago."

Ladun scanned the faces under the crowded canopy then asked, "Where is Tsola? I haven't seen him."
"He had to work," Zuri replied shortly. She felt a little awkward that Tsola was not there. He had come to the service of songs yesterday and made a brief

appearance at Ikoyi Cemetery when the body was being laid to rest, but he'd made his apologies and left for a big meeting that he'd said he couldn't miss no matter what.

Their relationship had progressed nicely in the last year plus, but the guy was a workaholic. She had gotten used to him not being there for important events her friends were having or cancelling plans suddenly because he had to fly to Abuja or Paris to attend impromptu meetings. At first, she used to get upset and throw tantrums, but Tsola reminded her each time that if she didn't want a busy man she would end up with a poor one and he had no intention of being poor so she had better get with the programme.

"It looks like Adesuwa and Tami have rescued Lara from her relatives," Ladun whispered. "Please tell that guy to move so there are enough seats for them." She pointed to a man who had placed his plates on the table and was getting ready to sit.

Zuri hustled over and pleaded with him to move to the other side of the table. He said nothing but eyed her as he reluctantly moved to sit elsewhere. Zuri and Ladun exchanged knowing looks and started laughing.

"Please sit down quickly, oh. This guy almost beat me for these seats," Zuri said as the three girls approached the table.

"Which guy?" Adesuwa laughed, as she scanned the table. "Aren't the tables assigned?"

"Don't worry. Unnecessary drama. He has vamoosed," Zuri responded.

"Trust me, it can't be worse than the drama Tami and I just experienced," Adesuwa shook her head as she sat down then scooted forward in her chair.

"Lara, your relatives are something else," Adesuwa continued. "Can you imagine that as I was going around giving the gift bags with souvenirs in them to each person, your uncle Festus's wife kept calling me back and saying, 'You haven't given my friends, or me! Are we not important? *Abi* it's only important Lagos people that you are giving!' I was weak for the woman, oh. I hadn't even gotten to her table yet."

"Adesuwa, please your own was good," Tami chimed in, looking disgruntled. "At least it was souvenirs! Granted just notebooks, plastic bowls, and key holders but at least they are gifts. Lara, I saw Aunty Nkechi and her church friends packing Jollof rice inside nylon bags and stuffing them in their handbags! You would think they didn't have food in their houses. Plus, they kept lying to the poor waiters that they hadn't been served food and telling them off each time."

The friends all looked at each other and burst into a fit of giggles.

Lara had a wry smile on her face as she said, "Leave my relatives alone, oh! This is mild compared to what they have done in the last couple of months. They have shown me pepper. I'm just glad it's over and they will all go back to their regular lives after today."

She turned to Zuri. "Did Tsola make it to his meeting?"

"Yes, I think so. I haven't spoken to him since we got here." It wasn't hard to tell that Zuri was disappointed that he wasn't here. "I'm sorry he couldn't be here, Lara, but you know how the boy is about his work. He loves you, though. You know that, right? He would have been here to support if he could have."

"My dear, he has been more than supportive," Lara rubbed her friend's shoulder soothingly. "Your boy gave me a cheque for one million naira at the service of songs yesterday. I was in shock when I opened it at home. Please thank him for me. You know I'm jobless right now, so every little bit helps."

"You're joking!" Zuri exclaimed, surprised. "Why does Tsola behave like this! You know he didn't even mention giving you a cheque to me."

Tami raised her brows and nodded with approval at the gesture. "Correct guy. He just performs, no need to make noise."

Ladun was grateful that Bode was not at the table at that moment. After he'd finished his meal, he'd left them to their girl gang banter and went to greet a family friend he'd spotted earlier. He might have been embarrassed because he hadn't been in a position to give Lara that kind of money right now but he had done the important thing and been supportive in his own way. Besides, they had all contributed as much cash as they could afford towards the funeral.

"Meanwhile, how's the job search going, babe?" Zuri asked, placing her hand over Lara's that still rested on her shoulder. "Any luck?"

"Man, it's tough out there! It's been a few months, but I've been distracted with funeral arrangements. I've sent my CV out to colleagues in the industry and I've gotten a few referrals and interviews but so far, I haven't found a good fit."

"Ah, ah! Which one is a good fit again?" Tami asked. "Is it not a job you are looking for?"

"*Abeg, abeg!* I'm looking for a job, but I don't want to enter one chance. It's either the wrong role, the company looks a little dodgy, or the pay cut is too much."

"You are proud, oh," Ladun laughed. "People are looking for jobs—any job, really, and you are here being choosy."

"I'm not being choosy, love. I just know my worth," Lara shrugged. "I may be jobless, but I've spent the last ten years building my career, my experience, and my skills, so I know what I bring to the table. I'll admit I'm running out of savings pretty quickly and I need to find something soon before things get desperate."

"I totally agree with you, babe," Adesuwa said. "The right fit is important. There's no need to jump from one job to another every six months. Plus, with all your experience, any company worth their salt will be lucky to have you."

Lara tamped down her worry and told her friends, "Anyway, I have an interview this week and it looks promising." She looked at the four women, grateful for their constant support. They had all been there for her in these gruelling months, every single one of them.

A few hours later, as the last guests left and the vendors were clearing out their belongings, reality started to set in as Lara looked at her phone, already filled with emails and text messages from vendors with their account details reminding her that the balance of their money needed to be paid. She looked up to see a Black Mercedes G-wagon driving into the compound.

Who is this one? Lara thought. The reception was over, and she was in no mood to start entertaining latecomers. It was dark which made it difficult to make out who it was from where she was sitting. As the figure drew closer, she couldn't believe her eyes.

Am I seeing things? Or is that Deji Suleman?

"Lara!" A familiar deep, sexy baritone voice called out as he approached her.

"Deji! Oh my God, it's you!" Lara exclaimed in shocked delight. "I thought I was seeing things. What are you doing here?"

"I was in a friend's office in Abuja this morning when I heard you lost your mum and that the funeral was today. I came to give you my condolences and pay my respects but unfortunately, I can't stay."

"Why, *now*? Stay for a drink at least."

"I'm on my way back to the airport. I have to be in Geneva in the morning." He handed her an envelope.

"Oh, thank you! It's a pity you have to run."

"We'll catch up when I'm back." He gave her a hug before returning to his car.

This was the first time she had seen Deji Suleman in at least three years.

She smiled wistfully, wandering down memory lane to their first meeting during a cocktail at the OTC Conference in Houston. He had been flirty, brilliantly entertaining, and they had definitely vibed. They had exchanged numbers, but then she found out he was a billionaire and was very married with at least two children. She had kept her distance, but they said hello at oil and gas events when they bumped into each other. It was an absolute shock to see him tonight. What was even more shocking was when she opened the envelope and saw a cheque for five million naira.

"Well done, dear," Bolanle praised, interrupting her thoughts. "It's finally over so now you can have some breathing room. You really tried. It was hectic."

"Thank you so much," Lara smiled sadly. "You've been great."

Bolanle Okusanya-Feyita was a third-generation funeral director of LTJ Funeral Homes and had been very helpful with information as well as allowing Lara to pay in instalments.

"I just wish you had taken a funeral plan years ago or had life insurance for your mum," Bolanle mused. "It would have made things so much easier and much less expensive. I tell all my friends these are things to think about as their parents start ageing."

"I know, oh," Lara said with regret. "But the truth is no one wants to confront death. I guess in my mind my mum was old, but not old enough to have died yet. I had imagined many more years with her, of her seeing me walk down the aisle and of her carrying her grandchildren." It still stung every time she thought about the fact that her mum was gone and would never experience any of those things with her.

"Anyway, I'm leaving, but I wanted you to have the invoice," Bolanle said.

"Thank you again for being so helpful and understanding, especially about the money. Don't worry I'll pay it all off very soon. Let me just get myself together."

"I understand." Bolanle was not unsympathetic to Lara's predicament, but she was a businesswoman after all.

"In fact, I just got a surprise gift of five million. I will transfer it to you as soon as I pay it in," Lara said.

"Thank you so much," Bolanle said. "I would appreciate that. Even though it is not my usual policy for payments to linger, I trust you because you've been so transparent and kept your word at every stage. It's refreshing." She gave her a hug before she walked away.

As she stood at the entrance on her own, she opened the envelope to reveal an invoice from LTJ breaking down the costs of the funeral.

Her eyes widened with shock when she saw the balance highlighted in red at the bottom of the invoice. Her head started spinning. The total cost was twelve point five million naira!

How? How did I possibly rack up this bill for the funeral? She had put down an initial deposit for two million naira and paid in smaller instalments during the months of planning.

"One point six million naira for a casket!" Lara shouted. She couldn't believe her eyes! Was this a joke? Was the casket made of gold?

She had a vague recollection of Aunty Nkechi insisting on the imported casket. In her grief, she had allowed her to have her way, not paying much attention to the cost. Between Aunty Nkechi and Uncle Festus, she had only received a begrudging single cheque for two hundred and fifty thousand naira, and she suspected that she'd only gotten it because they found out Aunty Ifeoma had given money to support her and they didn't want to look bad.

They needed to be able to tell their friends that they had contributed to their sister's burial. She knew asking them for more would be a futile mission.

There were other costs involved. The burial plot cost one point five million, but thankfully a part of her deposit had gone towards that. The marble head for the gravesite cost five hundred thousand, the hearse rental was one hundred and twenty thousand, decorations, lying in state and the wreath cost another one hundred and fifty k. The mortuary bill was another headache. It had cost fifty k for embalmment and two thousand naira per day to keep the body in the mortuary. With all the arguments between her mother's siblings, the body had stayed there for months and the list went on and on and on. They had all looked like small amounts at the time but together it was a monster bill.

Even with the generous donations from Deji Suleiman, Tsola, she and her close friends. She needed at least another eight million naira to clear her debts. This *gbese* was a lot.

****

Zuri

Zuri gazed out of the car window as Tsola parked his Range Rover in the car park beside the Lekki-Ikoyi Link Bridge. It read 05:43 AM on the radio clock and Tsola liked to run between half-past five and six in the morning before the sun rose to heat up the fit fam aficionados. There was the slightest hint of dawn as they reached the bottom of the bridge and combined with the streetlights and the obnoxious glare from the digital billboards that sat at the bottom of the bridge, their path was well lit. She didn't have the same zeal or stamina for running as Tsola did, but when she slept over at his house, it was easier to get up and go instead of dealing with the guilt of feeling like a lazy sod when he came back home after his run.

As they approached the tollgate, Tsola sped up and she didn't even try to keep up. He always ran a full two laps on the bridge, slowing down to keep her company as she completed her single lap for a few minutes before racing to the end. As she watched his deliciously athletic build embark on the journey to conquer the bridge, her heart lurched in her chest, and she felt the heat rise on her neck—and a few other places. It was crazy how he still had this effect on her after almost two years of dating. Tsola was tall, dark-skinned, a bona fide member of the Idris Elba sect of the beard gang, and he had tight muscles on every inch of his body.

She came to the end of her run and approached the bottom of the bridge where Tsola was already doing a series of stretches as he cooled down.

"Well done, babe," Tsola smiled as she jogged up to him. "You are improving. Your stamina and your time are definitely better these days. At least I didn't have to wait for you for ten extra minutes at the bottom of this bridge," he said teasingly, as he poked her in the ribs with his index finger.

Zuri gave him a teasing glare. "Stop, *jo!* If you like don't wait, one of these billionaires will collect your girlfriend on this bridge. Then your eye will clear," she joked.

"Ah, look at this girl! You don't know that I'm almost a billionaire?" Tsola laughed. "My dear, you should be worried about your competition on this bridge—the women that are wearing half tops, who can run faster than you and are flirting with your boyfriend."

Zuri glared at him.

A grinning Tsola continued cheekily, "Ah! Are you angry? You see, you can start it, but you can't finish. You are lucky I love you and I don't have eyes for any of the women trying to finesse their way into my bed," he said as he took her hand in his and kissed the back as he led them towards the car.

As they joked, Zuri mentally braced herself as she got into the Range. "I need to talk to you about something," Zuri said as she settled into the passenger seat. "It's not a big deal but I need to get it off my chest."

"I'm listening."

"Obinna and Teju found land that's perfect for the Yaba development. It's about sixteen thousand square metres and it has good road access and drainage."

"Sounds great. What's the catch?"

"Well, turns out the land belongs to the Sannis. Olumide's family."

"Right." His expression instantly flipped from interested to stony.

"The team has been dealing with their agent and the demands are becoming more ridiculous by the day. Can you believe they want to choose the construction company as well as get a hundred million naira upfront on top of the units we are offering them as part of the joint venture?!"

"I see." Tsola's tone was glacial.

"Mr Tunde wants me to lead the negotiations because I have a prior relationship with the family."

There was an uncomfortable silence.

Say something," Zuri said softly.

"What would you like me to say?" Tsola voice was tightly leashed, but there was something off in his tone as he continued, "That I'm uncomfortable with the fact that you want to use your relationship with your ex-boyfriend to negotiate?"

"Tsola I'm not using my relationship with my ex to negotiate," Zuri replied firmly. "My boss thinks we have a better chance of getting better terms because I have a prior relationship with the family."

"Same thing."

"Tsola, it's work. I'm trying to be upfront with you about it."

"What do you want me to say, Zuri?" He snapped. "We both know that entitled shit is going to use this as an opportunity to get back in your life."

Zuri understood Tsola's irritation because, over the course of their relationship, Olumide had tried a few times to get back with her. He constantly pushed at her boundaries in ways that were completely inappropriate; hugging her a few seconds too long when he bumped into her and Tsola at a party, and occasionally sending unsolicited gifts of flowers and jewellery. Tsola found him disrespectful and couldn't stand him.

"Babe, you just have to trust me. Olumide might do inappropriate things because he is who he is, but you have to trust that I won't let him cross the line."

"Zuri, it's not about trusting you. It's about not putting yourself in a compromising situation with a guy you already know has inappropriate intentions. If you are waiting for me to say I'm okay with it because its work, you'll be waiting a long time. Let Obinna or Teju lead the negotiations. If you weren't there that's what would have to happen isn't it?"

"Yes, but I am there. You just have to trust that I can handle myself."

"If you respect me or our relationship, you'll let Obinna or Teju deal with Olumide," Tsola said with finality.

"I don't want to fight."

"Neither do I. You wanted my opinion, that's how I feel about the situation."

"I've heard you," Zuri said flatly and turned to look out the window.

They sat in silence for the rest of the car ride to Tsola's house.

****

Zuri

As she stepped out of her car, Zuri smoothed her CP Woman skirt and rifled through her bag to find her sunglasses, even though the entrance to Shiro was only a short distance from where she was parked and would have to take them off as soon as she stepped into the restaurant. She felt like a million bucks and her Dapmod shades always gave her that extra ginger that made her feel like a badass.

The five friends had made it a point to meet at a restaurant at least twice a month so they could all catch up in person. Between WhatsApp and Instagram, it was easy to forget that you hadn't actually seen your friends in a while, and this would be the first time they were meeting up since Lara's mum's funeral.

She was greeted by their usual friendly waiter and followed him as he led her to their favourite window-side table. She scanned the room to see if she knew anyone dining. Lara and Ladun had already arrived. The rest of the room was filled with expatriates, no one she recognised.

"Hey, loves!" Zuri breezed in and air-kissed both women before she sat down.

"Ah, ah! You look nice," Lara said. "You didn't come to play with anybody today. Nice bag! Is it new?"

"Yes, oh!" Zuri placed her new Chanel bag on the table. "But you should see the Birkin I'm about to order."

"It's lovely! Present from Tsola?" Ladun said, her face lighting up.

"Nope, present from me!" Zuri was gleeful. "My reward for closing the financing deal for Richmond."

"Hmm. You seem to be rewarding yourself a lot these days," Lara said, as she perused the menu.

Ladun laughed.

"Is that shade?" Zuri said.

"Nah, babe. Just facts," Lara responded. "In the last couple of months, you've bought everything from Jimmy Choo and Louis Vuitton to Balmain. then the other day you said you were saving for the Birkin that Banke showed y—"

"Ah, ah! Are you counting my money?" Zuri cut her off sharply.

"Not... exactly. I'm just saying slow down," Lara replied. "When you tally everything you've spent, do you have the equivalent in savings and investments? In the words of Jay-Z, you can only afford something if you can buy it twice!"

"Leave Zuri alone, *jo*," Ladun chimed in. "Is it your money?"

"See me see trouble, oh!" Zuri retorted defensively. "Of course I have savings! But don't I have a right to spend my hard-earned money? I'm just rewarding myself for working really hard on that deal."

"Okay, Kim Kardashian!" Lara laughed. "First of all, the deal you closed puts money in Richmond Development's account, not yours. Second of all, I'm just saying be cautious so you don't regress into old habits and ruin all the work you've done to get out of debt. Look at me. One day I was buying Chanel, paying international school fees and the next I was jobless and looking for assets to sell. I was saving and investing, I thought I had financial security but in the middle of my crisis I realised I had not been saving and investing enough, especially in comparison to my income."

"I'm being cautious, ma," Zuri replied, a touch defensive. "I save towards these things I'm not borrowing to buy them, thank you very much."

"See, you are getting upset over a few simple questions because you know I'm right," Lara said. "I'm just asking you... after you bought this bag which is roughly the equivalent of five million when you convert it to naira, do you have five million left in your savings?"

Zuri had the grace to look a bit sheepish. "Uhm, I don't know."

"Actually, the reality is to spend five million on a bag you should have at least ten times that in assets because you are not Kim Kardashian. The babe is worth approximately three hundred and fifty million dollars, so when she spends fifteen thousand dollars on a bag, it basically a blip!"

"Okay, oh, Lara Forbes," Zuri snorted cattily.

"I'm serious. The most ironic thing is that she probably gets a lot of these luxury items for free from the designers because she's a celebrity and people like you who don't earn one per cent of what she earns want her wardrobe."

"I feel like you are being judgemental. Do I have to be as rich as her before I treat myself to a few things?" Zuri clapped back, annoyed.

"Listen, I'm just saying money in your account doesn't necessarily mean you can afford the bag. Yes, I'm proud of you for not going into debt spending more than your salary every month. You are saving, but don't just save to spend, save to build. I'm just worried you are spending more than you are building assets."

Lara words gave Zuri pause, but she sat there, stubbornly silent.

Sensing that she was ruining the mood, Lara laughed and tried to defuse the situation. "Anyway, let me shut up. I can barely afford this meal right now with all the *gbese* on my head. So you guys are paying, FYI."

"I *gatchu*," Zuri laughed. "Judgemental broke ass! *Abi* I should save the money for your meal too."

"If I slap you, *ehn*," Lara teased back.

"Tami is late," Ladun observed, changing the subject. "I'm not surprised, but

I wonder what is keeping Adesuwa. She's usually the most punctual one of us."

"Thank you, Sam," Ladun said as their waiter brought a bottle of sparkling water and glasses with ice and lemon, which they hadn't ordered, but he instinctively knew they needed. "You are always on point. *Abeg*, no vex. Please help me take a picture."

"No problem, ma," Sam said with a smile. He was used to his part-time photographer duties for their crew.

"Please take one from that angle as well," Ladun pointed, giving him directions. Their posing and posturing got them amused glances from a few guests, but this had become normal. Thanks to the advent of social media—Instagram in particular—their generation felt the need to document every single event or adventure, no matter how minute.

"If it's not on the 'gram, did it really happen?" Zuri laughed.

"Tami and Adesuwa are now at least twenty minutes late," Ladun said glancing at her watch as the spirit of mischief took over her.

"Instead of calling them, let's post one of the pictures on Instagram, tag them and use the caption to call them out for their lateness," she suggested.

Just then, they saw Tami walking towards the table.

"You are very early, oh, madam," Zuri said with mock disdain.

"Abeg, leave me, *jo*. You won't believe the day I've had!" Tami flopped into her seat, clearly exasperated.

Zuri rolled her eyes. "Tam Tam! You are always late, leave story," she laughed. "My only surprise is that you are here before Adesuwa."

"Trust me, this was different. Let's just say I had a meeting with my accountant that didn't go so well. And the traffic was horrendous!"

"Isn't it always!" Lara sipped on her sparkling water and reviewed the menu trying to decide what to order.

"Adesuwa was on Adeola Odeku street, last I checked, so she should be here any minute," Tami explained.

A few seconds later Adesuwa walked in, gracefully collapsed into her seat and said to the waiter, "I'll just have the chicken salad," she ordered, looking frazzled. "I'm so sorry for being late guys," she said apologetically. "It's been a hell of a day. Plus the traffic was insane."

"Are you okay?" Lara asked as Sam took their menus away after taking their orders. "I'm starting to worry about you, hun. You've been a bit distracted these days."

"I'll be fine! I've just had a lot to deal with. Actually, I have something to confess," she said as she looked at their faces. "Not to confess per se because it's my life, but I feel guilty that I've been keeping it from you."

Tami and Zuri laughed.

"Ah, ah! What did you do Adesuwa?" Ladun said. "Spill!"

"Okay, okay!" Adesuwa inhaled deeply, nervous. "Soji and I have been back together for two months." She hid her face behind her hands. "On a trial basis!" She insisted.

"What?" Lara exploded. "You can't be serious. After everything, Adesuwa."

The rest of the girls looked at each other, aghast.

"There's more," Adesuwa said. "He took one million from our joint account that was meant for SJ's school fees and still hasn't given an explanation why. Now I don't know what to do. I even tried to ask his mum for advice, but you know how that goes. She said he's a man and I shouldn't be questioning him."

She looked at their shocked faces. "Listen, I don't need your judgement right now. I need your help."

Her friends were accustomed to Soji and his mother's antics by now. Even when her son was doing something fundamentally wrong, she continued to blindly support him. It hadn't done him any favours. His awful behaviour would be clear to everyone else, but his mum would find some village wisdom or twist a bible scripture to justify his actions. If it wasn't so terrifyingly awful, the whole debacle would be actually quite amazing to watch.

"Forget Soji's mum for a minute. I'm still trying to wrap my head around why you took him back. Let me see... the man cheated on you with an eighteen-year-old, stole all your money, left you in debt and then ran off with his child mistress," Lara counted off on her fingers. "Explain to me, Adesuwa, how does this decision make any sense. Now you are surprised that he took SJ's school fees."

Lara hissed and turned her face away, hand on her cheek. "I have nothing else to say."

"We moved past all of that because if I'm really honest, I don't want to be divorced. I'd rather work on my marriage and try to have another baby. I told him frankly that besides good behaviour, he would have to go through the IVF process again. It was one of the conditions for us getting back together and he agreed.

Tami, Zuri, and Ladun exchanged looks and all reached out to hold her hand. It was tough watching Adesuwa go through all of this. Her husband's infidelity, issues with her mother-in-law, secondary infertility; it was like life refused to give her a break. They could only be thankful that she was no longer secretive about her struggles and could talk to them openly. Now they could support her.

"Although, now, he refuses to contribute financially to the process. He says he doesn't have money!" Adesuwa continued. "And guys, this thing is expensive. I feel like I just got out of the hole paying off his debts and now I seem to be sinking into another one. But I want this so badly. Is it so wrong to want to fight for my marriage?"

"Adesuwa there's fighting and there's allowing yourself to be used," Lara said pointedly.

"Listen, I saw Soji at Cocoon on Thursday night," Tami told them. "And their table was not a small boys table, oh! Like I'm talking at least ten bottles of Veuve Clicquot! I couldn't even count the bottles of Rémy Martin they kept bringing to the table. How in God's name can he say he doesn't have money?" She asked.

"Usually, Soji will tell you he didn't contribute, that his friends are the ones that bought the drinks," Adesuwa said shaking her head. "But this time he actually had the effrontery to use one million from our joint account to pay for drinks at that lousy place."

"But that's the part I don't understand, Adesuwa," Zuri said in consternation. "Why does he still have access to your money?"

"You guys take it easy," Ladun tried to cool the conversation down. "He is still her husband."

"So?" Tami rolled her eyes.

"I don't know. I just thought he had changed." Adesuwa's dejected shoulders drooped even further. "I wanted to show him that I trusted him."

"After what he did the last time?" Lara said with disbelief.

"I never said I had forgotten about that," Adesuwa replied.

"But you still gave him access to your money?" Zuri tilted her head forward pointedly. "After paying off his debts?"

"This was the reason I didn't want to tell you guys," Adesuwa said defensively. "I don't need the judgement."

"No one is judging you, Adesuwa." Lara struggled to hide the anger in her voice. She lost. "Actually, I take that back. I AM judging you! I judge you for enabling this man's bad behaviour. Even if you decide you want to be married to that demon, at least be smart with your money!"

"Lara, calm down! Your blood is hot, oh!" Ladun soothed. She agreed with them, but she could sympathise with the difficulty of Adesuwa's situation.

Soji wasn't just a boyfriend, he was her husband and the father of her child.

"Sorry, but I agree with Lara on this," Tami said. "This is financial abuse, Adesuwa. You need to break free."

"Easy for you to say," Adesuwa lashed out with contempt. "You aren't married."

The conversation was spiralling into a shouting match and accusations. Zuri felt like she had to intervene before it got even more heated and lines got crossed. She had known that statement would trigger Lara and Tami.

"Please let's talk about something else," Zuri said.

There was an awkward silence.

"So, uh, Tami. What were you doing out on a Thursday night?"

"My friend, be quiet!" Tami gamely took the baton from Zuri's question, doing her part to lighten the mood. "Were you not my partner in crime in the waka until Tsola came into the picture? Plus, you know Thursday nights at Cocoon with DJ Sparrow are always *lit*!"

"I'm still your partner in crime, Tami," Zuri injected more humour that she was feeling into her voice. "It's just that these days I only have the energy to go out on the weekend. I can't imagine going out on a weeknight and having to go to work the next day."

"Please, are you minding this one? We are no longer spring chickens," Ladun chimed in. "Those days of partying from Thursday to Sunday like it's two thousand and four are long gone! And none of us can keep up with Tami. Besides we are employees, she's an entrepreneur! When you are the boss, I guess you can work when you feel like it. I, on the other hand, hate my God-forsaken new job," she groaned.

"I wish that was the case," Tami sighed. "At least you are getting a steady salary. I'll admit when I first started this entrepreneurship journey it was because I didn't want to answer to anyone. I wanted to be my own boss, call the shots, work in my own time."

"Ah! My own time!" Ladun sighed. "Words I may never hear again because of that witch at work, Belema. You guys I miss waking up at ten in the morning. I wish I was my own boss."

Lara and Zuri laughed.

Zuri gave her an amused look. "Ladun! Being your own boss is not about waking up at ten. You just need to find purpose in your work, babe. I personally think you haven't given that job a chance. I've met Belema and she's not that bad."

"Exactly," Lara said. "I've told her she needs to change her perspective. She's just waking up and attending work. Her mind and soul are not there."

"*Abeg*, leave me," Ladun said as she rolled her eyes playfully. "Which one is attending work again?"

"Trust me I learnt the hard way," Tami said. "Waking up at ten became skipping work a lot because it was just a hobby, but even you guys have to admit that I've changed. I've been busting my ass in the past year to build this business. Still, I feel like I must be making all the wrong decisions because I can't seem to catch a break. Every time I think I'm taking a leap forward a ton of bricks come tumbling down."

They all nodded their heads in agreement. Tami had really turned a corner and now spent her time constantly implementing new ideas to grow her business. In fact, Irawo was now easily a top ten Nigerian fashion brand, as soon as she decided to focus on it more and actually do the work, her star began to truly shine. Brides wanted her to design their wedding dresses, celebrities wanted her creations so they could stand out on the red carpet. Everybody was after Irawo if her three hundred thousand followers on Instagram and multitude of global customers were anything to go by.

"Oh, honey. You are doing well. These things take time," Zuri said.

"She's right, you just have to be patient," Adesuwa said. "But what exactly is the issue, dear. How can we help?"

"It just feels like I'm failing at every turn. If it's not the generator that breaks down, then customers are not paying. Maybe I should just give it up because this business is not for me."

Sympathetic, Zuri's tone softened. "Now you are being dramatic, Tam. I know I said take it easy, but nothing can be that bad, it's just business and everyone makes mistakes. You just have to dissect the problem and look at what went wrong. What you could have done better and do your best to improve going forward."

"I wish it were that easy!" Tami said. "My accountant just told me that we have no cash! And let's just say after this, the 'Bank of Daddy' will be closed for a while."

"Your dad has always supported all your endeavours, Tami," Zuri laughed. "He's not going to stop now!"

"Trust me, he is definitely going to stop supporting my business financially," Tami said. "He told me categorically that if he didn't see any profits from this last one million he gave me that would be his last contribution to my 'hobby'. There's a huge demand for my work, especially on social media but for some reason, I'm just not seeing the profit. I don't know what to do anymore!"

"Guurrrlll! It's not easy. Entrepreneurship is tough but I'm sure you'll figure it out," Adesuwa said. "Maybe you should talk to someone. A consultant?"

"Don't worry, jo! You've come this far." Lara said. "You'll figure it out. In fact, I know one business coach. He's really good. I'll send you his number."

"Thanks, babe," Tami said. "I'd appreciate that. I need all the help I can get."
"Meanwhile, I have gist," Lara whispered conspiratorially.

"O ya, spill!" Zuri leaned in to hear more. "Is it about a man?"

"New toaster?" Ladun asked.

"Not exactly," Lara tore a piece of bread and dipped into the olive oil on the table. "Remember that guy, Deji Suleman. The one I met at the OTC in Houston, like three years ago?"

"The billionaire that turned out to be married?" Adesuwa asked.

"Yup! That one. He came to the funeral and gave me a cheque for five million naira."

"Ah! Stop it!" Tami squealed. "You are lying! Just like that?"

"Erm, Tami. He's a billionaire," Adesuwa said. "That's not a big deal for him. The real question is what does he want in return?"

"Madam, calm down," Ladun said. "It's her mother's funeral. It isn't out of place for him to give her money towards it. Must he want something?"

"Well to be fair he used to fancy her, So there's a real possibility he wants something," Tami said.
"But let's give him the benefit of the doubt."

Zuri chuckled.

"Those funeral costs were not a joke," Lara sighed. "His generosity was not unwelcome."

"Just be careful, *sha*, Lara," Adesuwa continued. "These men always want something in return. Remember that he's married."

The girls' attention turned to Sam as he came to the table carrying a tray with decadent chocolate desserts they hadn't ordered.

"Compliments of Chef," he announced as he presented the treats with a flourish.

All the girls mouthed their thanks to the chef as he waved his back. He always treated them like rock stars every time they visited.

****

Zuri

The room was freezing cold. Zuri opened her eyes slowly and for the first few seconds, she wasn't quite sure where she was. The white blinds and the grey sofa in the corner felt familiar but it certainly wasn't her home. It took her brain a few seconds to adjust then she realised she was in Lara's house. As she threw the duvet back, she saw that Lara's side of the bed was empty.

She must have gotten up earlier, Zuri thought, as she tried to find her bedroom slippers so she could walk around the house to find Lara. As she walked down the hallway, she admired the artwork that lined the walls. Lara always had such a good eye for art, they always seemed like random pieces she had picked up over the years, but they always came together so nicely. She favoured modern African contemporary art and even her favourite galleries Terra Kulture and Rele Art Gallery had her on speed dial, so they could tell her when they had new collections.

As she approached Lara's living room, she heard soft sobs.

"Hey, babe." Lara started, jerking her face up at the sound of Zuri's soft voice. "Are you okay?"

Zuri had spent a few days at Lara's apartment precisely because of moments like this. She had been worried about what was going on beneath Lara's steely exterior. To an outsider, Lara seemed fine and was getting on with it, but Zuri knew her friend. She had been dealing with a lot it and was bound to take a toll. Even if she didn't open up or talk about her feelings Zuri wanted her to feel like she had her back.

Zuri had never seen Lara this broken. Lara was the friend you went to when you wanted advice about most things, relationships, money, et cetera. But for the first time, Zuri wondered just how Lara handled the financial responsibilities that came with being a daughter, sister, and the breadwinner of her family.

She didn't even have anything close to Lara's obligations and the fear of not being able to pay her bills almost crippled her, so she couldn't even begin to imagine what her friend was feeling.

"I'm fine, just trying to figure some things out," Lara looked up from her phone and tried to wipe the tears streaming down her face.

"What's wrong? You look seriously upset." Zuri probed. "Are you thinking about your mum again? Talk to me. Is it the bills?"

"Chai Zuri, calm down!" Lara snapped. "You are being dramatic. Yes, it's partly the bills but at this precise moment I just got some disappointing news."

"Lara, I'm just trying to help," Zuri said softly, taking no offence.

"Sorry darling, I'm just a little irritated and quite frankly frustrated!" Lara said as she put her face in the palms of her hands in despair.

"Talk to me," Zuri said, as she soothingly rubbed Lara's back.

"I don't know how I'm going to raise the cash I need to pay off all this debt with no source of income." She straightened her back and then slumped right back into the sofa. "I've been to a hundred interviews, but I can't seem to find a job. The companies that want me can't pay and the companies I want, don't want me. I just got another email now which was basically a polite rejection. Zuri, I'm just tired."

"Girl, you'll find something soon," Zuri said reassuringly. "You still have more interviews lined up, your resume is in the hands of some very influential people. There's hope, you just have to keep pushing."

"I know, I know," Lara said, "but every time I look at these bills, especially the ones from the funeral, I kick myself because I don't know how I allowed my relatives who don't feed me manipulate and pressure me into having this elaborate funeral."

"Man! The worst part is they've now gone back to their lives and left you holding the bag," Zuri said. "Anyway, what has passed has passed but honestly, Lara, you need to make sure this doesn't happen again because you remind me of my mother."

"What do you mean?" Lara asked, confused.

"Hmmm. My mum is financially responsible in every other way, but family members and their sob stories are her kryptonite. She made a lot of money in her life but succumbing to the pressure of constantly being everybody's problem solver kept her broke. She ran all her businesses successfully but when I think about all the assets she could be living off now if she hadn't spent all her savings paying other people's children's school fees, hospital bills etc. And the annoying part is sometimes she did it to the detriment of her own finances by going into debt. It makes me so angry because when we fell on hard times, we had no one to run to. All the people she had helped couldn't help her. I'm just saying you need to be careful."

"You know what?" "I can't even argue," Lara laughed brittlely. "Because I allowed them to emotionally blackmail me into this whale of a bill. Now I am jobless none of my relatives are in a position to help."

"Do you have anything else you can sell in the meantime? Land, perhaps?"

"I tried to sell off a piece of land I've owned for years in the Badore – Ajah axis, but none of my real estate agents have been able to find buyers. It's been three months now and it's not looking promising. All the prospects that we've gotten have come with one story or the other. It's either they don't have the money complete and want to pay in instalments or they are waiting on a loan from a bank to come through. It's exhausting!" She began sobbing again.

"Lara, try to calm down. I know it's not the same thing, but I went through this a little over a year ago, remember? Even if I didn't have your assets or your income, and my bills seem trivial compared to what you have on your plate, I understand how you feel! It's like your whole world is sinking and you have no control."

"Precisely. That's exactly how I feel, and I'm crippled by fear! Zuri what am I going to do? How am I going to solve this mess?"

"One step at a time, babe. One step at a time. I think I should set up a meeting with Omosede. She's good at things like this."

"Actually, that sounds like a good idea," Lara said looking up.

"But first things first," Zuri said earnestly, as she held on to her friend's hand. "Lara, you are one of the strongest people I know, so don't let fear overcome you. Panicking is literally the worst thing you can do. You need to sit down and write down everything you have that's of value and their estimated worth, all your assets, everything you owe, all your debt and the estimated value. Let's even see if we can negotiate some of it down. This way we have a true picture of your financial health before you go and meet Omosede."

Lara looked at her friend. She was grateful. "Thank you for being here. Thank you for insisting even though I was being stubborn about being alone."

"You know I *gatchu!*" Zuri said playfully, as she pulled Lara into a side hug.

I can't believe this is my life right now but I'm so grateful for my friends, Lara thought. Zuri, Tami, Adesuwa and Ladun were always there for her no matter what. They had held her hand through her mum's illness and even the madness of the funeral. It was funny, her mum always said the true test of friendship was when bad things happened. She always insisted that it wasn't about who you hung out with, went to parties with or enjoyed yourself with, true friends mourn with you when you are mourning and celebrate your successes when you are celebrating. Lara always argued with her that it wasn't that serious but in death, she could finally agree with her.

But she knew she had to soldier up—it was make-or-break time.

SMART MONEY LESSON:
FINANCIAL ABUSE IS A THING!

Financial abuse is typically defined as unauthorised use and control of a person's money, property, or other valuables. It usually occurs between two intimate partners. Sometimes it's subtle, with the perpetrator gradually taking control over bank accounts and financial transactions using manipulation and emotional abuse as tools but other times it can be obvious, violent, and threatening.

Adesuwa is an educated, strong woman in the workplace but when it comes to her marriage she comes across as weak because of how she allows her husband Soji to "finesse" her when it comes to money. In her case, even though she is financially prudent, she goes into debt over her husband's bad choices and condones his unauthorised access to her income to spend on frivolities.

Her response to his behaviour is mostly underpinned by certain cultural mores and pressures, the 'Your husband is the head of your household, you shouldn't question him' rhetoric. There's an expectation for women to be understanding and accept behaviour that can jeopardise the present and future financial wellbeing of the family.

This sort of covert financial abuse can play out in several scenarios. For example, women who have become secret female breadwinners but still have no control over their finances because their husbands control the spending and resists "giving" his partner control over the money she earns. There is a thin line between being a supportive spouse, willing to pick up the slack when a partner loses their job or goes through a hard time in business and being used for your financial resources. This can go both ways; women who are financially abusive obtain access to their partners' finances which may lead to the unauthorised use of credit cards, misappropriation of assets, etc.

Another insidious form of financial abuse we don't discuss but reigns supreme in Africa is the financial abuse from relatives. In the first book 'The Smart Money Woman,' we touch lightly on the fact that Lara may earn a lot but is cost-burdened by her family members. Although, it is not an uncommon story in Nigeria for people who feel indebted to their families to put themselves in financial harm to cater to their relative's needs, this form of financial abuse really hit home when I went on a book tour across Africa.

From Tanzania, Kenya, Ghana to South Africa, many women strongly identified with Lara's predicament. In South Africa, they call it 'the black tax'. I heard first-hand accounts of women who were first-generation university graduates post-apartheid, who get their first jobs and are burdened to take out loans and credit cards to then repay their family for making sacrifices for their education, by paying for their current lifestyle expenses. The dilemma here is that these women feel a responsibility towards their families, now that they have means but the consequences are that they put themselves in severe debt even before they have a chance to climb the career ladder.

These unwise decisions have implications, as it reduces their ability to build assets that can protect their financial future and can frustrate their day to day working life because they are forced to live from paycheque to paycheque.

We are Africans, so family is important and any well-brought-up child has a desire to make their family proud by supporting them financially, especially in cases where the family has made sacrifices for them to get where they are.

There is a sense of responsibility and sometimes guilt. Many African millennials find themselves in situations where there are no limits to the proportion of their income that goes their family and as such, they begin to pay for their families' wants instead of needs. Consequently, they end up with no savings, financial safety net, or assets to fall back on in the event that they lose their source of income.

Lara could have had a simpler funeral, but a toxic combination of her sense of duty and her family's emotional manipulation put her in an unnecessary financial situation. This became worse when she lost her job and had no relatives to turn to.

It's important to that we put on our own oxygen masks before we help others because money in your account does not always mean you can afford to give. Sometimes short-term thinking leads to long term consequences. The truth is simple: You are not required to set yourself on fire to keep other people warm.

EXERCISE:

1. Track how much of your income has gone towards meeting the needs of relatives in the last 12 months.

2. Compare the value of your generosity to relatives to the value of your savings and investments within the same period.

3. Set spending limits for giving, then create a budget that allocates your limited resources effectively. For example, I earn ?100,000 a month, therefore I will make a commitment to put 15 per cent of my income towards assisting family and friends.

4. Set personal guidelines for yourself for what kind of requests are eligible for your financial assistance.

5. Create an eligibility checklist with questions that pertain to your lifestyle and belief system. These are examples but feel free to add your own.

   a. Is this request a want or a need?
   b. Is this request contributing to an asset that will help to generate a future income or is it towards an expense or a liability?
   c. Is this request life-threatening? For example, required for medical care?
   d. Is it time-bound? Or do I have more time to plan towards this request?
   e. Will giving financial assistance at this time jeopardise my ability to pay my own bills and cover necessities such as rent, electricity etc.?
   f. Am I separating my emotions from logic while making this decision?

6. It is not always possible, but make an effort to give in a way that helps the beneficiaries to generate their own income so they are not dependents forever. E.g. money towards education, learning a skill or towards starting a business.

7. If you can afford it or save towards it, set up a revolving fund for family members. A pool of cash, specific members of the family can tap into when they want to start a business. With specific guidelines about how much each person can access, for how long, how business plans are approved, and the maximum period required to pay back. This way the fund can replenish itself every time family members pay back and family members can keep each other accountable for paying back because if one person doesn't pay back it affects another's ability to draw from the funds. This system gives family members an opportunity to fund their ideas instead of relying on one or two persons within the family for financial assistance repeatedly. It may not be easy because of varying personalities and attitudes to money but if done right, it works.

8. Financial assistance for medical reasons is a top request from family members in Africa. If you are a breadwinner that has to deal with these requests regularly, it might be advisable to set up medical insurance with a Health Maintenance Organization (HMO) for your extended family members, as this might be a cheaper way to deal with small medical emergencies.

CHAPTER 3

RESTRUCTURING THE BUSINESS

Tami

Tami stood in the middle of her atelier in full crisis mode. The worst thing that could possibly happen a fortnight before one of the busiest Lagos wedding weekends, aside from the atelier catching actual fire had happened—two out of her three tailors had quit!

No notice.
No sorry.
No goodbye.

They had just collected their salaries and not shown up for work. This was a nightmare! She had two brides and about eight bridesmaids to fit alongside *aso ebi* for at least eight wedding guests.

At this point, she wasn't sure which outfits had been completed or which outfits had even been started. All she could see was her least qualified tailor's confused face, the tailor's assistant Basirat hopping in a corner whimpering '*E gbami*! Ha! What we are we going to do?!' over and over again instead of being proactive.

Tami closed her eyes for a few seconds grinding teeth and resisting mightily the urge to slap some sense into the girl. She was so angry. Angry at how disloyal they had been but mostly mad at herself because she should have known better. They had both worked with her for more than a year, and it had lulled her into a false sense of security.

Her thoughts were interrupted by the sound of her phone ringing. It was Zuri. In the middle of a mini-meltdown earlier that morning, she'd texted Zuri, who'd been in a meeting, then sent a text to their group chat. Three hours post cry-fest, she was calmer but still with no solution.

"Hi, Zuri."

"Oh, thank God! You sound calmer." Zuri's relief poured through the phone.

"Anyways, good news first. I called the two tailors I use in case of emergencies. Remember those young boys that live on my street? They have agreed to be your machinists for the next two weeks. I've sent them transportation money and your address. They are on their way. You can negotiate with them when they get there."

"Oh my goodness! Thank you so much, babe. You are the best!"

"Also, Lara says she got the number for an agent who can get you a pattern cutter to work as a contract worker in the meantime, so check your phone. She's in a meeting but she says she loves you and you should calm down."

"Besties come through! You would laugh if you saw me right now. I'm standing in the middle of the atelier just being a hot mess! I haven't made a single decision since I got off the phone with you and the two *dokpemus* I have here are also just staring at me, clueless. Zuri, honestly, I just want to go back home and crawl under my covers and maybe summon the energy to deal with this tomorrow."

Zuri cracked up. "Don't do that, my love. Trust me, you can do this. By the way, I didn't get the full gist of what happened."

Tami took a deep breath, walked out of the atelier and into her tiny office.

"That Bekeme girl poached my tailors!" Tami groused. "I got to work this morning and noticed that two of them weren't in. I thought they were running late, but two hours into the day they were still not at work, so I started calling and sending messages. No response. Then I noticed my third tailor, Gabriel, looking at me suspiciously and so I knew something was up. I grilled him, and he spilt the beans."

Tami gave a rundown on what Gabriel had said and that the two staff members had collected money on the pretexts of a sick child and suddenly pregnant wife. "Like, I'm weak for these people. Why tell such extreme lies?"

"Who does that? Put sickness on your child because you want to lie? Bekeme must be paying oil and gas money!" Zuri commiserated.

"Ahhh! Wait for it! The salary difference is fifteen thousand. I mean, to avoid this drama I would have happily increased their salaries, but that's the thing with these people. There was no communication. I had no idea they were not happy."

"But did you call Bekeme to confront her? You guys are friendly, *abi*?"

"Confront her, *ke*? There's nothing she would love more. She's probably watching to see if I can recover from this blow. This is why I like to keep these industry people at arm's length. At best she's a frenemy I say hello to at events and maybe take the odd Instagram picture with."

Zuri laughed. "Do you remember that makeup artist, Wana, whose two best hands left to set up their own thing, after apparently stealing from her and poaching her clients? You see I expect that from Nigerian staff but the part I don't understand is the friends and clients who then go to the traitors' new store to patronise them under the guise of, 'It is cheaper' BS. The thing is most of them are entrepreneurs who run their own business, so they have staff. You know that their decision would be a lot different if they put themselves in Wana's shoes."

Tami frantically typed an email to yet another customer informing them of a slight change to their next appointment date as she listened to the misfortunes of Wana as told by Zuri.

"Man! That thing blew my mind, oh. At the time, I wondered how her business would cope because she had been training those girls for years and I heard a lot of her clients ported. At first I was like, 'But they are not slaves, now. It's okay for them to go and start their own thing.' Then I heard they stole from her. Nobody says they have to work for her forever, but how you leave is extremely important. The ironic thing is they'll probably soon figure out that running their own business is not beans," Zuri ended with a sigh.

"You know!" Tami agreed. "It's not beans at all! I'm not going to let this throw me. Bekeme will probably lose those tailors the same way she got them. It's going to be difficult to get new tailors and train them. Again."

"My dear, it's not easy! You just have to roll with the punches. Doing business in Nigeria is tough, especially when dealing with staff. The other day I interviewed someone who had a computer studies degree with no real-life experience with an actual computer."

Zuri launched into a tirade about the ills of the Nigerian educational system, so-called graduates with degrees but no actual education and the chaos it causes for employers.

"They are so focused on the certificates that they forget the actual learning. I figured it out when she couldn't do basic things with Excel, and sadly I wasn't even fazed because I am so used to these inconsistencies. When I hire these days, I focus on the people with the best attitude and training potential, so I cannot even imagine what it's like for you dealing with tailors, who have even less education." Zuri ended her rant and took a deep breath.

Tami sighed. "Girl! I don't even know. I'm just going to focus on the *gbese* in front of me now. I'll be sleeping in the office this weekend, at this rate."

"One step at a time babe, one step at a time," Zuri soothed as she got off the phone.

****

Lara

Lara glanced at the bouquet of pink roses that had been delivered that morning from her favourite florist in Lagos, RF Gardens. The flowers had come with a note from Deji Suleman.

Congratulations on your new job! Let's celebrate. Have dinner with me, his note read.

This guy is persistent, Lara thought.

Since the funeral, besides the large cheque he had written to offset some of her mother's funeral costs, there had been a series of thoughtful gifts sent to her house and office. They ranged from expensive jewellery—a Van Cleef & Arpels bracelet, which cost upwards of three thousand dollars with a note that said, *Lara, you deserve beautiful things*—to food from Salma, her favourite lunch place in Victoria Island. The note said he had seen on Instagram that she was a regular there, which made her smile.

The week before she had also received a flower arrangement at home with a note from Diamond and Pearls Travels saying *All-expense paid trip anywhere courtesy of DS.* When she called him to say thank you, he said she deserved a break after everything she had been through with her mother's illness and subsequent death.

Until now, Deji had not asked for anything in return, but she wasn't a child; his generosity would not come without a price. Even though he hadn't said or done anything specific, she was sure this was all a ploy to get her to date him which would have been lovely if he wasn't very married. The expensive gifts were lovely, but she didn't let them get to her head because Deji was a very wealthy guy; he could afford such largesse, and his bank account wouldn't even feel a pinch.

Lara's thoughts were interrupted by a soft knock on her door.

"Come in," she called.

It was Amaka, her assistant. "Sorry, ma. MD just called an impromptu meeting in the conference room for senior management staff," Amaka informed her quietly.

"For what time?" Lara queried.

"Now, ma," Amaka responded. "Some of the other VPs are already there."

"Okay, I'll be right there." Lara rose from behind her desk and smoothed her white Style Temple pantsuit. She had chosen this slightly edgy ensemble because these days, she needed a boost to cope with her new work schedule.

After months of interviewing and sending her resume throughout her network, she had finally found a job she was excited about. She had taken a business development role at a boutique indigenous company, Oasis Oil and Gas.

It was ironic that despite all the interviews she'd attended, her ideal job fell into her lap quite by chance after speaking up during a session at an industry conference she had participated in with a former colleague. Her now boss, Pere, had been speaking on the panel and, impressed by her insightful questions, had asked to talk to her during the lunch break where they had set up a meeting for the following week.

She got the job on the spot. It had meant a significant pay cut from her previous role as well as a change from oil trading to business development, but she was excited about her career prospects.

As she walked into the conference room, she tried to hide her nervousness behind a smile. She found a seat next to the MD's chair at the head of the table and closest to the door, trying to gauge the temperature of the room. Was this a good or bad news meeting?

"Good morning Ladies and gentlemen," Pere boomed, announcing his presence as he strode theatrically into the room.

Lara was amused by the dramatics of it all. Pere would have had a great career in acting if he hadn't made so much money so early in his career. Still, his positive vibes seemed to indicate it was a good news meeting.

"I am pleased to announce that Oasis Oil and Gas won the bid for our very first deep offshore asset." The room erupted in applause. This was excellent news for everyone in the company. Six months ago, Oasis had bid seventy-five million dollars for a deep offshore asset which was a significant departure from their strictly onshore deals.

That's a huge win! Lara thought. When she'd started, she had been sceptical about whether they would be able to win because they had zero experience with drilling offshore and the competition had deeper pockets.

Which probably means we've paid too much for the asset, Lara suspected. *No matter. We can recoup the money down the line, depending on what we find. The important thing is we have the block.*

The excitement in the room was palpable, and everyone had broken into side conversations. She could hear Chinedum from finance telling Segun that their bonuses next year were bound to be *lit.*

Lara looked at one of two other women in a room mostly filled with men, which wasn't surprising when you got to this level of management in a company like Oasis. Starting out, women made up almost half the workforce, but as she climbed the ladder, she'd lost most of her female counterparts to marriage and babies. They had all gone on to start their own businesses or become fulltime housewives so that they had more time to raise their kids.

She wanted to ask a question but didn't want to dampen the mood. As bold as she was, she always felt like a duck when she was in a room like this—calm on the surface but feet paddling furiously underneath.

She was going to ask her question anyway. "Excuse me, sir."

Pere turned to face her and nodded for her to proceed with her question.

"I assume the plan is to farm out part of our equity in order to bring the block to production?"

"Yes," Pere replied noncommittally.

"I just wanted to know if we had any international partners on board yet, and what is the minimum work programme commitment the government requires on this asset?" Lara relaxed her face to present a pleasant exterior so she didn't look too abrasive.

"A sharpshooter," Pere replied, impressed. "Straight to business before we even have a chance to celebrate our small win."

She could hear murmurs around the room and could almost see some of the men giving each other knowing looks. She didn't care. She had learned early on in her career that no matter how intimidated she was, she needed to speak up when she had a valid contribution.

"For phase one, they've given us five years," Pere expounded on the details of the deal. "We have to acquire and interpret five hundred square kilometres of seismic, map out the subsurface, identify an optimal drilling location and drill one exploration well."

"Sounds fair." Lara jotted notes furiously as she tried to write down all the essential details.

Lara's phone notification light flashed. There were several messages from Tami and Zuri. They seemed to still be dealing with Tami's tailor emergency, but she couldn't leave the office right now. She had an idea she needed to run by her boss first, and if she didn't corner him as soon as the meeting was done, there was a real possibility that she would lose her shot because half the time the man was on a plane somewhere and she didn't have time to waste. This was her time to be aggressive about earning more.

****

Adesuwa

"Mummy please can you read it again," SJ said.

"No, darling! It's time for bed," Adesuwa refused gently. "It's past your bedtime, and you have school tomorrow."

"Pleeeease, mummy," SJ pouted, adding his adorable puppy eyes. As tempted as she was to give in, she knew that it would only lead to even more begging for extra time up. Besides, she was tired. It had been a long day at the office, and she still had to have a difficult conversation with Soji before she went to bed.

As she tucked SJ into under the covers and switched off his lights, she heard Soji's footsteps on the stairs. He was back from whatever he had done that day—they both knew it was not work.

She hadn't confronted him about the money he had spent at Cocoon from their joint account weeks ago. She had wanted to, but the thought of the emotional gymnastics that went into discussing money issues with Soji had stopped her. It wasn't worth the drama, she had thought at the time. Although her silence seemed to have translated to acceptance because Soji's spending from their joint account had gotten progressively worse and she was still too afraid to confront it, until today.

Today, she had done a tally of the amounts he had withdrawn over the last month and to her horror, they had been getting progressively larger. Thirty thousand here, fifty thousand there, and then payments that were for five hundred thousand and more, all unexplainable. She had tried to pay their rent the week before and the balance in the joint account meant she had to liquidate some stocks to meet the obligation. She was tired of living like this.

"Hello, my love," Soji said, as he threw his blazer and briefcase on the sofa in their bedroom.

"Good evening," Adesuwa's clipped response slid right over his head. It seemed like he was in a good mood.

"Ah ah, why are you squeezing your face?" Soji tried to sweet-talk her out of her mood.

"Am I?" Adesuwa asked coldly. "Sorry. I didn't mean to, I was just thinking."

"Thinking about what now?" Soji smirked. "You are always thinking!"

"Well, someone has to!" Adesuwa remarked as she folded clothes with sharp movements that betrayed her temper and put them in the wardrobe.

"What does that mean?" Soji said, sounding offended.

"It doesn't mean anything." Adesuwa reined in her anger, knowing that he could use this to pick a fight, and she needed him to be receptive.

"I made spaghetti Bolognese for dinner," Adesuwa volunteered. "Do you want to eat upstairs or downstairs?"

"Spaghetti again?" Soji complained. "I've told you I don't want to be eating carbs at night. Can't you make a salad or something?"

"I had to cut the grocery budget this week," Adesuwa explained. "There was no money for extras like lettuce and cheese."

"Fine," Soji said, sounding irritated. "Just set it up downstairs."

As she set a place for Soji, Adesuwa began to think of ways to discuss the issue with him, so it didn't turn it into a destructive argument.

I'll just keep my voice as calm as possible, Adesuwa thought.

The best thing was to stick to the facts and focus on what she wanted to gain from the conversation, which would be his changed behaviour. However, she knew that chances were that Soji would get defensive and hurl insults at her.

Soji walked down the stairs and settled into his chair at the dining table in silence. As Adesuwa served his dinner, she contemplated confronting him while he ate but decided he would be in a better mood after his meal.

"Soji. I wanted to talk to you about something." She watched him walk towards the television to set up his PlayStation 4.

"What?" He sounded distracted, irritated, and not the least bit interested in what she was trying to say. "Please, I just want to wind down for the day. I don't need drama tonight."

"It won't take long, but it's important," Adesuwa grimly continued.

Soji looked at her for a second, then went back to playing his game.

"It's about our finances," Adesuwa continued. "I'm worried that there's a lot of unexplained debits going out these days and it has made it hard to pay our bills."

"What unexplained debits?" Soji asked, still playing his game.

"Well, there was the one million at Cocoon the other week," Adesuwa said.

"I guess it's not so unexplained then," Soji said. Besides I told you I was celebrating closing a deal with my friends. Don't worry, I will pay you back the money when the deal pays out.

Responsible people usually wait till they've actually gotten the money before they start spending money they don't have to celebrate a deal that hasn't materialised yet, Adesuwa thought. However, she kept her thoughts to herself because she knew pointing this out to Soji would only add fuel to the fire.

"Okay there was another half a million, and I didn't—"

"Wait!" Soji said, cutting her off. "Is this your plan? To emasculate me by tracking everything I've spent in the last couple of months?"

"I'm not tracking you, Soji," Adesuwa retorted. "I'm just concerned. It's been a struggle to keep up with paying the bills. I just wanted us to talk about it and make adjustments."

"It's not your fault," Soji sneered. "It's because I've been going through a tough time. You want to rub it in my face. After, you will say we are a team. My money is our money, but when I spend it, you'll come to me with this crap. You are just manipulative! I don't need this!"

He grabbed his keys and stormed out of the house.

Adesuwa sat there in silence until she heard him drive through the gate.

Well, that was a disaster, she thought. She'd known he would throw a fit to evade her questions, find a way to make his bad behaviour her fault. But she was tired. She didn't know how much longer she could deal with this. However, she knew that tomorrow she would open a separate account and put her money there. Soji couldn't keep spending money he did not earn on things that were irrelevant to the family's wellbeing.

****

Tami

It was the constant pings from her phone that startled her out of deep sleep.

Ooo-oh! It's too early for this! Tami thought as she reached for her phone. It had been a really long week. The crisis with her tailors had really messed with her production timelines. Even with the contract tailors Zuri and Lara had hooked her up with, things were still tight.

She hadn't slept for more than four hours since Thursday because she had to stay in the studio to supervise and make sure everything was perfect. They'd barely made their deadline, but she was just grateful they fulfilled all their orders just in time. But all she wanted now was sleep.

I can't believe I forgot to put my phone on vibrate.

It must be a client because none of her friends were crazy enough to call her at this time unless it was an emergency. She squinted blearily at her phone screen and saw a bunch of Instagram mentions and WhatsApp messages.

What has happened now?

The only time she got mentions like this was when it was her birthday or when a huge celebrity had worn her dress, and all the blogs carried it.

CELEBRITY FASHION DESIGNER, TAMI OF IRAWO DESTROYS BRIDE'S WEDDING

She jerked fully awake and jack-knifed out of bed.

Oh my God, oh my God, oh my God!

This was a disaster. The story in the blogs read that after a bride had paid half a million naira to Tami for a custom-made dress, the dress had ripped at the back while she was on the dance floor with her husband because it was made of cheap fabric!

She looked at the photos on the post. There was a photo of herself on the left side and a photo of a distraught bride on the right. It turned out to be Amaka, her bride from weeks ago, who kept changing the design and fabric of her dress up until two days before the wedding. Tami remembered her weight had also fluctuated north from the time she had commissioned the dress till the night before the event. Tami was in shock because no one complained to her and the wedding was weeks ago. Why now?

They were dragging her in the comment section. Comments ranged from 'All you people that want to use big-name designers, they are just deceiving you, they'll use cheap fabric then charge you an arm and a leg', 'Other customers also complained', to some people even calling her an *ashawo*! The vitriol poured in post after post.

Her thoughts were interrupted by an incoming call from Zuri.

"Babe. Just saw the mess on Instagram?" Zuri said. "Are you okay?"

Tami sobbed.

****

Tami

It had been a long week. Between pulling out all the stops trying to sort out the scandal *and* the production crisis she was dealing with, Tami was beyond frustrated. She was losing money left, right, and centre. Clients were cancelling their orders, some had asked for a refund. She was in survival mode, putting out fires daily, but she knew that could only work in the short term. She needed a long-term plan if Irawo had any chance of survival.

As she put her bag on the bed and changed to her flat slippers, she glanced at her watch—it read a few minutes past eight. She was exhausted and was really looking forward to unwinding by watching a few episodes of 'Billions', a Showtime series she had become obsessed with, and going to bed early. No luck, though. Her mum was waiting for her, and she knew no conversation with her mother would be swift. She resolved to give her short and sweet answers so she could at least keep the conversation to a twenty-minute maximum.

"Hey, Mama!" Tami said as she walked towards her mum, who was behind the stove stirring a pot of stew. She wrapped her arms around her mother, her fingers interlocking round the older woman's gently rounded tummy. Tami's head sank into her mother's back as she took in that scent that reminded her of home—a mix of her mother's favourite Estée Lauder scent, one she had been wearing since the 1980s, combined with the herbs and spices she was using to cook her infamous red stew.

"Tammmii!" her mum squealed with delight. "It feels like I haven't seen you all week. Are you running away from your mother or are we quarrelling?"

"Ah ah, Mummy! How? Can one run away from their best friend, the sugar in my tea?" Tami teased.

"*Wayo* girl! Go, *jo!*" Mama Tami laughed as she turned around to give Tami a proper hug.

It had been a tough couple of weeks and Tami had hardly been home. Trying to resolve the crisis with her tailors and fulfil her customers' orders meant a lot of late nights and early mornings. This was the first time she had been back home before her parents were in bed.

"It was a hard week, Mama. You know what I've been going through with my business," Tami whined in a sing-song baby voice.

"Your father has been looking for you. He says you have been avoiding his phone calls and sending him text messages that you'll call him back but never do, and that you'll see him at home, but we know how that has panned out."

Tami's felt dread creep over her. With all her problems at work, she had been avoiding her father and the row they were sure to have over Irawo and its continual losses. She knew her dad was probably the best person to give her advice, but she also felt like he would never see her as anything more than his little girl who was playing at business. To be fair, she had given him reason to think that way in the first few years of business because she had never really taken the whole thing seriously until eighteen months ago.

These days her talks with her dad were painful. Although she had been working really hard to grow her business so Irawo was no longer dependent on his handouts, all her strategies seemed to be failing at this point. She couldn't bear the disappointment he tried to hide in his voice but showed so clearly in his eyes.

"He is in his study! Go and greet him," Mama Tami instructed sternly, interrupting her daughter's thoughts.

She made the sign of the cross as she knocked on the door of his study. She loved her dad but more than anything and she hated to feel like she was disappointing him.

"Daddy! its Tami," she said tentatively.

"Come in," her dad called.

"Hello, Papa." She gave her dad a hug before she sat opposite him.

"I'm glad you finally made an appearance," he chided. "Gallivanting around Lagos, *abi*?"

"Not even!" Tami denied. "I have been steady hustling this week. I had to deal with so many different issues with my tailors; I almost lost all my customers because two of my tailors quit."

"Hustling, *ke*? Are you a drug dealer?" He looked slightly alarmed. "I've told you to stop calling yourself a hustler. It is so unladylike!"

Tami grinned at his old-school outrage. "Sorry, Daddy. I keep forgetting that you see the word differently. It's a generational thing."

"Madam, your generation cannot just redefine a word and give it their own meaning," he scoffed. "It is bad enough that I sent you to school to study engineering and you decided to be a fashion designer."

Tami stared at him blankly. She was tired of her father's constant reminder that she didn't decide to become an engineer and follow in his footsteps. She never had any interest in the course. She had just finished her degree to fulfil all righteousness.

"You are looking at me!" he groused.

"Daddy, I don't have much to say. Fashion is my passion, sir," Tami said. She always switched from 'papa' to 'sir' when she was feeling defensive in a conversation with her dad. He lectured her at least once a month, and no matter how many times they had the conversation, he remained unconvinced.

"Passion!" he spat the word out as though it was dirty. "You children of nowadays and your bullshit! Passion? Sewing clothes for socialites that won't pay!"

Tami wanted to roll her eyes but knew if her dad saw that he would answer with a dirty slap. That non-payment thing had happened once! A socialite had been trying to get out of paying for the *aso ebi* she had made for a wedding and Tami had made the mistake of sharing her frustration on the matter with her father. At the time he had been sympathetic but now he did not hesitate to throw it in her face when he wanted to make an argument for why she should apply for jobs at an oil and gas company.

"I am now convinced that you want to be hungry and poor and I'm done indulging this frivolous hobby!" he lectured. "When you are tired, you will go and get a job."

"Okay, Daddy," Tami soothed.

He wasn't having it. "Okay, *abi*? You wasted the school fees I paid and now you are wasting the millions I've given you for this Irawo nonsense. Seven years and I haven't seen you turn a profit! The business cannot even stand on its own without my money."

"I'm sorry, Daddy. I'm turning that around now. I admit the first five years I didn't really know what I was doing but in the last eighteen months I've really stepped up I promise," Tami pleaded.

"Hmm! That's what you said six months ago when you convinced me to give you another one million to restructure your business," he sneered.

"Am I wrong? How much profit did you make from the world-class fashion show you put on?" He mocked.

"None." Tami had the grace to look ashamed, but still, she deflected. "I made a loss. It wasn't my fault. Things just didn't go as planned, but I'm fixing it."

"Your passion has to feed you, my dear," his piercing stare was filled with frustration and annoyance. "If you were not living under my roof, eating my food, and basically getting pocket money to keep your business afloat, how would you survive? How would you pay rent? Live this lifestyle you love so much?"

"I don't know." Tami couldn't feel any lower. Why did he have to rub it in? It was bad enough she had to deal with haters in her industry, but it hurt to come home to this kind of criticism from her own father, who was supposed to believe in her more than anyone else.

Seeing the look of despair on her face, her father seemed to pause for a minute, as though to consider his next words carefully.

"Tami! I know it seems as though I am being hard on you, but it's for your own good. You are a highly intelligent girl! I love that about you, but with this fashion thing, it seems like you are wasting your life."

"Daddy! How can you say that? I am not. It is my passion, and I'm trying to make it profitable! These days you never even recognise my efforts!" Her frustration welled up and threatened to spill over. "I've been putting in so much work, and I've stayed the course instead of giving up! You should believe in me more than anyone else."

"Don't be silly. Of course I believe in you, Tami, but I have thrown millions of naira at the problem hoping you would figure it out. No matter how much money I give you, there doesn't seem to be any progress."

He stared at her intently.

"I'm afraid we've reached the point where we have to ask ourselves if this is the right course! Maybe you are not good enough at this to make money from it. In fact, let's be practical, how many Nigerian fashion designers have become millionaires? Tell me."

Tears started to well.

"There's no need to cry, Tami. I'm just giving you constructive criticism. I want you to succeed, and if we need to find another career path, I'd rather you do it sooner rather than later."

She was silent, and the tears were now streaming down her face profusely.

"This is business, Tami! Why do you have to get so emotional? This is definitely something you get from your mother," he scolded.

"In fact, this is Abeke two point oh!" He said as he shook his head. "Your mother is a lovely woman and a great wife, but I don't want you to repeat her mistakes in business. Unfortunately, history seems to be repeating itself with you. Me throwing money at a series of failed businesses started at your mother's whim that don't amount to anything but hobbies."

Her father got up and started pacing the room, pausing every so often to point and gesticulate.

"How much have I invested in your business in the last six-and-a-half years? Five million? Ten million naira? Do you know how many entrepreneurs would kill for the opportunity to gain access to capital of ten million interest-free?"

"I'm sorry to have disappointed you!" Tami sobbed as she listened to the lecture.

"No need to be sorry, Tami. I just wanted to let you know face to face that I will no longer be supporting your business financially. I put a roof over your head, feed you, and I have paid your school fees, which is the best any parent can do. From now on, you will have to figure things out by yourself."

SMART MONEY LESSON:
RUNNING A PROFITABLE BUSINESS

Social media has glamorised entrepreneurship, but the reality is that globally, it remains challenging. It can leave you broke, stressed, and questioning your sanity. In Africa, there is the added stress of operating while dealing failing infrastructure and limited access to capital—and all the other niceties that are available in better-developed countries. However, it can be a beautiful nightmare when it works, because difficulty and problems often equal opportunity, and we have plenty of all three here.

An entrepreneur finds a problem to solve that people will pay them for, for a profit. However, the road between idea and profit is littered with obstacles. Let's use Tami's business and the fashion industry in Nigeria to highlight a few mistakes entrepreneurs make.

The Business Model Is Broken
If you ask entrepreneurs in Africa why their business is struggling, three out of four are going to cite lack of capital as the issue. While this is sometimes true because money can solve a lot of issues, the truth is sometimes, the business model is broken.

A business model is a framework that helps you understand how the different activities within the business come together to create value. The entrepreneur may have figured out a problem to solve, but not how to make money from it. And, if your business model doesn't work, money won't solve the problem—it might even make it worse. A hundred-thousand-naira problem could quickly turn into a million-naira problem because cash was raised but the money was applied in a way that did not positively impact the bottom line.

In Tami's case, she got seed capital and subsequent funding from her father, but it has still not led to her business being profitable. This could be for a few reasons. One of which could be spending on a fashion show which is great in terms of branding and positioning but does not lead to sales. In the end, the question is what is the return on investment (ROI)?

In Nigeria, the fashion industry has grown tremendously, but this has not resulted in profit because the model is broken and there are big gaps in production and distribution. Let me explain: Internationally, one of the major reasons for a fashion show is to showcase the designer's collection to buyers who have large distribution networks. For example, buyers from Selfridges, Saks, Nordstrom, etc. send representatives to fashion shows. A buyer sees pieces within a collection they think they can sell and places orders for them (e.g. 100 pieces from a collection, 200 pieces for a design), which translates to revenue for designers.

Here, however, the fashion shows look great but there aren't many buyers; certainly not ones with significant purchasing power. In cases where an international buyer may be interested, many designers have no production plan to cope. Which means even though a buyer wants 100 pieces, the supply is simply not available due to issues of funding, poor planning, consistency in quality and sizing.

Production issues also come into play when it comes to the issue of influencer marketing. Ready-to-wear designers give clothes to celebrities to help generate sales because the idea is to convert the influencer's audience into customers. However, this strategy is usually not effective because of poor production planning.

For example, Toke Makinwa has two million followers and is a fashion influencer. Tami gives her an Irawo dress to wear to an event well-covered by the press. The pictures are reposted on several digital platforms, people want the dress, and the enquiries start rolling in. Customer A calls Tami to order the dress in a size 12. Tami says sorry we are out of stock, but we can make it for you within a week. Because the expectation is ready-to-wear, this frustrates the customer experience.

So, my question is, out of stock means out of what amount? 10 pieces, 20 pieces?

Although the worry many designers have is inventory risk, a better strategy would be producing 100 pieces. Give one piece to an influencer, you know can convert the audience into customers and have a ready supply of 99 pieces to sell when demand has been drummed up. Otherwise, a designer just ends up making free clothes for celebrities with no ROI aside from brand visibility.

Even on a retail level, the capacity for production and supply is an issue. Nigerian fashion designers have honed their customer acquisition strategy by showcasing their designs on platforms like Instagram. Like Tami, they have drummed up the demand that is required but do not have the supply or capacity to meet said demand, causing dissatisfaction and a backlash. This can be a good problem if operational efficiency is improved or a bad one if it continues to frustrate the customer experience and eventually tarnishes the brand they have built.

Vanity Metrics Versus Value

Social media is a huge driver for many SMEs. It has created a low-cost platform for businesses to increase their visibility and grow their brands. It is easy to get carried away by vanity metrics such as the number of followers on Instagram, number of likes per post, number of registered users or downloads. These are fantastic because they show signs of traction. However, it's important to distinguish between real metrics and vanity metrics because If you only track vanity metrics you can get a false sense of success. We must remember that there's a difference between customers and the people who like your posts on social media. Your customers are the people who pay for your goods and services and this is important to note because likes are great, but sales are what sustain a business.

Visibility is a currency, but again the real question is, how does it convert your audience to customers so that visibility leads to sales or generates revenue?

Customer Profile

Have you clearly defined your target audience? It's important to identify your ideal customer. Give them a name. Where does Sidi live? Where does she work? How much disposable income does she have? What does she do for fun? What other brands does she engage with? What are her pain points? Why are they buying your product? What problem does it solve for them? Sometimes we make the mistake of thinking people are buying a product purely for functional reasons but you must also ask yourself what are the emotional reasons people buy your product for and how can you leverage on that. So for example, a mobile phone can be a communication tool or a status symbol. Not knowing who you are targeting, why they are buying and their ability to purchase the products or services you create can affect whether your strategy will work or not. If you don't have an accurate picture of who your ideal customer is, it will be difficult to determine your customer acquisition strategy or a sales strategy. You may have a brand, but can you sell?

Accounting Systems

There are businesses that generate high revenues but are making a loss and the business owners don't realise it because they don't keep accurate records. Sometimes it is because they don't separate their personal finances from their business finances, and sometimes its because they rely on their bank balance and only start to probe when they are low on cash. This often leads to a decision to raise extra capital in the form of debt or equity to keep the business afloat but sometimes you don't need a loan, you need to organise your accounting system.

An accounting system captures your daily transactions and qualifies them, i.e., sales and expenses. Sometimes it is not even about having fancy accounting software. It could just be as simple as manually keeping track on an Excel sheet of what you've sold, where you've received cash in exchange for goods versus who owes you money for goods sold and who you owe (e.g. your suppliers who have given you raw materials on credit) and the cost of things you've paid for. It also helps with working capital management. It helps you determine when the money you owe is due and when you can expect payments you are owed. It is important to keep track because even when you introduce an accountant its easier to organise things.

Making Assumptions Instead of Interpreting Financial Statements to Make Decisions

Many businesses make the mistake of going through their day to day operations making assumptions instead of learning to interpret their financials to make decisions. Understanding your cash flow statement, balance sheet and profit and loss statement can help you identify strengths and weaknesses of the business to determine where changes need to be made.

Cash Flow Statement
Your cash flow statement is an analytical tool that tells you how the company has brought in cash and which expenses it has spent those funds on during a given period. It is important because even though a business has assets, its survival is dependent on its ability to cover its expenses in the short term. A business that consistently brings in more cash than it spends is considered healthy.

A cash flow statement is typically divided into three parts: cash from operations, cash from investing, and cash from financing. Cash from operations shows cash that has been generated from the company's core business transactions. Cash from investing shows money that comes from businesses outside of the company's core operations and cash from financing refers to cash from financing activities such as loans or equity investments.

Balance Sheet
A balance sheet represents a snapshot of the company's financial health at a certain point in time. Interpreting it can help you see if you have taken on too much short-term debt or if you have invested too much capital in inventory. It can also be another test for short-term liquidity and cash available for daily operations.

Profit and Loss Statement
A profit and loss statement measures a company's financial performance. Many businesses experience a lag between the time they provide a good or service and when they get paid, which could sometimes lead to your business having a healthy

balance sheet but be short on cash. Interpreting this statement can help you make decisions like set trade credit policies (i.e. customers that have credit with us must pay within 14 days) or can help you see that customers are not paying. It could also be useful in helping to measure return on assets and measure how much profit the company is generating for each dollar of assets.

Internal Processes
Many small businesses lack internal processes, and this often leads to a combination of loss in income and the business owner being a slave to the company. This creates a situation where, due to the owner's inability to delegate, nothing works without them being physically present. To build a business that can outlive you or even work without you being physically present, you need structures. You must create a system that breaks down tasks in every aspect of the business, production, marketing, distribution etc. From when you create a product or service to when the customer makes a payment.

If you are an employee you have a job. If you are self-employed you OWN a job, and a true business owner OWNS a system, where other people work for them, which means if you leave the business, it will still run without you and grow without you. This is the goal but most times we confuse self-employment with business ownership.

EXERCISE:

Map out your business model

- Which of your business activities are revenue-generating? Which ones generate the most revenue, and how can you amplify them?
- Which costs and expenses contribute directly to generating revenue?
- Map out internal processes for your business and identify the loopholes (CEOS need to put themselves in these two mind frames. If you were a customer, where would your experience with the business be frustrated? If you were a thief which loopholes provide an opportunity to steal?)
- Which indirect costs can you control or cut out?
- Build an ideal customer profile.
- Ensure you have up to date financial statements.
- Set monthly and quarterly profit goals.

CHAPTER 4 INTRAPRENEURSHIP

Ladun

"Okay. Now that we are all here, let's get started," Belema said.

As the meeting began, Ladun looked around the conference room. There were two other recruits from different teams—Dotun, the account manager that typically handled liquor brands, and Ibrahim, who was probably the best graphics designer in the creative team.

They both nodded and smiled their welcome. Ladun smiled back.

This should be interesting, she thought. She had never worked directly with either of them, but they seemed nice enough.

"I've put this team together because I just landed a new client and I want the campaign to go in a different direction than what we typically do at Taurus," Belema said. "It has to be epic! I have recruited you three because I need people who think differently from most people here."

She paused and looked around the room.

"Ladun!" Belema continued. "Last week you referenced the influencer marketing strategy employed by the South African Tourism Board, and even though Mrs Ebhonu shut you down, I liked the train of thought."

"Thank you, Belema," Ladun replied. "I appreciate that. I honestly think influencer marketing is the new wave, but no one else at Taurus seems to think so."

"No, I agree with you," Belema smiled. "Most of the management at Taurus don't realise it yet, but consumers have changed. Back in the day, all you needed was your logo and an advertising campaign that included TV commercials with models or the actor du jour, ads in print, and radio jingles to do the job. In 2019 though, people buy into stories, not logos. They don't care about the model that's showcasing a product or service. It is easier to convert them into customers when they buy into the stories of real people who are experiencing your brand. I love the idea of influencers for this new campaign. Even though I'm not quite sure about the conversion rate from audience to customer, I'm intrigued enough to want to try it out. I want the campaign for this new client to be experiential and they look like my best bet."

"Who's the new client, boss?" Dotun asked.

"The Hargrave group," Belema replied. "Heard of them?"

A chorus of noes emitted from the staff.

Belema laughed.

"They are a hotel group with a pan-African vision." She paced the room slowly as she delivered a brief rundown.

"In the last few years, they've renovated old boutique hotels by leaving what is spectacular about them and modernising the rest. They have hotels in Lagos, Abuja, Kigali, Accra, Nairobi, and Johannesburg. They recently renovated a beautiful hotel in Cape Town and are keen on the Nigerian market. They want their hotels to be the destination of choice when Nigerians travel to countries where Hargrave has interests. However, our focus in the next ninety days is showcasing the latest jewel in their crown—The Princeton Hotel and Spa. It is a five-star luxury hotel located near the V and A Waterfront in Cape Town, and it has beautiful views of the working harbour and Table Mountain. It also has a pool and top of the range spa treatments."

"So, guys. How do we sell this?" Belema challenged, propping one hip on the table.

"How have they launched their other hotels in the past?" Ibrahim asked.

"Good question," Belema responded. "They've typically gone the traditional route—put on a big event, circulate the pictures in print media, create a commercial, buy ad space on TV and radio to announce they have arrived."

"So why don't we just do that, then?" Dotun asked.

"Well, I only landed this account because I told them I would be able to deliver something different," Belema replied, not breaking a sweat. "Besides, we are not ruling out traditional media entirely, I just want an approach that will create an organic buzz that leads to real conversion."

"I see," Dotun said, sounding sceptical.

"What approach did you have in mind?" Ibrahim asked.

"Well, I was hoping we could use an influencer strategy," Belema explained. "Similar to what the South African Tourism Board employs when they take Nigerian and Ghanaian celebrities to South Africa and use them to experience all the delights the country has to offer."

"Interesting. How does that work exactly?" Ibrahim looked unsure.

"My own is that this sounds very expensive!" Dotun interjected. "South African Tourism Board is basically a government agency. Does Hargrave have that kind of marketing budget?"

"Hargrave has a twenty-million-naira budget," the challenge in Belema's voice was clear. "I'm sure we can make it work."

"Even then, the South African Tourism Board takes celebrities like Bolanle Olukanni, Idia Aisien, John Dumelo, Jackie Appiah, Orezi, and Emmanuel Ikubese. They are bungee jumping, riding in helicopters, going on safaris, and eating at fancy restaurants and they are there for about ten days," Dotun argued.

"Belema, they do so much. A twenty million naira budget—which I presume still includes regular ad buys for TV, radio and print—is not a lot," Dotun continued.

"Sorry, oh! I'm lost," Ibrahim chimed in. "How do you know the details of the activities they do when they get to South Africa? Are you friends with any of them, Dotun?"

"What?!" Ibrahim said as every head swivelled to stare at him in shock.

"Helloooo?! Instagram much?" Dotun responded.

"I am not on there, oh," Ibrahim said, straight-faced. "I guess I don't keep up with these things."

"You work in advertising and you are not on Instagram?" Belema said, amused. "There's so much wrong with that statement, but let's not even get into that now."

"I have a Twitter account, but that's about it," Ibrahim said. "I'm a private person. I'm not interested in taking selfies and sharing my life with the world."

"Instagram is not just about selfies, my dear," Belema replied. "But more importantly, it's our job to know how to use the different social media platforms so we can leverage them to advertise our client's products and services."

"Exactly!" Dotun said, rolling his eyes. "Anyway, I followed their last trip, and it looked like they had fun, and it definitely sold me on the whole South African experience, but I still think it's an expensive strategy to employ for a hotel."

"I want to hear less about what we can't do and more about how we can make this happen," Belema dismissed, trying to move the conversation forward.

"Ladun you haven't said much. Anything to add?" Belema prodded.

"Anything you decide is fine," Ladun replied.

"What does that mean exactly? I'm asking for your opinion, Ladun."

"Okay. I think the whole influencer marketing angle would definitely work for a hotel. I also agree with Dotun that the approach could be expensive, especially when you factor in the fees that these big influencers charge."

"Exactly!" Dotun said.

"Again! I want to hear less 'we can't' and more 'this is how we are going to it'," Belema was beginning to sound exasperated. "I thought I was bringing the best and the brightest together on this project, but so far, I am not impressed."

" Okay, I have a suggestion," Ladun offered.

Belema turned to face her. "I'm listening."

"What if we use a mix of influencers? Not necessarily A-list celebrities, but influencers who have a decent following and high engagement. That way, it would be cheaper, and we may not even have to pay influencer fees. They would just be happy to come on a five-star trip, and they could experience the hotel a week before its grand opening."

"But doesn't that defeat the whole purpose?" Dotun said. "Brands use celebrities for a reason. Bigger numbers mean bigger engagement and bigger conversion."

"Ladun?" Belema said, looking at Ladun, waiting for her to counter.

"Not necessarily!" Ladun became more animated as she thought through the possibilities. "You see, these days there are all kinds of influencers in different sectors who have become thought leaders in everything from cooking, raising children, personal finance, travel, and even medicine. They may not have entertainment-type numbers, but they have a high engagement with people who really listen to them. Besides, the majority of the people who follow the entertainers in Nigeria can't afford what we are selling. They'll like the pictures and comment but the real question, is are they the target audience our client is looking for?"

"I like where this is going," Belema mused.

"I think we need a more targeted approach," Ladun continued. "We can find influencers who have a decent following not necessarily a million followers on Instagram. Maybe start with a baseline of thirty thousand followers, but have consistent content and an engaged community that actually buys what they are selling."

"Like who?" Dotun said.

Ladun was blank for a second, and then it hit her.

"My friend Tami, for one. She's a fashion designer. She has about three hundred thousand followers on Instagram. I think she would be open to something like this."

"Okay! We're getting somewhere," Belema said as she looked at the time on her watch. "Ladun, I want you to come up with a dossier by Monday with a list of possible influencers, their profiles their numbers and why they would be a great fit. Once we've decided on who will work best, we can flesh out the plan."

"Dotun, talk to your guys," Belema continued. "See which brands would be willing to partner with us to sponsor some of the activities. Also, you need to get on the phone with airlines, let's get one of them on board to either cover the cost of the tickets or at least subsidise it."

"Yes, boss. I'll call South African Airways first," Dotun said. "I think they would be open to something like this." He stood up from his seat, ready to leave the meeting.

"*Oga* Ibrahim," Belema turned to the graphics designer. "Please figure out how Instagram works before our next meeting on Monday. You must get a feel of the platform so you can participate productively in these meetings."

"That's all for now, everyone," Belema said as she picked up her cell phone to check a message that had just come in.

"Ladun, please stay for a minute. I'd like to discuss something with you," Belema said.

"Sure," Ladun answered apprehensively.

Belema looked to where Ladun was seated and said, "You look worried. Don't worry, I don't bite. I just wanted to have a chat with you."

"Okay." Ladun grimaced. *Does this girl have a problem with me? She told me to join this new team, and I joined, no questions. Now the babe is singling me out. So irritating!*

"I think you need to speak up at meetings," Belema said. "I've noticed in quite a few meetings that you are mostly mute."

"Mute?" Ladun asked, offended. This girl was obviously trying to be rude.

What did she mean by mute? She thought. This was especially annoying because Belema was at least three years younger than she was. She was not her mate, and outside of this office, she wouldn't be able to speak to her in this manner. She was tired of trying to stomach all the snide remarks and blatant disrespect from people in this office who two years ago would have never been able to speak to her, not to talk of have the opportunity to ask her inane questions like why she was mute.

"Now, you look offended. I'm only trying to say I think you have a lot to contribute because the little you do say in meetings is smarter than most of the people in this office, but you back down too easily! As soon as someone disagrees with your suggestion, you retreat."

"I'm not offended," Ladun said, with a plastic smile. "Thank you for the feedback. I'll do my best to speak up," she said as she got up to leave the conference room.

"Lean in!" Belema called out cheerily as Ladun left the room.

****

Lara

"Is he having a meeting?" Lara asked Pere's assistant, a distracted Bisi obviously taking a personal phone call in the middle of the day.

"Ada, hold on," Bisi whispered into the phone. "No, ma. I think he's reviewing term sheets. Let me tell him you are here." She picked up the intercom.

"He says you can come in," Bisi said as she gestured towards the door.

Lara took a deep breath as she walked towards his office. She had been trying to get a meeting with him for weeks, but he had been in Switzerland finalising a trade agreement, and she didn't want to discuss what she had to say over the phone. She knew this was going to be a big ask and if she had any shot at getting a favourable response, it had to be a face-to-face meeting.

Her heart always skipped a beat when she entered Pere's office. The room spanned the length of the entire fifteenth floor; so big you could fit a two-bedroom apartment in the space. There was an intimidating mahogany desk that sat at the centre of the room and a sitting area with brown leather couches and a wood coffee table made from a section of a tree trunk that both sat on a tan goat hair rug. The sitting area and the well-stocked bar occupied the entire left side of the room. On the right side of his office, there was a dining table that sat eight, which sat below the gigantic chandelier and a bookshelf that covered the entire right wall. Pere's office smelled of money and was the epitome of old school luxury. The double floor to ceiling windows overlooked the Lagos Lagoon and brought in a light that softened the masculine textures.

"Madam, this one you have been looking for me the last couple of weeks and can't tell me what you want over the phone. Am I safe? Should I be scared?" Pere joked.

"Ah, no, sir. Scared, ke?" Lara laughed. "You know anything I bring to you that's good for Lara is also good for Oasis. Trust me, you are going to love this."

"Clearly, this is a money matter," Pere laughed as he closed his computer to give her his full attention. "I hope I can afford this proposition, Lara."

"Trust me, you can," Lara said. "It's really simple. I have a few leads and I'm pretty sure I can get us international partners for the RM24 in six months instead of twelve."

She said this with a confidence she didn't feel, but she knew Pere didn't respond to weakness or doubt. She had to show strength, even though she wasn't exactly sure how she was going to pull this off, seeing as she was still new to the role. Still, she needed him to agree to her terms first before she took on the challenge.

"Hmm. Sounds interesting," Pere said. "I would definitely like to start making money back on RM24 sooner rather than later."

"And you will," Lara said. "I have a few leads, and I'm floating the idea that we are willing to farm out fifty per cent of the equity. That way, we not only get about thirty-five million dollars back from the bid amount, but we will also still own fifty per cent of the well."

"And they'll provide financing for the drilling of the well as well as build local technical capacity?"

"Yes, sir."

"It sounds like a tight timeline, but of course I would be incredibly happy if you could make this happen. But I know you, Lara, what do you want in exchange?"

"Two per cent." Lara laid her cards on the table and looked her boss dead in the eye.

"Ah! Two per cent, Lara! Just carry gun! Madam, that's a lot of money."

"Yes, it's a lot of money I'll be saving you when you have a final agreement in six months instead of twelve. Plus, the terms I'm laying out mean we'll be making a profit even before we see one drop of oil. I'm asking for two per cent of the profits, sir! In the grand scheme of things, it's not that much, but it's enough to motivate my hustle!" She ended with a confident smile.

Pere looked at her assessingly. "Let's do one point five, and you have a deal."

"Okay, sir," Lara agreed.

"You know what I like about this?" Pere said. "It's based on performance! I don't have to worry about putting money in your pocket if you don't deliver." He stretched his hand out to shake on it.

Lara stood up and clasped his hand. "You'll have my agreement by the end of the week."

"Agreement?" Pere looked confused.

"Yes, sir. Let's put this in writing so there's no confusion when the money comes!" Lara said. She had gotten to know Pere reasonably well. He was a great guy, but when it came to money, she knew she had to protect herself before he had a change of heart. He could revise his interpretation of what had been discussed in this meeting.

"You are angry, oh," Pere laughed. "That's fine. Let your lawyer draw up the agreement and let me have a look before you send it to legal."

****

Zuri

Zuri stared at the message she had drafted to send to Olumide for the hundredth time. She had been going back and forth on whether or not to set a meeting to discuss a joint venture with Richmond developments.

After her conversation with Tsola, she had made several feeble attempts to convince Mr Tunde that they should find another piece of land for their development, but he had resisted. Teju and Obinna had second and third options, but she had to admit they were not as well suited for the development as the Sanni's land.

"I don't understand why you can't just call the Sanni you know," Mr Tunde had argued. "You said you had a prior relationship with them, and I was confident you would bring this home for us! What changed?"

"It's complicated," Zuri had muttered, but he had given her a look that said *get it done. No excuses.*

As she stared at her phone again, she decided it was best to call him instead.

"Zuriiiiiii, love of my life! The one that got away!" Olumide exclaimed as he picked up the phone. "To what do I owe this pleasure? *Abi,* you have broken up with your boyfriend?" He remarked cheekily.

"How are you doing, Olumide?" Zuri said as she rolled her eyes. She knew this was going to be a long road, trying to get him to work with Richmond while politely dodging his advances.

"No, I have not broken up with Tsola," Zuri said. "I'm calling about business. Business that will put money in both our pockets."

"That's too bad," Olumide responded. "But go on. What business are you bringing my way?"

Zuri spent the next thirty minutes explaining the situation with Richmond, then set a meeting for drinks the following week. She had tried to persuade him to set a lunchtime appointment, but he insisted on meeting after work hours because he was busy. Or so he claimed.

What can I do? She thought to herself. *I need something from him.*

****

Ladun

"Let me call you back," Bode said as he dropped the phone.

He peeked through the window and watched as his wife locked the doors of her Toyota Corolla then headed towards the front door. He smiled. It always amused him that after ten years of marriage, through the ups and downs, she still did it for him. He had never met another woman he was more attracted to than Ladun. He had always favoured full-figured women, but it wasn't just the curve of her waist or the way her hips moved when she walked. It was a combination of everything about her and the way her mind worked, blowing him away every single time.

It wasn't that she was a brainiac, it was something more practical... the way she was able to problem-solve even in tricky situations. He admired that she was quick on her feet in situations where most people would freeze, always bold, and would always come up with the most creative solutions. Weirdly, he had come to rely on her for that particular skill for both the little and big decisions they faced.

When his dad died and all the mayhem over his estate had begun, there was a voice in the back of his mind that consistently whispered, 'Ladun will leave you'. He had never voiced his fears, but he acknowledged that they were real because even though his wife was resilient, there was a part of him that doubted she would be able to deal with the financial upheaval in their lives.

The first time he met Ladun was at an end of year beach party his boy Kunle had thrown at Bode's family's beach house—nicknamed Eko Miami—located on a private island off the coast of Lagos. Guests could only get there by boat, it was a thirty-minute ride that took you to one of the most luxurious locations on this side of the Atlantic. The beach house had been one of his favourite properties owned by his family. Bohemian on the outside, it had three upscale bedrooms with ultra-modern facilities on the inside as well as an elevated infinity pool that overlooked the beach. Parties at the beach house were legendary! Only the best Lagos DJs, the champagne seemed unlimited, and outdoor activities included everything from quad bike riding and table tennis to kayaking and jet skiing, which usually kept guests there from ten in the morning to whenever the crowd gave up.

The first time he'd noticed her, she had been in conversation with a group of women when her laugh had drawn him in. He had turned around to see who it was when their gazes clashed.

Even then she was thick, with a killer hip-to-waist ratio. She had luscious dark skin that glistened in the sun, as though she had sat in a bath of *ori* before she left her house. He stared her down as he usually did when he wanted to signal to a girl that he fancied her and most girls looked away shyly, but not Ladun.

She had stared right back, and her eyes had had him completely arrested. Later on, he'd realised it some of the effect was due to the green contact lenses she'd worn but regardless, he had never met a more confident woman. It wasn't her clothes because she was dressed simply and even looked slightly out of place with the girls she came to the party with. Her confidence did not come from being the thinnest girl in the room with a four-thousand-dollar handbag or designer sunglasses. It was just something about the way she carried herself. Later that evening, he had tried to talk to her, but she dismissed him, leaving him stunned. She had not been rude, but it had been a polite brush off like he was not important, a feeling he was not used to. He was Bode Ashoni, good looking on the best of days and more importantly, he was an heir to the vast Ashoni Empire.

I mean, fine boys like us, na dem dey rush *us,* he had thought. His eyes followed her every move at the party, and it had taken him at least two weeks to find her number. No one in his social circle knew her because she had tagged along with a friend of a friend who worked in her office. When she finally agreed to go on a date with him, he felt like he was in high school again. He planned their first date with the precision of an experienced Casanova and the excitement of a sixteen-year-old boy.

Bode had been a bit shocked when he asked where he could pick her up, and she had sent an address in Ijesha. The thing was, most girls he dated were spoiled rich girls who lived on the Island. He had been on a few dates with girls who lived on the Mainland, but on the first couple of dates, they often sent him an address in Ikoyi or Lekki where they could be picked up. One girl who lived in Iyana Ipaja had even gone as far as to lie that she lived in Lekki Phase One. Eventually, he'd found out it was her friend's house. He didn't really care where she lived; he just thought less of her for lying about it. Ijesha was a bit out of the way, but it impressed him even more that she wasn't fronting about where she lived in the typical Lagos girl fashion.

He had borrowed his father's Mercedes and luckily his driver knew her area well, so her place hadn't been that difficult to find, being that those were not the days of a Nigeria-friendly Google maps.

He still remembered the red dress she wore like it was yesterday. It had hugged every curve on her body.

The babe is set, he'd thought at the time. In the car ride to their destination she had asked him where they were headed, and he'd replied it was a surprise as they drove on to the private tarmac where a few of Nigeria's wealthiest families parked their planes.

Ladun held his hand and said, "I'm not sure where we are going, but I don't own an international passport."

He had looked at her and smiled.

"Don't worry, you don't need it." He had been amused and even more impressed by her matter-of-fact statement.

His family owned a fractional share of a Gulfstream, and he had called ahead to make sure the pilot was on standby, and the plane was fuelled and ready to go. The jet was mainly available to him for work trips and the occasional holiday with the boys, so if his father found out about this tryst, he was going to kill him. Even for Bode, this was a frivolous expense but as he glanced at her, holding her hand and leading her up the aircraft steps, he knew it was going to be worth it.

"Good evening, Mr Ashoni," Captain Osa said, welcoming them aboard the aircraft. "We'll take off in twenty minutes," he continued as the stewardess led them to their seats.

As they settled down in the leather seats, he peered at Ladun trying to decipher if she was impressed, but he honestly couldn't tell. She had an expression on her face like she was amused, not impressed or excited just calm, not as though she experienced this every day but was amused and entertained by the prospect of the experience.

"So, are you a spy?" She smiled mischievously. "Or does the jet come with immigration privileges as well?"

He laughed. "You are hilarious! No, I'm not a spy, and the jet doesn't come with immigration privileges. Private jet or not, we must all show our *pali* when we fly internationally."

He paused and examined her face. "We are not flying anywhere, *per se*,"

Bode told her. "Just flying around the airspace for an hour and a half. I've ordered a meal from my favourite Italian restaurant in Lagos. It's a tiny hole in the wall in VI, it's not popular, but I love the food and the wine selection. I took the liberty of ordering for you. I hope that's okay? I would have called to ask your preference, but I didn't want to spoil the surprise."

"Thank you." Ladun looked pleased. "I can't believe you went through all this trouble for me."

"I like you."

"You can't like me, Bode. You don't know me," Ladun replied quietly.

"Well! I liked you enough to want to impress you at great cost to me because my father is definitely going to kill me when he finds out I took the plane out and wasted jet fuel on a date," Bode lamented.

Ladun laughed. "Yeah! He should kill you. This is a rather elaborate date for a woman you don't know. But I have to say I am impressed."

"Well, you'd better be."

He liked her.

She was quiet, but she'd looked at him so intently as though she was peering into his soul. He couldn't explain it, but just the way she looked at him turned his world upside down. It was funny, but that night he'd known she was going to be his wife.

As Ladun got to the top of the stairs, she found Bode sitting on the sofa. He was supposed to be watching the tennis that was on TV, but the sound was muted, and she could tell he wasn't watching, his mind seemingly far away.

"Hello, handsome!" She cooed as she kissed him on the lips, bringing him back to reality.

"Hey, babe!" Bode responded, raising his arm and reaching for her waist, drawing her closer from behind him.

"Which of your girlfriends were you daydreaming about?" Ladun teased.

"Hmm! Just reminiscing about one *correct* babe I met when I was twenty-five years old," Bode responded.

"She must have really been one hot babe, for you to still be thinking about her more than ten years later."

"I can't even lie, she was!" He said dramatically, staring into space as though he was trying to conjure up the image of her.

"That goddess waist was something else!"

He ducked as she punched him in the shoulder

"*O ga, oh,*" Ladun said exclaiming in Yoruba.

"You know how I feel about hips now," Bode said, mock seriously. "I basically stole my father's private jet to impress her on our first date."

"Ahhh! And Baba Ashoni did not kill you? You should have *kuku* married her, oh," Ladun teased.

"I did," He said, pulling her into his arms. "And it was the best decision I ever made. She changed my life forever."

"Really?" Ladun said softly as she placed her head between his shoulder and the nape of his neck.

She always wondered how he cradled her 200-pound body as if he was carrying feathers. Bode was muscular and tall but had a slim frame, and she was heavy.

"The thing is, I thought she was going to leave me," Bode whispered in her ear.

"Why?" Ladun said, confused. "Why would she leave you? You are the best husband in the world."

"Well, for starters, she married a billionaire's son, and now she's stuck with a guy that's not sure where his next paycheque will come from," Bode said.

Ladun raised her head to look him in the eye. "You are serious?" She said as she searched his face for a reaction. Was he joking or were these real fears?

Bode was silent.

Ladun lowered herself to the ground and knelt down between his thighs as she held his hands in hers. "Bode, is this how you really feel? You think I'm going to leave you?"

"The truth?" Bode replied. "Yes, sometimes."

"You think you can get rid of me, so easily?" Ladun teased, trying to make the situation lighter. "I'm from Ijesha, oh! That's where you met me, remember? I fell in love with a sweet guy who would do anything for me and my children! What more could a girl ask for?"

"You might be from Ijesha, but you got used to the trappings of billionaire life pretty quick," he laughed as his fingers pulled on her left cheek.

"Before, *nko!*" Ladun laughed as she eyed him up and down. "I'm a fast learner. Besides, even though I wasn't born rich, God made me for better things. I was not meant to suffer. He made me for enjoyment. *Abi,* you don't know the meaning of my name, *ni?*" She poked him in the ribs.

"*Oladuni mi,*" Bode said.

"Yesssss! That is me!" the words came out with an exaggerated Yoruba accent. "Bode, my name literally means 'wealth is sweet to have'. This situation is temporary, my love. Life has dealt us a blow, but we are still here, we are still young, and there is plenty of time to become billionaires. In the meantime, we just have to learn to adjust. Plus, I married the smartest Ashoni brother and all the moves you are making in the fintech space now are going to pay off!"

Bode looked at her with a big smile on his face.

"This woman, *ehn!* Are you shading my brothers?" He laughed.

"I didn't say anything, oh," Ladun laughed. "Besides, at this rate, we are going to have to rely solely on you to take us back to billionaire status because I hate my job! And today that Belema girl got on my nerves. It took everything for me not to give her a piece of my mind."

"How was work?" Bode asked sarcastically. Since Ladun started the job, she had complained bitterly about her co-workers and more recently, about the boss's daughter, Belema.

"Listen, Bode, the company sucks! They are stuck in how they used to do things twenty years ago. Meanwhile, we are in twenty nineteen!"

"Then share your concerns with them, love," Bode suggested as he had many times before.

"Do they listen?" Ladun said. "I've tried to explain to Mrs Ebhonu many times that the consumers we are trying to reach with our ad campaigns have changed. The way they consume content has changed, the type of content they connect with has changed, what influences them to try a product or service has changed," Ladun exclaimed. "But what do I know I'm just a reformed housewife!"

Bode chuckled. "Babe! But that's the point! You are their target audience. You used to personally consume some of the goods and services they are trying to sell, so you have good insight into the consumer's perspective."

"You would think so, but I'm tired of talking."

"What did Belema do to you today?"

"Ha! Madam Belema thinks she can just come in and turn the company around in five seconds. I mean, she formed a new team today to work on a new client she just landed and had to drag me into it, with no consideration for any of the other work I had on my plate."

"Why did she need a new team?" Bode asked.

"Ask me, oh! She said she wanted 'new thinking'," Ladun said, using air quotes to emphasise how silly she thought the prospect was. "She wants to launch an influencer campaign around this new hotel in Cape Town, that's looking to attract Nigerian customers."

"Sounds interesting. Haven't you been saying influencer marketing is the new wave? But the company would never go for it because they are too traditional in their thinking! This should be a good thing, no?"

Ladun glared at him. She had been married to this man for long enough to know when he was attempting to gently steer her in a particular direction, so she could see her situation from a different perspective.

"What are you trying to say, Bode? Just spit it out, jo! I can see what you are doing."

Bode Laughed. He didn't know why he bothered because she always caught him, but this was still a better approach because you couldn't force anything down Ladun's throat. You had to nudge her slowly until she came to the right conclusion.

"Well, I just think you have a flair for advertising and branding if you just gave it a chance. I worry that you are too worried about the internal politics and rigours of working a nine-to-five job instead of worrying about creating value."

Ladun sighed. "The question is, will they let me?"

"I know you hate to hear this, babe, but that's the wrong attitude! It doesn't matter what you think they'll let you do. You have to think about what your goals are and what problems you are helping your company solve on a daily basis. Trust me, working in the corporate world is just like running a business. The game is to convince people to do what you want by articulating the value you provide and convincing them to buy into it. Sometimes you are convincing customers, sometimes its other partners to work with you make something happen and other times its convincing investors to give you money to fund your ideas. In your case, it's getting the buy-in of your management on small ideas so that they allow you to execute bigger ones down the line."

"I guess you are right, but it's easier said than done, Bode."

Bode tapped the cushion next to him on the sofa and gestured for her to come and sit.

"I know it's hard, babe, but I know you can do this, my little problem solver," he told her bluntly, lifting her chin with his finger. "You just need to adjust your attitude. When it gets hard, most people think the key is to find another job or start their own business but the truth is, if your work ethic and follow-through is whack even in a job you hate, it's probably going to be whack in a new job or your own business because you haven't mastered the art of sucking it up and getting the job done."

Ladun smiled. She felt fortunate to have Bode as her partner in life; he knew just what to say to ginger her. All she felt was gratitude. Despite everything they had been through—the financial upheaval, the shame—their marriage had survived it all. If anything, it had even become stronger. In the ten years they had been together, they had had it relatively easy with a few minor disagreements over the years, but she had always felt like their love could withstand anything. The real test had come when Bode's father died. If she was honest, she had panicked a little in the beginning, but she had quickly shifted gears because Bode needed her, her children needed her, she couldn't afford to fall apart.

Maybe Bode was right. Maybe working on this Hargrave project with Belema was an opportunity to show top management what she was capable of delivering. Actually, if she was honest, a part of her needed to prove to herself that she could do this. She had been relying on the I'm-just-a-housewife-what-do-I-know-about-work line so she could deflect from what she was really terrified of—trying hard and failing.

I'll give it a shot! Let's see what happens.

SMART MONEY LESSON: INTRAPRENEURSHIP

As mentioned briefly in the first book 'The Smart Money Woman', there is a lot of conversation around the idea that if you want to be rich, you must become an entrepreneur. Not everyone is cut out to be an entrepreneur—if we all become our own bosses, who will the employees be?

Unemployment in Africa is high, so it's a welcome change that young people can create non-traditional avenues for income-generation. However, not everyone has the entrepreneurial know-how to build a team, develop structures, and ensure operational efficiency to help a business scale. We must start encouraging people to be entrepreneurial in their thinking even as a salaried employee. Those kinds of workers are value-driven, adopt critical-thinking methodologies, and use innovation to solve problems within the business.

Mark Zuckerberg may have had the idea for Facebook and founded the company but Sheryl Sandberg, Facebook's COO and author of 'Lean In: Women, Work, and the Will to Lead' has been instrumental in helping to build structures and scale the business. Not being the owner of the idea doesn't make her a less valuable employee. Being an employee doesn't always have to mean you will only earn a low or middle income. Dustin Moskovitz gave the example that if you joined Facebook as employee number one thousand, you would have made roughly twenty million dollars—a solid example of how helping to scale a business can line the pockets of employees as well.

Intrapreneurship is the implementation of start-up practices in large corporations to produce valued innovation. There's value in intrapreneurship and organisations need to start encouraging the entrepreneurial spirit of their employees within the company. People who innovate and contribute directly to the bottom line, especially in measurable ways should be paid more than people who just attend work.

You might be reading this as an employee who disagrees with the above sentiment because, in your experience, you work hard but don't necessarily have a commensurate income to show for it. Although this can happen a lot, especially in Africa, I'd like to ask that you consider some key points:

1. **Measurable Results**
   You don't get paid for the hour, you get paid for the value you bring to the hour. Now many of us tend to confuse effort with results. For example, Lagos traffic is legendary, and a typical employee can spend up to five hours commuting to work every day, and much as this is stressful, it does not directly contribute to the bottom line of a company. Which means an employer does not value it as much as they value activities that directly impact their profit margin. A business is a profit-seeking entity, and it's much easier to negotiate with an employer when you can measure your contribution to the bottom line.

   For example, an employee who can say, 'I brought in two corporate clients who contribute 30 per cent to our revenue every quarter' or one who can say, 'I work in an operational capacity but a process I created directly reduced costs by 30 per cent which improved our profit margin', ultimately has more bargaining power than an employee who says 'I work hard. I'm in the office from five in the morning to ten at night every day', but can't show measurable results. Sis, it could even be argued that you are in the office for that many hours because you are avoiding traffic or using free internet. It's not about how many hours you work; it is about measurable value.

2. **Specialisation**

It is crucial to develop a craft, a set of skills and expertise that you can hone over a lifetime. We get paid for the complexity of the problem that we solve—the more complex the problem, the higher an income you are able to command. For example, a general practice (GP) doctor gets paid less than a cardiologist. A GP spends up to eleven years gaining the required knowledge, but a cardiologist has to spend an extra decade on top of that. A bank teller has a different set of skills from an executive that structures transactions in the corporate finance department of the bank. This is not to say that we should make it a habit of piling up unnecessary certificates because there is a difference between acquiring the qualification just to say you have it and it being relevant to your career.

3. **Personal Branding as an Intrapreneur**
   Intrapreneurs often make the mistake of thinking that their personal brand is not important. However, the world has changed; everybody has a personal brand whether they build it intentionally or not. As an intrapreneur, what's your personal brand within your organisation? What do your boss and colleagues say about you when you are not in the room? Internally what are you known for? What tasks will your boss give you responsibility for because they trust you can run with it?

Understanding the answers to the questions can help you determine how to package yourself to amplify your strengths and target areas to improve on.

Many intrapreneurs tend to focus solely on improving on being good at what they do—great! Continuous learning is fundamental but you cannot simply put your head down and wait for recognition; you must be able to speak about your wins and achievements, taking rightful credit. In most organisations, the people who get promoted are not always the most skillful, they are the ones who not only have the skill but know how to make sure that decision-makers are aware of their contributions. They tend to have a voice and such they are seen first when opportunities arise.

Externally, your personal brand also matters. Now, I listened to a podcast recently that pointed out that if you don't take control of your narrative other people will do it for you because there's something called Google. Think about it, these days when you meet a person one of the first things you do is Google them, then try to find them on Instagram or LinkedIn, so you can figure out what they are about. Yes, social media might not give us an accurate picture of individual lives, but it provides us with a snapshot you can run with. The question is what do people see on the internet when they search for your name? What do you intentionally or unintentionally put out?

A strong personal brand that visibly demonstrates your work experience as an intrapreneur, your achievements, and how you are able to overcome challenges, ultimately speaks for you before you enter a room. This could make all the difference in your career trajectory. It could determine your next promotion or job opportunity.

One of my favourite examples of an intrapreneur with a strong personal brand is Bozoma Saint John because of how she owns her authenticity. She doesn't try to fit in—she owns everything that makes her unique and different from her blackness, to her hair and her personality and that's what makes her magical. She served as the head of global consumer marketing at Apple Music, the chief brand officer at Uber and is the current chief marketing officer at William Morris Endeavour.

There are probably plenty of branding executives and marketing officers of huge corporations who work really hard behind their cubicles, but the thing is we don't know their names. Now the thing is when companies are looking for a brand executive to help work on their brand, they'll probably see Bozoma first because of her strong personal brand. This is the difference between marketing and branding. With marketing, you have to go out to convince people to buy into your value, but with branding, you attract opportunities you may not have even known were available because you are a known quantity.

I once heard Bozoma speak at an event and talk about how she hasn't had to interview for a job in years because companies reach out to her to offer her positions. That is the power of personal branding.

Do you know the worldwide trends in your industry, global standards for what you do? Do you do research on what the equivalent of you does in a global company? Do you invest in building your hard and soft skills?

If you are a woman in a position of power in your organisation, you should make it your mission to foster environments that allow this kind of behaviour to thrive. It's good for employee retention and good for the businesses profit goals.

EXERCISE:

Negotiating your Compensation

1. **Create a Value Statement**
    Your value statement is the script you use to explain your resume conversationally. This is not about the list of tasks you've been assigned at a job, but how you compellingly summarise your accomplishments—particularly relevant when haggling for your promotion or transitioning to a new job. It should spell out the value you bring to the company and the impact your contributions have had to the bottom line, using measurable examples that make you irreplaceable. Value is NOT entitlement; Value is NOT deceiving yourself or inflating your accomplishments. It's an honest assessment of your contributions in one sexy value-add package.

2. **Formulate a strategy to communicate your value**
    Sometimes we fail when negotiating because even though we know our worth, we don't know how to express it in a way that convinces the other party that they need to pay for said value. You could be the most helpful, most hardworking employee but nobody does anything in business from an altruistic perspective. So what does your employer consider valuable? You need to make an employer see a direct correlation between your contributions and the company's bottom line. Your value statement should act as your sales script when you are pitching. It's a script that should be practised and refined regularly so that you are ready whenever the opportunity presents itself.

3. **What Does Compensation Mean to You?**
    Here's a little secret about working in a nine-to-five job:

compensation does not have to be purely cash remuneration. You need to define what fair compensation for your time looks like for you. Sometimes it's about training opportunities, flexible work hours, and in a start-up or small company, it could also be equity. If the business cannot afford to pay you market value for your contributions, it is worth having a conversation about getting compensated for your labour in part ownership of the business instead.

4. Research What Your Peers Are Earning in the Industry

You can talk about what you deserve all you want, but your compensation also depends on what a company can afford to pay you based on their size and balance sheet. Do your research about what industry standards are. In Africa however, this is slightly tricky because the information is not as readily available and even with primary research, Africans tend to be secretive when it comes to disclosing how much they earn. It is worth making friends with people in comparable positions within your industry to find out what they take home in income because knowledge is power, and sharing information with your peers can help you establish your baseline.

5. Make a Plan to Deal With Rejection

Rejection happens to even the most successful people and despite knowing your value. The key is to fail forward. Getting feedback on why you got the "no" this time and incorporating your learnings the next time you go in to make a request. Just like with sales or raising capital sometimes it takes twenty noes before you get the yes, so don't let noes discourage you—learn and move.

CHAPTER 5

LIVING YOUR BEST LIFE

Zuri

Zuri sat at a table by the window, her attention split between watching the door at Z Kitchen waiting for Banke Gbadebo to arrive and checking her emails. They had initially been casual acquaintances but Femi, Banke's husband, had been doing a lot of business with Tsola in the last year and they had found themselves socialising a lot more.

It was a Saturday afternoon, and they were supposedly meeting for a late lunch to discuss Banke's new business venture. Truth be told, she was really here to show off her new Hermès Birkin bag to someone. Anyone. It had arrived the week before, and she didn't feel great talking about it with her girls after Lara scolded her for her spending months before. It was a naughty purchase, but she couldn't help it. She loved everything about the bag and how superior it made her feel, and only Banke could understand. Plus she had gotten it at a bargain price from Banke's personal shopper.

"Oh my God! You've launched it already! I love it!" Banke squealed as she dropped a brown Togo leather Birkin on the chair in between them, then signalled a waiter to bring a menu. "It's gorgeous! I love that you chose the red, it definitely compliments your skin tone."

She ordered a starter and a main dish and asked that they be quick about it. "Don't judge me. I'm starving," Banke laughed as she placed her order. "It's been such a long day at the store, getting the workmen to do everything to my specifications. It's so exhausting dealing with these people, and I can't wait till the store is finally ready. We will shake Lagos!"

"I'm sure it'll turn out great," Zuri said supportively. "You sound like you have it all under control, so why did you need my help?" She asked.

"Darling, I mostly wanted to catch up," Banke replied. "But I also needed help sussing out the competition, and I know you know a lot of them because of your work with the short-stay apartments."

"Oh, you mean which interior designers do good work?" Zuri replied. "Well, I love DO II designs, and their diffusion line Icora is stunning! I could reel off a list of some other good ones, but to be honest, the person you should for sure try to get a meeting with is Aunty Ifeyinwa Ighodalo. I'm still amazed by how she's been able to create such high-quality furniture at such affordable prices."

"Meeting, ke?" Banke scoffed. "Please, just give me the lowdown. I don't want my competition to see me coming."

"Uhm, Aunty Ify is not your competition, darling," Zuri laughed. "Do you know how long she's been in this business for? I meant, get a meeting to ask for advice."

Banke had recently decided to start a luxury interior design business, she said would give luxury living in Lagos a new face. She found it amusing that Banke was constantly starting new businesses without much evidence of success in the previous ones. According to her, she was a serial entrepreneur, but the fact is, she never stuck with any of her ideas long enough to truly call them a business. She got excited in the initial stages and would talk about nothing else for months but as soon as it got difficult, she dropped it like roasted plantain fresh off the grill. Then she would go mute until she decided to start the next business.

Zuri honestly wondered how Femi was funding these ventures. Since she'd known Banke, she had started a fashion label, bakery, catering business, crèche, and most recently, a mummy and me website that combined advice with selling children's clothes and toys. It was hard to keep up.

"My love, a little advice," Banke said, interrupting Zuri's thoughts. "I hope you don't think it's too presumptuous of me, but we are friends, so it'll be terrible if I didn't tell you the truth. I think it's rather tacky for you to be wearing a Marc by Marc Jacobs watch when you are carrying this beautiful Birkin bag."

Zuri was taken aback for a few seconds as she stared at her wrist. "I love this watch," she said, "and besides, I can't afford a Rolex right now."

"Girl, you can't be rolling with me and talking like a broke person," Banke mocked. "What do you mean you can't afford it?"?

"Do you know how much a Rolex is, madam? Besides, I've been overspending lately. Lara will kill me if she hears. Zuri laughed. She's already been riding me about my expensive purchases.

"But Lara is broke, darling!" Banke said cattily. "Didn't that company she works for just fold up? Not to gossip, but I heard that she's had trouble finding a new job. Is that who you really want to be taking advice from? She's probably jea—"

"Banke, let me stop you right there. I've always taken advice from Lara and I always will," Zuri said, trying but failing to keep her disgust in check. "Yes, the company she worked for folded up, but did they also tell you that she's found a better job? She's far from broke, darling. Lara is one of the smartest people I know, and she always lands on her feet. Besides Banke, the difference between you and Lara is that Lara is spending her own money and has assets to back it up. You, honey, can't say the same because you spend your husband's money and have no assets of your own to speak of."

"Please don't insult me, oh" Banke responded in shock. "I was only giving you some helpful advice. Anyway, if you can't afford it yourself then we need to work on getting Tsola to buy you one," she said, changing the subject.

"Again, I can't afford it, Banke, and I certainly can't ask Tsola to buy me one," Zuri replied, rolling her eyes.

Wake up, oh! You can't have a boyfriend as wealthy as Tsola and be saying things like that, darling. You can afford anything he can afford, and I assure you, Tsola Preware can afford a Rolex."

"Tsola may be able to afford it, but I certainly don't feel comfortable asking him to buy me one," Zuri pushed back. "If he gives it to me as a gift, great, but I wouldn't ask for something like that."

"You are so naïve," Banke laughed. "I have so much to teach you about affluence. You are on the arm of one of the wealthiest bachelors in Lagos. You had better look the part."

As the conversation veered on to other things, Zuri couldn't help feeling a little insecure. She realised that every time she hung out with Banke, all they seemed to talk about was how to purchase the next symbol of social status. Banke tended to criticise everything she owned; if it wasn't her car, it was her choice of a designer bag. According to Banke, Gucci was now so pedestrian that it would never be worn by anyone with taste.

"OMG! You'll die when I show you the Cartier bracelet I got. It's divine. I saw Sarah Langa wearing it on Instagram, and I just had to get it." The boasting and posing went on and on.

Zuri stretched her lips in a polite smile. "It's lovely."

She listened to Banke ramble on about her taste, her friends, her newest big-ticket purchase, she realised that the woman had become a caricature of what she saw on Instagram—lost people following every trend on the horizon. Zuri reckoned Banke's fixation with the accumulation of "things" and preoccupation with social status was a distraction from something else that was going on deep within.

I love beautiful things, Zuri thought to herself, *but I can't let myself be around people who pressure me into buying things before I can afford them.*

It was a slippery slope, and she could now see that her association with Banke had slowly led her down a path that was triggering old money habits.

****

Zuri

It had been a long day hanging out with Banke. Late lunch had turned into drinks, but now she was exhausted. Zuri whisked her Hair by Kuku wig off and flung it on the bed with a massive sigh of relief. She caught a glance of herself in the mirror and laughed at how she had transformed from slay queen to Ekaette in five seconds. The cornrows beneath her wig needed to be washed and redone. Tsola always mocked her to no end when he saw her cornrows anytime she took her hair off in front of him. He called her his 'village girl', and she always acted like she was offended, but secretly she loved that they had gotten that comfortable with each other and that they could be themselves.

As she contemplated taking a shower before she got into bed, her phone began to ring. It was ten at night, and she wasn't in the mood to talk to anyone this night unless it was Tsola.

She looked at her phone. It was her mum.

She knew the consequences of ignoring her mother's phone calls would be incessant WhatsApp messages saying things like, 'Have you abandoned your mother? You are now too busy to speak to me, *abi*? After I carried you for ten months!' and so on and so forth. Her mother was the most dramatic person she knew aside from Tami. She still wasn't quite sure who was in first place.

"Hello, Mummy! Good evening," Zuri greeted.

"My dear, good evening, oh! How are you?" Mama Zuri responded, sighing dramatically.

"What has happened again?" Zuri wondered. Her mother always "acted drama" just before she lamented about something.

"Mummy, is everything okay?" Zuri asked.

"Yes, oh, my daughter. Everything is okay in Jesus mighty name," Mama Zuri replied, exhaling slowly again. "How come it took you so long to pick up? Are you with Tsola?"

"No, Mummy, I'm not," Zuri replied as she rolled her eyes.

"Ah ah, I hope you guys are not quarrelling?" Mama Zuri said anxiously.

"No mummy, we are not!" Zuri exclaimed. This woman was a trip and a half. In one breath she would say 'No sex before marriage, oh, Zuri!' in another breath she would be asking funny questions. With Tsola at this time of the night? If she had said yes, she was sure it would have elicited another kind of sermon.

"Mummy, how is everything? How is Benin?" She asked in an attempt to change the subject before the conversation inevitably turned to marriage, and she didn't have power for that one this night.

"Hmmm!" her mother said with yet another deep sigh. "We are managing, my daughter, but things are tight."

"Mummy, what happened again. I sent you two hundred thousand naira last month. You can't possibly be broke again," Zuri lectured.

"Did I tell you I'm broke?" Mama Zuri said, raising her voice. "I'm not broke in Jesus name. Please don't speak negative things into my life. I just said we are managing."

Zuri knew better than to argue with her mother. It was already ten fifteen, and they still hadn't gotten to the koko of the matter yet. This could take all night if she decided to argue.

"Okay, Mummy. Sorry," Zuri said. "What happened to the money?"

"I used it to sow seed in church," Mama Zuri replied without a hint of remorse.

Zuri looked at her phone. Was this woman for real? She thought.

Her mother had asked her for money last month, saying that she didn't have enough to pay the bills, so Zuri sent her money to pay the bills as well as some extra cash. Now she was saying she used it to sow a seed in church! A seed was typically Nigerian Christian speak for giving money to the church or pastor and tying it to an expectation from God. It was the modern-day equivalent of the sacrifices mentioned in the bible.

"Mummy, which seed again?" Zuri said. "How many seeds do you plan to sow this year?" She asked sarcastically.

"Is there a limit? Fear God, oh, Zuri. Fear God! Besides, it's because of you I'm sowing all these seeds."

"Because of me?" Zuri asked, but in her mind, she knew the answer to this question.

"Yes, *now*! So that Tsola will propose quickly. Or do you think I'm playing here! You people have been dating for over a year now! It's time to get married! I know the Lord will help him make up his mind soon," Mama Zuri proclaimed.

"Mummy! God's time is the best. You can't keep sowing seeds on top of this marriage thing and expecting me to send you money to replace it," Zuri sighed. "As soon as the words came out of her mouth, she knew she had made a mistake."

"*Eh hen*! Zuri!" Her mother complained. "So you are now telling me what to do? It is not your fault. Everything I am doing is to protect your future, so you will finally settle down with a good man and have children. But instead of you to thank me, you are busy complaining. *Osalobua*! What did I do to deserve such an ungrateful child? In fact, Zuri, you are selfish! You don't want me to see my grandchildren, *abi!*" She was wailing gusto, and the guilt trip had been turned up to eleven.

Zuri tried not to laugh out loud. It was incredible how her mother could go from zero to a hundred in five seconds. She should be nominated for an Oscar for her dramatic performances.

"Mummy, I'm sorry!" Zuri said as she reached for her computer to transfer one hundred thousand naira to her mother's account. "You know I didn't mean it like that," she said, still trying to placate her.

"I have heard! You never mean it like that," Mama Zuri lectured sarcastically.

"Mummy, have you seen the alert?" Zuri asked. Her mother was silent, but she heard the alert come through on her mother's end, and her mother's "Humph" and begrudging thanks told Zuri she'd put out the fire—at least for now.

Zuri ended the call with her mum and was scrolling down her Instagram feed when a DM from Banke popped up with pictures of Rolex watches. Zuri rolled her eyes but had started to scroll through the images when she got a debit alert showing the transfer she had just completed, as well as her account balance. Looking at her balance, Zuri winced. At the rate at which she was spending these days, despite a twenty per cent increase in her monthly salary coupled with the bonuses she was raking in each month, she might soon find herself in a situation where she was over her head again.

In the past couple of months, she typically avoided looking at her account balance because in the back of her mind she knew she was spending a little too rapidly and something in her didn't want to confront her habit. She just wanted to focus on her growing success at work and enjoy the benefits of it. Two years ago, when she had suggested that the Richmond create a new division that would provide an online platform matching the firm's clients with property, interior designers and furniture makers and furniture stores. She had been a little fearful at the beginning because not only would she be the youngest division head at the company, she was launching an online platform that most of the other top management players were sceptical about.

In no time, it became popular with clients across the world and also helped to ease new customer acquisition because clients referred more people and everyone wanted the ease of not having to worry about interior design or furniture after they had leased or bought a property.

With its growing popularity, Zuri decided to institute a subscription model that brought in a substantial income, as well as the fees and commission they gained from vendors for the privilege of having access to Richmond's clientele. Her department had become a rising star at Richmond, a fact that Zuri was very proud of.

She stared at her account balance again.

She had been avoiding it, but it was time to do some quick math to assess where she was with her personal finances because it would be a pity to have come this far in her career with no real monetary value to show for it. After her financial mishap two years ago where she had found herself in debt, unable to fix her car or pay her rent, she had become really good with sticking to a spending plan because there was a real fear of being in that position again.

Although she stayed consistent with dividing her income into three parts—seventy per cent towards her living expenses, twenty per cent towards her long-term financial goals and ten per cent towards her short-term financial goals. She realised that ever since she had started receiving the extra money from her salary increase and bonus, she was splurging a lot more.

She had made a promise to herself that she would put some of the extra income towards her long-term savings, but each month came, and she procrastinated and made excuses.

She would convince herself that she had worked hard so she deserved to splurge as much as she could but the whole year had gone by and she had done nothing to increase her savings, while her consumption had gone up.

She did a quick calculation. Her income had increased by about fifty-three per cent if she included her bonuses with her base salary increase, but her net worth had definitely not increased by that same percentage. Zuri began to think through all the high-priced items she had bought in the last few months.

She needed to make an appointment to see Omosede and get back on track after that last splurge.

****

Ladun

As she brought the wine out of the fridge to serve Lara and Zuri, she couldn't help but feel self-conscious about how different it all was. There was a time she had a home filled with live-in staff to serve the guests, but she put the thought out of her mind because she knew her friends didn't care. It was sweet how they made it a point to come and hang out with her at home; she knew it was a bit of a trek to this part of town from Lekki Phase One.

Bode had gone to pick the kids up from his mum's and taken them for ice-cream so she could have time to bond with her friends which was nice, because she needed the time to hang out.

"I have a bottle of red and a bottle of white," Ladun demonstrated one in each hand. "Who wants what?" She asked, as she placed the bottles on the table and brought out the glasses.

"*Abeg*, anyone," Lara said practically gasping between sputters of laughter. "Please sit down you have to hear what Zuri just told me. Did you know that Banke had the nerve to tell her that it was tacky for her to wear her Marc Jacobs watch with the Birkin bag? And that she doesn't roll with broke people. Wonders shall never cease."

"*Haba*, Lara!" Zuri laughed. "She didn't say all that exactly. She just said, 'You shouldn't say you can't afford stuff because it makes you sound broke.'"

"*Abeg*! Same difference," Lara said, rolling her eyes. "Don't even try to defend her."

"Tami gave me the tea the other day," Ladun shook her head, amused. "I was just waiting for Zuri to tell me how she reacted. Imagine the guts you have to have to say that to someone. I mean, even if you like luxury, there's nothing wrong with pairing it with affordable stuff. Is she in your pocket?"

"Hmm, she said I should ask Tsola to buy it for me," Zuri told them.

"That girl has no manners," Lara sighed. "Style is not about designer up and down. You either have it or you don't. Banke is one of those people that knows the price of everything but the value of nothing. She should be less worried about acquiring things and more worried about who she is becoming and the kind of contributions she was making to the world."

"Actually, I don't blame her. It is Zuri I blame because I don't understand this new friendship," Lara hissed. "Listen, we all like nice things, but you can't be making friends with people because of what they own or how they look. It's ridiculous! You now went to buy Birkin bag that we both know you really can't afford because you wanted to impress your new 'friend'," she said sarcastically. "*No go do pass yourself, oh!*"

"And *this* is exactly why I didn't want to tell you," Zuri said, rolling her eyes. "Small gist now you've started throwing shade." She was glad she hadn't bothered bringing up the unkind things Banke had said about Lara. Besides, she had already defended her, so at this point, it was moot.

"Okay, okay. Sorry," Lara teased. "I'm only half-joking. Let me not be a hypocrite. I own a Birkin, so I'm not saying there's anything wrong with buying one. I just don't want you to regress, and I can see old habits creeping in. Plus, friendship is about shared values, enjoying each other's company and helping each other become the best version of ourselves. What it's not? Being friends with people because of what they own! I can't imagine picking my friends because of what they can afford or not afford, that is just a set up for rubbish."

"I hear you, babe," Zuri sighed as she poured herself a glass of wine. "I'll admit I got a little carried away. I saw small extra money and my eye opened. I love the bag, but now I feel a little guilty because even though buying didn't break the bank, I know I'm not yet at a place in my life where I've truly earned it."

"See, the thing is, you can't let people like Banke or others on Instagram pressure you into doing things your income can't support because you might see their purchases, but you can't see their pockets or the assets they own. Banke has a rich husband that supports her, so while you are trying to keep up with her, ask yourself if you can keep up with her husband's net worth and the source of income that supports their lifestyle." Lara doled out the tough love with great advice.

"True," Zuri said. "I hear you but let's be real, it's tough to wait till you get *rich* rich to start living your best life. That could mean I'll be fifty before I can start living my real life, doing the things I want to do. Travel all over the world, go shopping without looking at price tags, eating at fancy restaurants, the works!"

"Right?" Ladun laughed. "I'm with you on that one. You only live once, man."

"Trust me I get it, I struggle too," Lara said. "However, I've learned that it's about balance. Real wealth is when your passive income can pay for your lifestyle needs. When you get to the point where the rental income you get from the property you own or dividends from your stock portfolio can pay for your trips to London or your shopping sprees. However, we all know it takes time to get there, and it's not easy to wait. It's also about defining what your best life looks like today, given your current income."

"*Abeg*! When it comes to defining your best life, we all want the same things, fancy cars, nice houses, exotic travel, and shopping sprees," Ladun laughed. "But *na money kill am*!"

"Exactly!" Zuri agreed.

"Yeah on the surface, maybe!" Lara mused. "But when you drill down to the basics, we all have different preferences. Think about it, if I put all the things you just mentioned on a list of things to splurge on and asked you to rearrange them in terms of a scale of preference, all our lists would look different."

"You are right, *sha*," Zuri laughed. "Bags and shoes would probably be at the top my splurge list, but Tami would put clothes above car, shoes, house, travel, and food. You would probably put travel above everything else because you love to see the world and you would be content with looking nice but not having anything new in your wardrobe."

"You know what?" Ladun said. "Me, I still want everything on my list, but if I had to choose only one thing to splurge on it would probably be living in a nice house, followed by driving a high-end car. Those are the things I miss the most. I don't even miss buying clothes that much. It was a nice-to-have, but I miss the way my old house was decorated and having live-in staff to take care of things."

"And Adesuwa's list would probably look similar to Ladun's, to be honest," Lara laughed. "But my point is, it's about balance. Yes, it'll take time to get *rich* rich but in the meantime it's about defining what your best life looks like right now, prioritising the things that truly bring you joy, being realistic about how much of it your current income can support and not letting Instagram or the Banke's of the world dictate your purchases."

"Can I confess something? Sometimes I see something on Instagram, and

I'm tempted to buy it not because I truly like it but because of what it signifies if I own it too," Zuri confided. "I know I'm the spendaholic in the group but am I alone in this or does this happen to anyone else?"

"My dear, we are all tempted by fancy things," Ladun laughed. "In the past, I've been known to buy a pair of shoes or Brazilian hair I didn't even like just because it was on-trend at the time, but I guess now I'm learning that it's about discipline. It's okay to be tempted as long as I don't act on it."

"Yup!" Lara chimed in, "I'm just saying we have to hold ourselves accountable for our financial health. You can have nice things, but not all at once. As you've bought Birkin now, you understand that you have to soak garri for a few months, *abi*? No more splurges for a while. It's time to double the hustle."

Zuri agreed emphatically. "I'm telling you, oh. I need to work harder and invest more aggressively because my real life is expensive. Your girl has expensive taste."

"At least you are being honest with yourself," Ladun said, sounding just a little down. "When I think about my former life, I wish I had put money in assets that would be generating an income for me now because things are so tight. I haven't been this broke since before I met Bode, but it is well, *sha*. I just wish I wasn't too poor to start investing, but I don't earn nearly enough to even think about putting anything aside."

"Babe, just start!" Zuri encouraged. "I've been there. It sucks at first, but you have to start putting something aside *small small* and concentrate on finding more ways to earn."

"Yup!" Lara said. "Just start saving at least ten per cent of your salary. And babe! You can't waste your time thinking coulda, woulda, shoulda. You have to focus on what moves you should be making *right* now. You have a good job. Apply yourself, babe, and start getting creative about how you can make more even within your company."

"I'm trying, oh. I'm trying!" Ladun joked.
"Not hard enough, my love," Lara teased back. "Listen! You guys I'm determined to make bank this year, and we all have to step our game. I'm not

quite there yet, but I have a plan. In fact, I've adjusted my financial infrastructure. Since I got my new job, I've been using fifty per cent of my salary to pay down my debt. I've cut out all unnecessary expenses until further notice and its working. I'm almost done paying."

Zuri cheered. "Wow! That's amazing! But you've always been strong-willed, *sha*."

"*Abi!*" Ladun agreed.

"I've also put a hold on giving financial assistance to family members till further notice," Lara continued. "I've opened a separate account and set a budget that determines how much I can give each month because I cannot come and kill myself because I want to help my family. My siblings have had to go and look for jobs to look after themselves. They are grown. It is time."

"Man!" Zuri said. "I wish I could create a budget for my mum. I love her to bits, but her own financial demands are never-ending. Can you imagine that she's been using the money I give her to sow seeds in church!" She groaned. "I don't even mind, but she'll finish sowing seed, then come and hit me up for more money to replace what she's spent."

Lara was wistful as she thought of her mum. "I know the feeling. My mum used to do that, may her soul rest in peace. You need to set a budget, *sha*, before you end up in my situation where I let family members overrun me with their demands to the detriment of my financial health."

"Bode is the same with his mum," Ladun laughed ruefully. "He can't say no when it comes to her."

"We love our parents, oh, but we must set boundaries otherwise it gets tricky," Lara replied.

"You've really been thinking about this," Zuri said. "I love how focused you are. You'll be back on track in no time."

"Ah!" Lara laughed. "When bills were chasing me up and down, how won't I be focused? I am determined not to be a slave to my bills. I just decided I had to change my mindset. I'm not a victim, I'm smart, and I have skills, so I know

that this financial downturn in my life is not permanent. But it's more than that. I'm hungrier for financial success than I ever was. I even went to negotiate with Pere to give me two per cent of a transaction. Long story, but it is dependent on if I'm able to bring international partners on board."
"Are you serious?" Ladun said. "Did he agree?"

"He did, oh!" Lara responded. "He agreed to one point five."

"You just gave me an idea," Zuri said. I should set up a meeting with Mr Tunde to negotiate commission on the Yaba development project because that could be excellent extra income."

"Yes, girl!" Lara cheered. "You definitely should. We are not playing any games this year. This money must be made, so let's keep encouraging each other."

"I wish I had something to negotiate too, but I'm so new at my job, no one even listens to me," Ladun said dejectedly.

"Again, that's the wrong attitude babe," Lara said, taking Ladun's hand. "You have to make them listen. Just start focusing on being a value addition, stop being afraid to speak up. You may have been a housewife for so many years, but you are super smart Ladun. You have to keep pushing."

"Man!" Zuri said. "You've just gingered me! I have to start aggressively investing again before I end up in the poor house."

"Ah!" Lara smiled. "How do you know? There are a few investments I've been looking at, things I can hopefully do with my money when I'm back on track. One of the biggest things I realised when I was unemployed is that I was too passive with my investments, with my money in general, really. I always thought that just because I earned a good salary and had job security, I was safe but going through all the hassle this year really made me wake up."

SMART MONEY LESSON: YOU CAN LIVE YOUR BEST LIFE AND STAY IN YOUR LANE

I loved meeting new people on my first book tour for the 'The Smart Money Woman' and hearing about the practical steps many women had taken to improve to their financial lives because they had read the book. Some women had bought land, started building their stock portfolios or invested in treasury bills, and I was genuinely impressed and humbled.

However, if I'm honest, one thing that irked me was when I heard people say "Ah! Arese, I didn't buy this bag, or I didn't go on holiday this year because of you." I didn't like the idea that people thought they were being judged for their purchases or that I was saying count every penny and don't spend money on the things you like.

There's a difference between being cheap and being smart with your money. My philosophy on money has always been rooted in self-awareness. I want women to really pay attention to who they are, what they like and what truly brings them joy and develop money habits that are not dictated by other people's expectations, driven by social status symbols or peer pressure. I believe in staying in your lane and only doing the things that your income can support.

The key to guilt-free spending is setting up financial systems that allow you to know what you can afford when you can afford it. In the first book, we discuss using a spending plan that divides your money into three parts 70 per cent towards living expenses, 20 per cent towards long-term financial goals (i.e. assets) and 10 per cent towards short-term financial goals (i.e. splurges). After paying for necessities and investing towards building assets, with what you have left, you are entitled to buy whatever you like. It's your money! So if that means holidays to the South of France, spend there! For some people it could mean fashion, for others it could mean fancy cars. But it's also about understanding what you have to cut out to balance the spending. You can't treat yourself more than you hold yourself accountable to your goals. You need to keep yourself responsible for being disciplined enough to build your future.

It is no one's job to judge other people's spending patterns; we all like and value different things. What is considered "frivolous" and "expensive" is relative. If Sade flies business class to Miami and spends 10,000 dollars shopping, she could also have 20 times that in assets and a source of income that will replenish it quickly. But Femi, who earns two hundred thousand a month but buys the latest iPhone for a thousand dollars, using up all his savings with no assets might see Sade's holiday on Instagram and call it frivolous.

When it comes to building wealth, tunnel vision is so important. It's not our job to count other people's coins or judge other people's purchases. The energy you use to figure out what the next person is doing and cursing them out on social media with your friends is energy that you are taking away from doubling your hustle and making your dreams come true. Sometimes, the most powerful thing you can do is to be patient while things are unfolding for you.

Set boundaries, get comfortable with saying I can't afford it right now. You have to learn to say no to things that aren't right for you or friendships that require you to overspend to keep up. Anyone who makes you feel bad for prioritising your financial health isn't someone that should be in your life.

For a lot of people, social media has increasingly become a spending trigger, but I believe that social media is not the problem; it's how you choose to interact with it that can be the problem. Instead of interacting with pages or people that derail you from your goals, learn to use it more intentionally. Follow and engage with people that inspire you and teach you things that can help to foster your growth, learn about your industry, and generally give you positive vibes. It's okay to aspire to have a particular lifestyle or level of success but let's stop using it as a tool to engage in negativity, bitterness, and hate.

EXERCISE:

1. Define what living your best life looks like for you then create a scale of preference for your lifestyle goals.

2. Set a budget and a spending limit for each lifestyle goal.

3. Identify your spending triggers. What types of people, items, events, or platforms do you engage with that jeopardise your financial health?

4. Optimise your accounts by automating your investments, setting up direct debits and having separate accounts for different goals. Most people fail when it comes to their savings because they have global savings and put all their savings in one account, regardless of whether they are for short-term or long-term goals.

CHAPTER 6   ASSESSING INVESTMENT OPPORTUNITIES: RISK AND RETURN

Tsola

"Good morning, Mr Preware," the receptionist greeted as she took his briefcase. "How was your night?"

"Good morning, Helen," Tsola responded. He had lived in Nigeria for many years now, but that question still made him laugh. It just seemed so intrusive.

Like, what is your business with what I did last night? He thought. However, he knew she meant well; it was just the Nigerian way.

"They are waiting for you in the conference room," Helen informed him.

As he walked through the bullpen, he could feel the energy of the Zuma Capital team. It was always a proud moment to see his people working hard either in their cubicles or in teams. Zuma employed about twenty-five people across their Lagos, New York, and Johannesburg offices. He still marvelled at the fact that they had some of the brightest financial minds working for them. He, Ebuka, and Folake had fought a few wars and many times it seemed like the bigger the size of the deal, the more obstacles they had to overcome. The fact was, doing business in Nigeria had taught them to get comfortable with a certain level of uncertainty.

As he strolled into the conference room, his partners had already started the meeting, judging from the raised voices emanating from the meeting room

"How's it going, people?" His cheerful greeting fell on deaf ears, and he could tell that this was going to be a tough meeting to decide whether to go ahead with the entertainment fund or not. He shrugged his Mai Atafo jacket off and placed it on the chair next to the head of the conference table, and immediately felt goose pimples creep up his arms.

"Folake this is your doing, I'm sure," Tsola remarked as he shivered. The air conditioning was cranked all the way up. "This place is cold, oh!"

She wasn't even listening because she was busy arguing with Ebuka and Morayo, their research analyst.

"I'm telling you, Ebuka, I don't think the risk involved is worth it," Folake said. "These Nigerian creatives are too flaky to be bankable. A friend of mine who invested in a record label about five years ago is currently in several lawsuits with at least three of his artists. They start with nothing, and an investor spends good money building their brand, paying for cars, houses, producing their albums, paying for international and domestic flights, and all that jazz. Then when they blow, the story changes and suddenly someone who has invested millions of naira becomes the villain. Is this something we want to get involved in? it all sounds way too emotional for me!"

"You have a point. The risk is immense," Ebuka said as he mulled over her argument. "However, I'm more interested in the fact that the overall value of the Nigerian entertainment and media sector is significantly lacking in value compared to other markets. The numbers are not great, and if the numbers are not that sexy, I'm not sure Zuma should be taking the risk."

"Well, Price Waterhouse Cooper's entertainment and media report for 2017 through 2021 says the combined estimated value of the music and film segments of Nigeria's E and M sector is about three point two billion dollars, which is pretty significant," said Morayo, reeling out the facts.

"Madam, that's just an estimate of the overall industry," Folake scoffed.

Ebuka wasn't having it. "I read the same report, Morayo, and you're making my point for me. You see, that estimate is significantly lower compared to other markets. South Korea's is estimated at eleven point two billion, and even South Africa in our backyard is estimated at nine billion. So why not take my money there? Again, I'm more worried about revenue prospects being too small compared to the risk."

Folake leaned back in her seat. "Let's even analyse the potential revenue that you are talking about, Ebuka. How much in actuals have individual entertainment projects brought in? Actuals, oh, not projected. Even the first

'Wedding Party' film which was all the rave reportedly brought in five hundred million naira with an estimated initial investment of sixty million. In terms of risk, what if that was a one-off? How many Mo Abudus and Kemi Adetibas are there in the Nigerian entertainment industry? How many can actually do those numbers consistently?"

Ebuka considered her words, raising templed fingers to his lips.

She continued, "Plus, I'm not interested in one-offs. For it to make any sense for Zuma, especially in terms of the time and man-hours that would be involved, I would be more interested in investing two million dollars in ten projects of its kind. However, the real question is, would each of the projects generate the same level of revenue? And what is the opportunity cost for Zuma? if we invested that amount of money in infrastructure or oil and gas, the revenue would be significantly higher, with much less risk."

Tsola watched and listened with amusement. Of course, all their arguments were valid, but he still believed building this fund could be very lucrative for Zuma in five to seven years with the right structure and the right strategy.

"All your points are valid, guys," Tsola interrupted. "I'm surprised none of you brought up the infrastructure and distribution challenges that make it difficult for entertainment in Nigeria to be as scalable as South Africa and South Korea. First of all, they have more cinemas and a population with a much more substantial purchasing power than we do."

"Yes! Another angle," Folake interrupted. "And, I didn't even talk about the liquidity issues and the limited exit strategies for an industry like entertainment."

"Madam, let me land," Tsola said as Folake rolled her eyes. She was brilliant and could argue different sides of almost every scenario, but of the three of them, she was also the most risk-averse. She only ever fully settled into risk when it was calculated as well as tried and tested. But Tsola's motto has always been no risks, no returns. They didn't make the big bucks in this market by playing it safe. You had to have the audacity to take the risks, albeit calculated ones.

Tsola nodded his head as he made his point. "Listen! I agree that the numbers are not as enticing as we would usually like, but I think we should consider that not only is Nigeria in the fairly early stages compared to most, there is empirical evidence in both the movie and music industry of what is possible numbers-wise, and the industry has gotten this far even with the limited infrastructure and financing support available to them."

"I hear you, Tsola, but potential is not profit, mate," Ebuka said. "And we are certainly not in the social enterprise business. We don't do the work we do to be charitable, we do it to make money."

Tsola had to laugh. Ebuka could undoubtedly be more capitalist than most capitalists, and he did have a point.

"Hear me out, my brother. I only talk of empirical evidence because some of these Nigerian creatives have done the unthinkable with little or no support. That shows me proof-of-concept. Let's steer the examples away from movies and look at music for a minute. For example, Eko Hotel, which has been the most popular concert venue for years, can host up to six thousand concert goers. Artists like Davido and Wizkid have consistently sold out the venue. They've both done the same for the twenty-six-thousand-capacity Eko Atlantic. These numbers are relatively small if you compare it to South African rapper, Casper Nyovest, who has consistently sold out their soccer city stadium. Reports say he sold sixty-eight thousand tickets for his last concert. My point is, there's something here and every pain point you've mentioned has pointed to a pain point in the sector that smells like opportunity to me."

Tsola paused for a minute to let his point sink in.

"So. Do we invest in setting up our own record label co-owned and co-managed with people who have the technical capabilities in the music industry but limited access to capital and business know-how? They can focus on the creative side, and we focus on capital raising and business structure to ensure that money is made on all sides. Or do we invest in the infrastructure that's set up to cater to music concerts that have hundred-thousand-person capacity but can also be manoeuvred to cater to smaller-sized concerts? Or, with regards to distributing visual content, do we invest in building cinemas to improve the scalability of content or invest in digital streaming platforms, so we not only capture the diaspora market but the rest of Africa? History has shown that there is a huge demand for Nollywood by Africans everywhere."

The wheels were turning in Ebuka's head as he listened. "Actually, some guys I went to business school with are killing it because they invested in digital entertainment in multiple Asian markets. Revenues are currently around the three-hundred-million-dollar range. It's quite impressive."

"Again, guys, that's a different market. They have the purchasing power and internet penetration as well as infrastructure to support that kind of growth, but I kind of see your point," Folake said.

"Look, people. With the right kind of thinking, strategy, and structure, we can make this work," Tsola stated. "But more importantly, I'm going with my gut on this one. We will make money. I think we should take a multi-pronged approach and find creative ways to invest in everything from concerts, movies, and distribution infrastructure. I think we will optimise our investment if we tackle this industry from multiple angles even though we start with the minimum viable options for each, so we don't spend a million dollars on a project only to find that it's not profitable."

Folake came to a decision. "Alright, Tsola. Let Morayo and her team build financial models around all the potential ideas, so we can optimise financing and see what potential combination makes sense for Zuma in both the long- and short-term."

"Yes, ma, I'm on it," Morayo said.

I'll get on the Qataris," Ebuka said. "Knowing Tsola, we are probably going to need twenty million dollars for this. Go big or go home, right?"

Tsola grinned as he glanced at the screen of his phone. "Good work, guys! I'm glad we are on the same page. My wifey is calling, so let me take this. I look forward to seeing those numbers. Morayo, I trust you to run them as accurately as possible for every possible scenario."

He picked the call. "Hold on, babe," Tsola said into his phone, then covered the mouthpiece and said to the team, "Let the finance team know. I'd like to see a worst-case, mid-case and best case for each individual project and each possible combination of projects. We must manage our cashflows and cost expectations from the onset."

"Great meeting, guys! Keep me posted." Tsola got back on the phone to Zuri and walked out of the conference room.

****

Adesuwa

It was nine on a Saturday morning, and the house was unusually quiet because SJ was having a sleepover at Banke's house. The house always felt sort of hollow when he wasn't around. He was the soul and vibe of their home, but as much as she missed him, Adesuwa was grateful for the solitude. She could catch up on her reading, listen to podcasts, and generally just get her mind right. With everything that was going on with her marriage, she honestly needed the peace and quiet.

Her thoughts were interrupted by footsteps and heavy breathing. As she looked up from her book, she could see her nanny, Olivia, hovering in the hallway right outside the living room. It was as though she couldn't decide whether or not to come in.

Adesuwa closed her eyes for a second and took a deep breath. *There goes my peace and quiet.*

She knew that when her nanny started acting shifty, she wanted something. Olivia had been with her since before SJ was born and had always been a solid, dependable nanny-slash-housekeeper. And, she was hilarious. Adesuwa loved how she was with SJ and was grateful to have her, even though on some days it took everything not to strangle her, especially on days like this. Everything in Adesuwa told her that Olivia was about to say something that would annoy her.

"Olivia! What is it?" Adesuwa said without turning around. "Madam! What is it, oh? I don't have all day! Spit it out. What do you want?"

"Ma, don't be offended," Olivia responded, as she approached, rubbing her hands together in supplication.

Adesuwa rolled her eyes and tried not to laugh. She could never understand why the girl insisted on using that sentence as a preface for every conversation. 'Ma. Please don't be offended, I just wanted to tell you I'm going to throw dustbin downstairs,' or 'Ma, please don't be offended my cousin is getting married next month, I want to beg you to sew cloth for me. I'm doing bridesmaid for her.' Sometimes it was, 'Ma! Please don't be offended there's one wig you are not using again. You haven't worn it for a very long time. I want you to *dash* me'. The girl was a mess!

"I'm not offended, Olivia. Please, what is it? State your case."

"Ma, please I want to ask for salary advance," Olivia smiled sheepishly as she made her request.

"You've come again. Salary advance for what, please? The last salary advance you collected you lent your brother, and you have still not paid me back. *Biko*, what is this one for now?"

"Ma sorry, it's not like dat. I don't want to borrow anybody. I want to do investment."

Olivia's air of contrived confidence made Adesuwa laugh. "What kind of investment? And how much?"

"Ma, *e be one business like this. Dem say if I put a hundred thousand naira inside, in thirty days dem go give me forty-five thousand. So, I wan' put hundred k so that dem go give me four hundred and fifty k. They said all I fit do is pay the money into their account and then send them my account details. Dem go pay me after thirty days. Dem dey call am cash flip!"*

Adesuwa pursed her lips and stared at her. It was all she could do not to start yelling.

She took a deep breath. "Olivia, it's like your village people have sworn for you. *Dem don' find you reach Lagos, abi?* You want to use salary advance to do scam. *After, you will come and say they did you.* When you should know better."

"Ah! No, ma. *My people don dey do am since, and dem dey make plenty money.*"

"Which people? See, let me tell you something there is no investment like that. They will just take your money and run. *Na scam. Which business you don do before wey you put ten thousand naira and the business commot forty-five thousand, ehn? Tell me, now?*"

"*Ah ma, I no know, oh! Na my cousin talk say this company dey very reliable. She see am for Facebook, and dem get many many testimonies. E better pas to put money for this one instead of to dey put money inside all these big big banks. Even after one year, sef, na only small money dem go put for your account.*"

Exasperated, Adesuwa's voice was at a near yell as she told Olivia, "Madam, you won't hear now, oh! I'm telling you those things are fake! They use it to scam unsuspecting people like you. Listen to me. If it sounds too good to be true, it probably is. I've told you many times to save your money. When you manage to save small, you go and spend it on something silly or lend your friend money that you can't afford to lend. Or you send it to your village."

"Ma, this one is different. *I just wan' make money quick-quick.* I will pay back, I promise," she ended on a whine.

"You are not listening to me." Adesuwa lowered her voice as she tried to reason with her.

"I'm listening, ma."

"Okay. Open your ears because I'm only going to say this once. This cash flip is. A. SCAM. You will lose the money because the people who do these things are fraudsters. *If na so dem dey make money, I for don be billionaire by now. Abi you think say me I no get sense?*"

"Ah! No, ma," Olivia said.

"Okay, this is what I will do. *I go give you a* salary advance of one hundred thousand and—"

"Ah! God bless you, ma!" Olivia interrupted elatedly, her body posture losing its tension and a huge smile plastered on her face.

Adesuwa could tell she was getting excited. "Calm down, I never finish."

"I won't put it in your normal account. I will open a money market investment account for you." She watched, amused, as Olivia's face lost its excitement.

"*Wetin be that one, ma? I no understand.*"

"I no go fit speak all the big big *oyinbo* wey I go take explain that one to you. All you need to *know na say money market na better investment wey go protect the money wey you put and give small* jara *on top. Right now, dem dey give like twelve per cent interest every year. So I go put one hundred thousand for there, but I get condition!* You must add ten per cent from your salary to the account."

"Hah! Ten per cent, ma! My salary no go fit reach do anything again!" Olivia scrunched her face and grumbled.

"*E go reach!* You will learn to adjust. *Your salary na fifty thousand naira, abi? Ten per cent na just five thousand. So, just adjust the way you dey buy airtime all the rubbish wey you dey talk for phone, cut am! You fit spend the remaining forty-five k how you like. In fact, I go commot the five thousand from your salary every month, add am to the money market account. After one year, you go don add sixty thousand on top the one hundred thousand wey I give you, plus the small jara on top from the twelve per cent interest. Then we go fit find small land for Akwa Ibom to buy for you.*"

"Ah, ma. *That one good, oh!*" Olivia sounded excited again.

"*Shey you understand now? Na this one be investment. You go dey save small small, then buy something wey get value wey fit appreciate over time.*"

Olivia hugged her. "*God bless you, ma. Thank you so much, ma. I don dey talk am since say you be the best madam wey I don get since I start work!*"

Adesuwa rolled her eyes affectionately at the very obvious-but-sweet praise.

"It's okay! *O ya*, go away now. Please go and make me ginger tea."

****

Adesuwa

I'm so glad the class is over! I could barely keep up, Adesuwa thought as she gasped for air.

She and Lara were at their regular spinning class they made a point to attend every Saturday if they were in Lagos. Lara was convinced it was the only way to keep her hips in check and Adesuwa needed any excuse to get in some cardio.

"Why are you always late to the class?" Lara mocked as they cooled down together.

"Leave me, *jo*! I was only ten minutes late! Plus, I almost didn't make it with all the shenanigans I had to deal with at home today."

"What shenanigans, love? Soji again?"

"Nah! Is it not Olivia? She came to interrupt my solace this morning. Talking about, 'I want to get my salary in advance' to invest in one of those cash flip scams. So I basically spent my early morning alone time having a go at her."

She looked over to see Lara bowled over with her left hand across her tummy, laughing uncontrollably.

Adesuwa nudged her light-heartedly.

"Stop laughing, *jo*, " she said as she finished recounting the saga. "Can you believe that she fell for that lie? Talking about her cousin saw it on Facebook, and it's a reliable company. On the real though. I don't understand why they prey on poor illiterate people. It's so disheartening."

"Ah, see you! It's not just low-income earners, oh. Have you heard of Japan Silver?"

"No! What's that?" Adesuwa replied.

"Well apparently they invest your money in "silver"," Lara said, using finger quotes for emphasis. "They have different bands, so for example, you put in one and a half million naira then you have to bring two people who can put up the same amount of money. Then *those* people have to bring in another two people again with the same amount, making a complete table of seven people. The person who started the table then gets to walk away with three and a half million."

"Huh? I'm a bit confused. It sounds like a pyramid scheme. Please, what does silver have to do with it?"

"Man, that's what I asked as well, oh!" Lara cackled. "A guy in my office and I had a full-blown argument last week about this. He was trying to recruit people for his table and was convincing them that it was a solid investment. When I tried to explain that it wasn't an actual investment because they technically weren't investing in anything, omo! The guy vexed, oh!"

Adesuwa laughed. "You should have asked him the prices they were trading the silver for and what volumes that kind of money could buy. This country, ehn!"

"Ah! How do you know? I asked him, and he said he didn't know, but that the company assures that if you want to see the silver, they could send it to you. I was dying. I asked him to please request to see the silver because that was the only way I would believe! I didn't know what type of buying and selling of silver required you to bring in other people with money to make a return."

"Please, how did he respond to that argument please because... solid?"

"Girl, trust me, I didn't understand his explanation. It made no sense. I tried to explain from a different angle and asked him how many actual businesses in Nigeria made those kinds of returns in that type of time frame. It just wasn't realistic."

"He must not be very intelligent," Adesuwa mused.

"On the contrary. He got a first-class degree from UNN and has a master's in oil and gas economics. He is brilliant. He just clearly knows nothing about money or more importantly, what qualifies as a real investment."

"Wow! I have no words."

Lara continued, "You know what? I wouldn't even be mad at the people who are putting their money in, if their approach was, 'Listen! This is a scam, but it's a scam that could potentially have a big payout, and if it doesn't, I can afford to lose the money'."

"Exactly! Scam the scammers!" Adesuwa replied.

"I know some investment bankers who were like, 'Omo, let's put money down, chop and clean mouth before this pyramid scheme falls apart' and they've made like thirty million."

Adesuwa's jaw dropped. "Wow! Really? I hope it's not their clients they are selling it to, oh, because no matter how you cut it, someone will get hurt down the line when the thing eventually falls apart."

"Of course not! They were selling it to their friends, and they certainly weren't calling it an investment. They were upfront about the fact that it was a scam and that it was like musical chairs. Someone was going to be left without their chair in the end, and you just had to hope it wasn't you. And another thing is you have to be a naturally gifted seller to convince other people to join because it's actually how effective your sales pitch is that will guarantee if you get your money back with returns. I can imagine if a table has someone who doesn't know how to sell being stuck, everyone else on the table will be stuck too."

Adesuwa shivered dramatically and told Lara, "These people were really living on the edge, sha!"

"I'm telling you! But guess what? It seemed like people were setting up businesses within the scam. For example, let's say I'm a good seller, and you are not. In exchange for me helping you to convince other people to bring their own millions to your table, I would collect a commission from your return, let's say seven hundred k."

Adesuwa shook her head in disbelief at the audacity of the whole idea. "Wawu! People are brave, oh! *Abeg*, let me go. I have to go and get my son from Banke's house."

****

Zuri

Zuri glanced at her watch. It was eight at night, and Tsola was not back from work yet. She had told him dinner would be ready by seven, but she knew he was either stuck in a meeting or Lagos traffic. Still, it would have been nice to get a text to say he was running late. He probably forgot, and she had learnt to get used to his lack of communication when he was in work mode. Early on in their relationship, this was the sort of thing that would have upset her, especially because she had spent the last four hours slaving over a stove making his favourite meal—starch and banga.

Okay, I'm being dramatic. I wasn't exactly slaving, Zuri chuckled to herself.

Tsola's cook Ernest had helped. Everything would be bought, cleaned, and chopped so that when she arrived all she had to do was cook. She was just glad that Ernest had stopped being territorial in the kitchen. In the beginning? *Na war.* He would say '*Oga like am like this!*', and, '*Ah, ma! Oga no dey chop that one,*' every time she attempted to do something in the kitchen. That behaviour had been especially annoying because even though she knew how to cook, she didn't love cooking, but she made it a point to make something for Tsola at least twice a week. She was glad he wasn't one of those guys that thought being in the kitchen twenty-four seven made you wife material, but she could tell it made him happy that she made the effort.

She looked at her watch again, then sent him a text. *Babe, food is ready. Are you on your way?*

He responded immediately. *I'm almost at the gate, babe. Will be up shortly.*

Zuri smiled as she put the finishing touches to the table setting.

"Good job, man. You definitely brought this one home for us," Tsola said as he walked through the door. His driver, Lasisi, was close behind him, bringing in his briefcase and jacket.

"Thank you, Mr Lasisi," Zuri said as she took the briefcase and jacket from him. "Take for transport," handing him a worn one thousand naira note she'd filched from Tsola's pocket.

As she locked the door behind Mr Lasisi and proceeded to take Tsola's things to the living room, she saw he was still on the phone, rounding up the conversation with who she imagined to either be Ebuka or Folake, looking pleased with himself. They must have closed a deal today or hit a significant milestone. She could feel his excitement as she walked up behind him wrapped her arms around his waist and kissed the nape of his neck before she placed her head on his back.

"Abeg! I have to go, Ebuka. Wifey wants my attention. Let's catch up tomorrow."

He put his phone aside then turned around to give Zuri a slow, lingering kiss. "I missed you today."

"Really?" Zuri gave him a teasing side-eye. "It sure didn't feel like it. No text, no phone call."

He hugged her tighter as he joked, "You've started, oh! You know how it gets when I'm busy in the office. Just because I don't text or call, doesn't mean I'm not thinking of you."

"I know that." She poked him playfully in the ribs. "So, what's this good news? This one you are grinning from ear to ear."

"Ebuka just delivered good news. Great news, actually." He rolled up his sleeves, washed his hands, and settled down to the meal.

Zuri's eyebrows lifted. "Uhm? Are you going to share?"

"He got the Qatari's to commit ten million dollars to Zuma's entertainment industry fund. I thought it would probably take a few more weeks to convince them to come on board for this one because it's not exactly what they're used to investing in, especially in these parts, but my boy did it under a week! The only caveat is that we have to find other investors to match their investment and complete the twenty-million-dollar round."

"Ah! So, if you don't find another ten million dollars, they won't invest?"

"Yup! That's basically it, but I'm not particularly worried about the condition because this is normal. It's just a signal that they are extremely interested but wanted to hedge their risk by making sure other investors think the fund is viable as well. Given Zuma's track record, the Qatari's commitment, and the financial model and strategy documents that the team has put together, it'll be a walk in the park to raise the rest."

"*Na wa, sha*. You guys are g's at Zuma," Zuri was impressed. "It still amazes me how you convince people to give you that much money for your ideas. I feel like the entertainment fund was just an idea you thought about two months ago, and like magic, you've already raised ten million. I meet so many people who struggle with raising capital for their small businesses, and the money they are looking for is tiny compared to the numbers you are talking about. They are looking for small amounts like ten million naira or even one million, and they can't find a bank to support them or investors to invest in their businesses."

"Well, the thing is it's a struggle to find cheap capital in Africa, especially when you don't have money," Tsola explained. "The harsh reality is that the more money you have, the easier it is to not only get money but also negotiate terms with banks and investors. So most big businesses can negotiate loans for around twelve per cent, and that's still a high cost to operate a business here. But when you aren't rich, and you approach a bank, they'll probably offer you about twenty-two per cent exclusive of charges, and they'll want collateral that's worth about a one hundred and fifty per cent of the value of the loan you are looking for. Which, frankly, defeats the whole purpose because, if you had the money or collateral in the first place, you probably wouldn't come to the bank because it's expensive."

"Exactly! Look at Tami for instance. She's been trying to raise twenty million naira to scale her production and ready-to-wear line. Her ideas are pretty solid, in my opinion, but the banks clearly don't see it. Either their terms are unreasonable, or they say no outright because she doesn't have the collateral to back the loan, and her father has said no to putting up any of his assets for her."

"Hmm. She probably needs equity, not debt. I don't think her business as it stands can support debt sustainably, but she needs to be able to articulate her value proposition and understand the financials that underpin her business in a way that investors will find attractive because the bottom line is, banks want to make money and so do investors."

"True, but it sucks to watch her struggle. She's so passionate about her business. Irawo is basically her baby, and she's so eager to make it a high revenue-generating business and prove her dad wrong."

"Tell her to put her numbers and strategy together, and we can set up a meeting to look them over and discuss some options. Twenty million is not a lot in the grand scheme of things, and I know a few people who might be willing to invest in a fashion business. She should come to my office, and I'll talk her through it."

"Aww! Thanks, babe. She'll be super grateful," Zuri said, smiling.

"Can I ask a question, though?" Zuri said as she spooned more banga soup on his plate.

"Shoot!" Tsola said as he looked at what was left of his starch. He hated the fact that he was eating such heavy food at this time of the night, but it was delicious, and it made him happy that even though Zuri hated cooking, she made an effort because she wanted to make him happy. To be honest, he didn't really care if she never cooked because it was not relevant to him in a relationship, but he was glad she did.

"Do you ever get scared, babe?" Zuri asked sincerely.

"Scared of what?"

"I mean, in business? Taking on all this risk! Do you ever think about if it doesn't work out?"

"Of course I do! The thing is, though, that most of my risks are calculated. The difference between most people and me is that even though I'm optimistic about the returns on my investment, I also rigorously assess the downside. Most people get excited about the returns but don't prepare for the downside of the investment."

"What's the biggest risk you've taken that didn't pay off?"

"Babe, I've been in business long enough that I've made a lot of money and I've also lost a lot of money, but I would say it was when we raised some private capital for my father's agriculture business five years ago. Preware Industries had farms all over the country but mostly focused on fish and pigs. My dad wanted to expand into palm oil and cashew nuts, and the plan was to raise money to buy machines for production and packaging and produce large quantities that would not only focus on producing for a local market but, would also be export ready. It was brilliant. But you know my dad. He is superstitious about bank loans or giving equity to foreign investors, so he raised private capital mostly from his friends. I was on the board of his company as a non-executive director as first son, so I helped to raise part of it from my close friends."

"Wow, that's awesome, babe. I'm sure he was proud of you."

"Mmm-hmm. He was when it was going well, and I successfully raised part of the money. Then, I was his superstar. However, when things got tough it was a different vibe."

"How come? You've never actually told me about this." Zuri couldn't believe what she was hearing.

"Well, it's never come up! It's not exactly pleasant to talk about."

"I guess," she replied with understanding.

"Well, because of a series of unfortunate events, all the investors lost money." It was easy to see that Tsola still felt disappointed.

"There was a fire on the largest farm which destroyed sixty per cent of what had been produced and the insurance had lapsed meaning we couldn't recoup our losses that way. Then one of our shipments took an extraordinarily long time to get our palm oil and cashew to Chinese partners who were our biggest buyers. Half the inventory was contaminated by the time it got to China. Everything went to shit because of things we could have never anticipated at the time. It got worse when one of my father's business partners who he had known for thirty years and had invested about thirty per cent of the extra capital went apeshit, took him to EFCC and said his whole business was a scam."

"Wow! Really? But he was your dad's friend. Did your dad explain what had happened?" Zuri asked, shocked. She could not believe that a friend would have reported him to the Economic and Financial Crimes Commission.

"Babe! That experience taught me that when money is involved, there is no friendship in business. My father did everything to appease him, he pledged personal property, but it was not enough. In hindsight, his reaction was stupid because the man invested in a business. He didn't lend my dad money. If the returns came through as expected he wouldn't have shared the profits with my father. That was the first time I saw two facts about doing business in Nigeria. First, the media is a powerful force. If you allow the world to create a narrative for you and you don't volunteer your truth, it can ruin you. I watched the newspapers call my father a fraud after his supposed friend took him to court to liquidate his entire business that had been in existence for thirty years."

"What?" Zuri gasped, covering her mouth with the palms of her hand.

"Man! It was crazy!" Tsola shook his head as if to clear his mind of the memory. Also, it made me realise that in this country, you are guilty until you can prove yourself innocent."

Tsola breath hissed as he inhaled deeply, then let out the air in a rush. "The worst thing was what I had to learn about friendship. Some of the people I called friends who had invested in this business and logically knew that this wasn't my fault, started to call me a fraud and a thief and harassed me for years while I was fighting this battle with my dad to save his company and investor funds. But there were the miraculous few who had invested the most money out of all my friends who were so patient and understanding, most of all, helpful. It was shocking because they had the most to lose. I'm talking at least a million dollars each, but they acted like family and saw me through. The company was never the same again, but it taught me many things. This was a company that had paid my school fees and had a thirty-year reputation that went kaput in just a few months over a series of mishaps and an accusation of fraud that was never proven. People need to understand that there's a difference between a business going bad, and a business being fraudulent."

SMART MONEY LESSON:
HOW TO ASSESS AN
INVESTMENT OPPORTUNITY

People are always asking what a sound investment is. They are typically looking for something to put money in that has minimal risk and high return, which, as I explained in the first book, doesn't exist.

The rule is generally the higher the risk, the higher the return. However, high-risk investments need to be adequately evaluated because the possibility of losing your capital is very real. This is not to say stay away from them, but that the risk has to be assessed and calculated.

Aside from investing in structured financial instruments, a new wave is to invest in small businesses that have a high potential for growth. However, how do you assess said growth?

If your friend or family member brings you a business opportunity, how do you assess whether it is the right opportunity for you or a valid investment? Most people tend to go into these situations blindly and nine out of ten times they fail because:

a. they made a business decision based on emotions, not facts;
b. they did not understand the business or industry they were investing in because they did not ask enough questions or the right questions;
c. they did not do their own primary research; and
d. they probably had a short-term view instead of a long-term one.

Unlike financial instruments which usually have a specified tenor or time horizon with the risks spelt out, investing in a small business can be trickier. With treasury bills, you are told up front for example, that the tenor is ninety days, and your interest within the period is 14 per cent—the terms are clear from the outset. With the stock market, the market price of each share is clearly available on the day of purchase, i.e., Random Bank at ?28.09. Even though you can never predict which way the market will go (up or down) within the period you hold the stock, you have historical data on what range the stock has fluctuated within in the past five to ten years, how much in dividends and bonuses they have paid out, et cetera.

You know from the beginning that these could be high-risk investments, but it is usually a calculated risk because for companies to be listed on the stock exchange, they would have had to go through due diligence, have corporate governance in place, shareholders have access to their financials, and there is also a clear exit strategy. When you need to offload the stock to realise the value in cash, you can sell it on the stock exchange. With investing in a small business it is trickier because the risks are higher, the exit strategy isn't as clear cut because the market for buying/selling businesses in this part of the world is extremely limited.

I thought an interesting way to assess this would be to give you some insight as to how established private equity firms evaluate investment opportunities so you can draw parallels when you are analysing an opportunity on a smaller scale.

Private equity firms look for value in private companies with the long-term view that they will produce a solid return. This is usually a period of between seven to ten years. The expectation is that the value of their stake in the company will increase significantly with a significant future return on investment.

Investing in private companies is not easy because they are mostly illiquid, risky, and primarily long-term investments. So, when your friend brings you an investment opportunity. Here's a checklist of things to consider.

a. Do Your Due Diligence

Private equity firms will typically send in a team to do a comprehensive appraisal of a business to establish its assets and liabilities and evaluate its commercial potential before entering into an agreement. This will include taking an in-depth look at the prospective company's critical financial statements i.e. profit and loss statement, cash flow statement and balance sheet, as well as doing a top to bottom examination of the business that allows them to test their assumptions against the facts and provide a clear understanding of the business's value and growth potential.

b. Understand the Fundamentals of the Business

It is one thing to glance through the financials of a business, but it's also essential to understand how the company you want to invest in works. You should calculate the unit economics. These are some questions you should have detailed answers to before you decide to invest.

i.   How does the business make or lose money?
ii.   What is the value proposition of the business?
iii.   What problem are they looking to solve?
iv.   What is the size of the addressable market?
v.   Is there a clearly defined target customer?
vi.   What will be the primary acquisition channels?
vii.   Do they have the potential to be productive and profitable?
viii. How will the business generate revenue?
ix.   What is the cost structure? (Full costs, including marketing and distribution)
x.   Does the business have any cost advantages?
xi.   What is the forecasted budget, and does it seem reasonable?
xii.   What traction has the company achieved so far?
xiii. What near-term milestones have been achieved before the investment?
xiv.   What products or services make the business innovative compared to its competitors?
xv.   How effective is the team?

xvi.   What team members need to be added?

xvii.   What is the project promoter's experience?

xviii. Do you have faith that the CEO and the team can execute their vision and have the experience and ability to deliver results?

Ideas are a dime a dozen. It is in the execution phase that most people stumble.

c. Carry Out Your Own Primary Research

It is essential to do your homework outside of the information the investment prospect feeds you. Talk to experts. Find people know the industry the prospective business is in, either because they work in the industry or have invested in the industry. Ask questions about loopholes or regulations that can cause the business to lose money. As much as any business is a potential opportunity, it is crucial to protect your downside. Talk to customers about what they like or don't like about the product or service.

d. Understand the Deal

How do the business valuation and deal structure stack up against others in the industry? Is the valuation realistic? Given the capital structure, revenue, net income, risk profile and growth rate of the business? What are the financial terms of the deal? What investment amount is needed? What is the investment type: debt or equity? What's the agreed interest rate or rate of return? What's the tenor of the investment? Is the use of funds clearly laid out? What is the exit strategy: who will buy the business in five to ten years? Does the business have the potential to generate enough profits during the lifetime of the investment to pay back the capital and give healthy returns?

ALTERNATIVE INVESTMENTS

An alternative investment is usually a financial asset that does not fall into one of the conventional investment categories, although these typically include private equity, venture capital, art, commodities etc. Recently, e-currencies such as Bitcoin and cryptocurrencies have joined the mix. Now, while I am not suggesting that these are bad investments, I would like to include an observation and offer an opinion. Alternative investments are much higher risks which is why they often have a higher return. And, in the bid to make money faster, people put their money in because they have heard stories of others who have made a ton of money from it while forgetting that some may have equally lost a lot. It depends on the timing of your investment.

Now my question is if you don't have a substantial amount in savings, fixed deposits, treasury bills, land, or property, why would you risk all your savings on a riskier venture when you do not have a financial foundation? It is essential to understand that even though there is a potentially profitable upside, there is also a potential downside and the attitude to the money you put into alternative investments needs to come after you have asked yourself if you can afford to lose such a sum.

No one likes to lose money, but without being emotional, you need to ask yourself some tough questions before you jump in the deep end. Questions like, 'If I lose money from this investment, how will it affect my financial obligations? Rent? Mortgage? School fees?' The money you can afford to lose in such investments is money that won't affect your financial obligations or lifestyle. Things like bonus money you were not expecting, excess disposable income (money that's left after you've covered bills, investments, and core savings). People will put money they've set aside for rent in Bitcoin, get stuck, and say they were scammed. You were not scammed; you took a risk, and it did not pay off.

As much as there are many scams and Ponzi schemes out there, we need to start to understand that it is ultimately your responsibility to do your research as well as you can before investing. Even with all that, some businesses fail, and it is also important to note that a business that should have been a success but failed, is different from a scam where the intention was to rip you off from the outset.

HOW TO AVOID SCAMS

Greed and impatience are the root causes of falling for scams. You are looking to make lots of money in a brief period with no danger of losing your capital. These usually don't exist, and when they do, they are not opportunities that everybody and their driver will ever know about, because they are typically not open to the mass market.

If the return seems too good to be true, it probably is. Think about it: if someone is offering you a 150 per cent return on your investment, asking yourself how many businesses in Nigeria give that kind of performance should give you some perspective. Also, you should ask what exactly they are investing in. When there's no clear answer, this is usually a tell-tale sign of a scam.

If they ask you to bring other people who also have the same amount of money to invest as you did for you to make a return on your investment? This is also another signifier of a scam—a case of borrowing from Peter to pay Paul. Because it is not investing in anything (just moving cash around), this will only last for a while but is not sustainable. Some people will get paid and be the town criers for the benefits of the scam because they made money, but some will get stuck when the funds are no longer enough for pay-outs.

There's a difference between a referral system and a Ponzi scheme. A business can pay you a commission for helping them bring more clients. It could be a fee that's a percentage of the value of the business brought in, but this will typically have nothing to do with the returns on your investment because the fee will represent a customer acquisition cost to the organisation.

Bear in mind that it's not easy to make money. If it were, everybody would have it. Real investments take time, consistency, and patience.

CHAPTER 7

LOVE AND MONEY

Lara

Lara got in the lift, trying to calm her nerves and display confidence that she definitely was not feeling. It was as though her body was betraying her. She wasn't scared *per se*, but she needed her body to get with the programme.

"What are you doing, Lara?" She whispered to herself as the elevator doors swished softly open. She hated to admit to herself that she was anxious about this date.

Not a date, Lara. Deji is very, very married.

In the last couple of weeks, he had been very persistent about meeting up and frankly the more she thought about it, the more she didn't want to be seen with him. She had given every excuse in the book—she wasn't feeling well, her friends needed her, she was dealing with a sibling crisis, and her workload was taking up too much of her time—but he'd been persistent, and she'd finally caved.

Tonight though, she was exhausted. Her workload had doubled recently because she'd had to attend several meetings to lobby international partners for RM24, which involved back-and-forth travel between Lagos and Houston.

Even though he still hadn't explicitly said what he wanted in exchange for all his generosity, she knew at some point it would be time to pay the piper. She had no intention of dating a married man. She wasn't a saint, but she had gone down that road before and knew that it never ended well, especially with a man as rich and powerful as Deji.

As she walked into the restaurant, she noticed it was unusually quiet for a Thursday evening in Lagos. There should have been a bit of a crowd, but the room was empty. As she proceeded from the entrance to the dining area, her eyes scanned the room for Deji. He sat alone on a table that was set for two, typing on his phone. He looked up as he saw her walking towards the table and stood up to pull out a chair for her.

She was wearing a red Adeysoile two-piece—a midi-skirt that stopped an inch below her knee with a three-quarter sleeves top with a high neckline, cinched at the waist with a black and gold belt. She'd chosen her armour intentionally, something that covered her cleavage and legs almost completely, so he didn't get the wrong idea, but she wasn't trying to look like a nun either. She knew the outfit accentuated everything great about her slim-thick figure.

"Lara, you look stunning," he greeted, his gaze a bit too warm as he gave her a peck on her cheek.

"You don't look bad yourself," Lara replied. Deji was one of those men who looked so good you couldn't tell their age, which was probably a result of the combination of regular workouts with a trainer, a good nutritionist, and good genes. She had always guessed he was either in his late forties or early fifties. He was not the tallest guy in the world, but you couldn't call him short either, and his slightly greying beard gave him a distinguished air. He was wearing a grey suit and a white shirt that seemed unassuming and straightforward but the cut and fit told her that it was an expensive designer. On his wrist, he was wearing what looked like a simple watch, but Lara knew its value was the same as a down payment for a mansion in Ikoyi. It was a Richard Mille timepiece with a black leather crocodile skin strap that retailed for about a hundred thousand dollars.

"It's quiet here today," Lara noted to the waiter as she glanced at the wine list. The waiter smiled and was about to explain when Deji cut in.

"I bought out the entire restaurant because I didn't want us to be interrupted. I know you are worried about who will see you with me and I want you to be comfortable." He glanced up at the waiter who was paying a little too much attention to the conversation.

"Let's get a bottle of Dom Pérignon, the rosé," Deji ordered and dismissed him.

"Are we celebrating something? I was just going to order a bottle of wine."

"Yes! I'm celebrating the fact that I finally got the most beautiful woman in oil and gas to sit down to dinner with me. She is harder to get an audience with than the president."

Lara laughed. "Only the oil and gas industry? Deji, we both know I'm probably the most beautiful woman you know."

"My bad, did I say oil and gas? I meant the world."

"Seriously though, I haven't been avoiding you. It's been a terribly busy few months for me. I feel like my life has been in turmoil since I lost my mum, emotionally, physically and financially. I've had to focus on work and be more aggressive about creating opportunities to earn outside of my salary."

"You are too fine to be worrying about money, Lara." Deji turned up the charm as he reached out to hold her hand. "I've been begging you since to let me take care of you."

Lara carefully slid her hand out of his grasp and gave him a gentle smile; she wasn't looking to offend the man.

In exchange for what? She thought.

She had heard this one before from men of his means and even the ones that didn't have as much as he did. Their interest wasn't about her, but more about possession and control and she knew from experience that the situation would, in the long run, end up being unsustainable. Men like Deji would offer to look after you but what they were really offering was access to an expensive lifestyle without a means to become wealthy yourself.

She knew many women who thought they had hit the big time when they landed a rich, married boyfriend. They were spoilt by first and business class tickets, private jet travel, exotic hotels, shopping trips, and maybe even getting their bills paid, but years later they would realise they were trapped in gilded cages. The man had given them access to a luxury lifestyle but had not equipped them with the engine that helped generate the kind of income that allowed them to afford that lifestyle without his presence.

"Deji, that sounds lovely," she said as looked at him directly in the eye. She wanted to be absolutely clear about what she told him next, "but you are very married to a beautiful wife and have four children, and that's not the kind of complicated relationship I am looking to introduce to my already complex life."

"How does that matter, Lara? Yes, I'm married. In fact, I'm not going to lie and say I don't love my wife. I love my family, and I'm not trying to introduce anything that is going to jeopardise any of that."

"How will taking a mistress not jeopardise your family life?" Lara was genuinely curious.

Deji was not about to give up. "Listen, Lara. I like you a lot. I would even go as far as saying that I haven't been able to stop thinking about you for the last few months. And yes, I have a wife, but I also have the means to look after you."

Lara sighed, she'd known this conversation was coming, but it didn't make it any easier.

"Deji, you keep saying you'll look after me. I may be going through a rough financial time at the moment, but you must understand that I'm very capable of looking after myself. I know the girls you usually chase get excited by Hermès bags and business class trips but, Deji, these are things I can afford on my own."

"First of all, Let's be clear. I'd be offering you trips on my private jet, not commercial flights," Deji said with mock seriousness. "My girlfriends don't fly commercial."

Lara shook her head even as she chuckled. "So that's all you got from everything I said?"

"Pretty much," Deji laughed. "But, Miss Independent, you are too beautiful to be one of these man-hating, I can do it all by myself, Nigerian feminist types. You should have a man in your life that spoils you, so you don't have to."

"Sir. I know you are old school, but you do realise that this is 2019? and you should know what feminism actually means by now."

"Educate me," Deji spread his arms out beside him as he issued the challenge.

"I am proudly a feminist because I believe in equal access to opportunity, but let's not get it confused. I also want a partner who can provide and protect, and there are things I still fully expect my boyfriend to volunteer to pay for."

"Sounds like you want to eat your cake and have it too, young lady."

"Listen, a woman identifying as feminist and striving for financial independence doesn't mean she hates men. It just means she wants equal access to opportunities that can generate enough income to look after herself and pay her bills. I'm self-sufficient, which means, sir, that I can survive on my own income, so any gifts or financial assistance from a man becomes a value addition, not a means of survival."

"Fair point." He looked amused by her argument.

Lara was not finished. "Well just so you are clear, it would take a lot more than trips on a private jet for me to even consider being anyone's mistress. I'm happy flying business. Besides, I get to fly private occasionally with my boss. I'm more interested in if the married man can buy me real estate. A stock portfolio. Things that can appreciate in value and give me a sustained income even after the man's interest in me has diminished."

Deji seemed to take this as a challenge. "Interesting. So, are you saying if I buy you property, you'll be my mistress?"

"Deji, I don't want to be anyone's mistress. If you *dash* me property, I won't say no, but I'm not in the market for a sugar daddy."

"I'll change your mind. Just give me time."

"I'm flattered that you would go through all this trouble to woo me into being your mistress. I know you want to sleep with me, but I guarantee you that I'll be more beneficial to you as your friend." Lara began to wind up to launch her pitch for a partnership with his firm.

"I don't see how, but enlighten me," Deji's tone was dismissive.

"I'm more interested in doing business with you that will put money in both our pockets. That way I don't need you to buy me property, I can buy it myself."

"Lara. I'm an actual billionaire. What kind of business can we possibly do that will override what I actually want from you?"

"Hear me out." She could tell he was getting testy. Nigerian men rarely took rejection well, especially wealthy Nigerian men used to getting everything they wanted on a platter of gold by virtue of the money they could afford to throw around. She knew she had to handle this delicately if she would get what she actually wanted from this man.

"Deji, you are an extremely attractive man, and I'm not saying I'm not attracted to you. I'm just saying I'm more attracted to your mind and the way you do business and I'd rather put myself in a position to learn from you as well as bring you value without the complication of any romantic entanglements that we both know will become bothersome after the initial thrill is gone."

That seemed to soothe his ruffled feathers; she knew she was appealing to his ego.

"I actually had an idea in mind," Lara continued. "I'm sure you heard a few weeks ago that Oasis won the bid for RM24."

"Yes, I did. Congratulations. I know a few firms that really wanted that one."

"Thank you," Lara replied. "We own the asset now, but we don't have the technical expertise to bring the block to production. So, I struck a deal with Pere, and I'll get a one and a half per cent commission if I can get international partners on board in six months. We want to farm out fifty per cent of our equity and bring on partners that can help build technical capacity."

"Smart girl," Deji said with a wink.

"I'm speaking to a few firms in Houston and Geneva, but I want a partner that not only has the technical expertise but has also done some work in Nigeria. That way, they understand some of the peculiarities of working in these parts before they come on board."

"That's the right approach. Who are you talking to?"

"A few people," Lara said vaguely. "I'm really interested in partnering with Welch. I've been trying to get a meeting with them, but they are showing very little interest. I'm guessing Oasis is a smaller firm than they are used to, but this is a decent-sized block that we can both make money from. I know you have a good relationship with them and act as their local partner here, so I was hoping you could help to facilitate a meeting and nudge them in the right direction with regards to terms."

He looked impressed and more importantly, interested. "I see you've done your homework. But Oasis is a relatively small player in upstream, and this is your first offshore asset. What makes you think I'll stake my reputation with Welch for an upstart because I like their head of business development director's smile?"

"You won't be doing this because you like my smile, you'll be doing this because it's going to put a few million dollars in your pocket," Lara returned.

"I'm intrigued. Explain."

"A little bird told me that Mayfield Oil and Gas has just started a new division that focuses on upstream infrastructure. If you can get me the meeting with Welch and influence the terms in Oasis's favour, I can guarantee Mayfield the contract to build all the pipelines and umbilicals to bring the oil onstream."

Deji stared at her in silence for a moment, then broke into a smile. He had always been impressed by Lara's good looks and knew she was intelligent, but this! This was some next level shit. She had just negotiated her way into at least half a million dollars if the deal went her way, which he had every reason to believe it would. He had always had a weakness for beautiful women, but nothing turned him on more than the smell of a lucrative opportunity.

He broke his silence. "Well, the good news is, I'm very interested in this deal. If everything checks out, it'll be unbelievably valuable for Mayfield. The unwelcome news is, the way your mind works has only succeeded in making me want to sleep with you more."

"I'll pretend I didn't hear that last part."

"Pretend all you want, but just know I'm not going to give up. I'm only going to redouble my efforts. In the meantime, my team will be in touch to get details and value the project and estimated revenue for Mayfield. If everything checks out, you have a deal."

****

Adesuwa

"No, this boy is a tout!" Chukwuemeka guffawed in disbelief. "But we are going to deal with him. Does he think he can outrightly disobey the injunction and go on to have a show in Amsterdam?"

"The explanation from his lawyer was that the injunction barred him from performing songs he had produced under the label at shows in Nigeria," Adesuwa glanced around the room to gauge their reactions.

"Ade! I hope you told him that we are not fools, we have video evidence of him performing at a club in Amsterdam," Chukwuemeka proclaimed.

"Well, this is where it gets fuzzy, His lawyers say he wasn't headlining a show. It was a brief performance at a small club."

"Are they joking?! The boy is still under contract, so any songs, old or new, belong to our client. As long as he got paid for that performance, he is in breach. By the time we are done with him, he won't be able to afford the shithole Turmeric Records dragged him out from."

Adesuwa huffed in amusement. Chukwuemeka was the senior partner. He was usually more stoic when it came to the law, but he became a little dramatic when they were dealing with a high-profile entertainment case or with a high-profile Igbo person. In this case, it was both, so his dramatics were turned up to one hundred.

Their client, Turmeric Records, was suing their artist Big Chex. They had signed him in 2009, and together they had produced back-to-back hits that had made Chex a superstar. Everything had been great until six months ago when Chex hired a new manager who tried to get him out of his old contract with Turmeric and promised to negotiate a better deal. As egos prevailed, negotiations fell through.

Turmeric executives cited the hundreds of millions of naira they had invested in not just covering the cost of producing the actual records but the investment they had made in building Chex's brand, which included, the cars, apartments, his first-class travel, the expensive jewellery to help him keep up his music video persona and they were yet to fully recoup their investment. In their opinion, Chex was disloyal.

Chex, on the other hand, believed he had been loyal for the past nine years and had made all the millions the company had invested in him back plus returns, and he felt at this point they were being greedy and wanted his blood.

The thing was, the Nigerian entertainment industry had grown quite a bit in the last few years, but the structure was still fractured. The primary source of income from music in the early days was from the shows. For nine years Turmeric had insisted on a seventy-thirty split in their favour from the revenue their artists got when they performed at shows.

These days, the revenue streams had increased due to the broadened number of distribution platforms where he could earn royalties. Big Chex had tunes for days, so his music was streamed and paid for by Africans all over the world. Let's just say his eye had cleared and he needed his bank account to match his superstar status. Four years ago, Chex had tried to renegotiate, but Turmeric had insisted that their contract as it stood then was fair, citing the millions they had invested.

Honestly, she didn't blame him. She could see both sides and wished these artists would read their contracts before they signed and that these record labels wouldn't be so greedy and give some leeway.

But Chex wasn't her client, Turmeric was, even though she had no desire to send him back to the squalor he had started from. She knew she was definitely going to use him and his low-rent lawyers to wipe the floor in court next week. Chukwuemeka was right—he was in breach.

"These small boys of nowadays. So disloyal!" Chukwuemeka lamented dramatically. "After everything Silvanus and Chukwudi did for that boy, this is how he repays them?"

As he turned to wave at another senior partner. Adesuwa rolled her eyes. This could go on for a while, and she didn't have the stomach for his rambling today of all days. She looked across the conference room at the disinterested faces of the other associates in the room and the fake expressions of interest they reserved for senior partners who signed their bonus cheques. She could tell they were waiting for him to stop talking so they could round up the meeting.

Usually, in these situations her feelings were somewhere between slightly amused and frustrated because as much as Chukwuemeka was excited about the cases like this, he would typically jump into their strategy meetings, grandstand a little, and hand off the bulk of the work to his favourite Junior partner, Adesuwa. Then jump back in again to take all of the credit during the press conference or media interviews. It was his way; she was used to it, but today she couldn't control the irritated expression on her face.

Her phone vibrated loudly on the conference room table, interrupting the meeting.

"Sorry guys," Adesuwa muttered, as she picked up her phone.

It was a WhatsApp message from a number that wasn't saved on her phone.

Hello Adesuwa, my name is Sonia. I just wanted to let you know that I am carrying your husband's baby. He has suggested that I take it out, but I know he is simply scared because you refuse to give him a divorce. We are in love. He doesn't love you. He loves me. You are just postponing the inevitable.

Numbness descended on her as she reread the message, and her blood turned cold.

"Adesuwa, are you alright?" Chukwuemeka asked, looking concerned.

Her expression must have given her distress away. She wasn't sure how to respond, and for a few seconds, she stared at Chukwuemeka mutely, not saying a word. It was as though she was no longer in control of her mind or body.

"Is anything wrong?" Chukwuemeka asked again. At this point, all the lawyers in the room were staring at her.

"I'm okay. I have to deal with an emergency." She stood shakily, her dignity holding her together as she gathered her things and made her way to the door.

There were a few murmurs in the room as she fled, and she could make out that Chukwuemeka was saying something, but her ears were ringing, and her entire body still felt numb.

As she settled at her desk and sunk into her chair, all she felt was despair. It had been a tough couple of weeks between the latest round of IVF failing again, Soji not being able to come up with a sensible explanation for spending her money and compounding it by coming home at odd hours even on weekdays. Sometimes he didn't make it back till it was ten the next day.

Adesuwa was fed up, miserable, and at the end of her rope. She felt like everything was falling apart around her, and she had no control. She put both her arms on the table, lay her head down and stared at the floor, not noticing when Mrs Akhaba entered her office and sat down on the chair in front of her a few minutes later.

"Adesuwa, are you okay?" The gentle question startled Adesuwa out of her reverie.

She looked up. "I'm sorry, ma. I'm just having a bit of a day. Actually, if I'm being honest, it's more like a bit of a bad few weeks."

"What's the matter, my dear? To be honest, I've been watching you walk around this office like a zombie, the last few weeks. I thought it would get better, but it looks like it's getting worse."

Adesuwa was tempted to spew out all her problems. Mrs Akhaba had been a mentor for many years, but mostly with work-related matters. She was the only female senior partner at the firm, and even though Adesuwa felt like she could confide in her, she was a bit hesitant to cross the professional boundaries and share her personal problems.

The truth was Mrs Akhaba had an inkling that her marriage with Soji was not stable because of a few incidents that had happened over the years. The most prevalent one being her over-indebtedness to the firm because she kept borrowing money against her salary to cover Soji's debts and at some point Mrs Akhaba had called her into a meeting to caution and tell her that it could affect her track to senior partner because the reality was that her behaviour was being scrutinised more severely. Mrs Akhaba had noted something Adesuwa had always known but never said: When you are a woman in power, your mistakes are magnified. It wasn't fair, but it was true. She had to explain to her mentor that her debt was a consequence of her husband's indiscretions.

She looked at Mrs Akhaba intently, still contemplating what to do.

"Young lady, I'm sure at this point you know that you can talk to me," Mrs Akhaba's steady voice freed Adesuwa from her stasis.

At this point, she needed to talk to someone, anyone. She wasn't ready to tell her friends about this latest fiasco. She knew what they would say already, and she wasn't prepared for their judgement. Calling her mother at this point was pointless, she would only provide platitudes like to pray, fast and only God can change the heart of kings, but she didn't need inanities right now. What she needed was some practical advice.

As she downloaded the happenings of the last few months in graphic detail, Adesuwa became overwhelmed with emotion, tears rolling down her face uncontrollably. She was embarrassed but grateful that her door was closed and she was in the privacy of her office. It was the first time she had cried in front of anyone in a while, but she felt a sense of release because, in the last couple of weeks, she'd had to bottle up her emotions. She didn't want Soji to see any more of her tears, she'd needed to be strong for SJ, and she'd needed to pull it together for work.

"My dear, you may not like what I am about to say but I hope you listen," Mrs Akhaba advised as she held both Adesuwa's hands.

Adesuwa closed her eyes and braced herself for the I-think-you-should-leave-him speech she had heard from her friends repeatedly in the last few years.

"My darling, you are not the first woman to be in this situation, and unfortunately you will not be the last, but you are going to have to snap out of it. You are giving this man and this situation too much power over you."

"I wish it were that easy," Adesuwa responded. "I seriously contemplated divorce after his last stunt over a year ago, but you should have seen the resistance my parents put up. You would have thought he was the victim."

Her mentor shook her head. "My dear, I am not talking about divorce. I am talking about control over your mind."

Adesuwa looked at her sceptically. What was this woman talking about?

"I know it sounds counterintuitive, but you have to change your perspective and focus on the things you have control over! Focus on the things that make you happy. Right now, you are so focused on changing a man that cannot be changed. My dear, you are not Jesus Christ. The only thing you have control over is yourself, your mind, your happiness, your work not Soji or even having a baby. In fact, the difficulty you are having with that is probably linked to your stress levels."

"It sounds easier said than done, ma," Adesuwa responded.

"It's not easy, but it's possible. Happiness is a choice, control over your mind is a choice. One that you have to take every day otherwise, you let this man run you mental. I speak from experience."

"I've been married for thirty years, and if I'm honest, I was miserable for twenty. I made a deliberate effort to focus on my work instead, after I got tired of running from pillar to post, looking for a solution to my marital woes." Her quiet tone spoke of regret and old wounds that had healed.

"You see, my husband was not just a womaniser he was also a drunk, and it was difficult to deal with his excesses. I sought help from pastors, family members, so-called marriage counsellors, until I realised that what I needed could only come from within me not outsiders. I didn't divorce him, but I left him alone and focused first on my work, then on my children, and then on discovering the things that truly make me happy. The things that bring me, Imelda, joy! And it worked like magic."

"What makes you Adesuwa happy? This weekend, sit down and write in a journal. What makes Adesuwa happy? Outside of being a lawyer, a mother, a wife, what defines you?"

It was her first 'Aha!' moment in a while. Adesuwa realised that she didn't know the answer to that question. She was blank. She actually didn't have a clue what made her happy. If she was honest, she had tied a lot of her happiness to Soji and Soji's behaviour. For the last few years, everything had been about how much happier she would be if only he would behave. If only he could just muster enough discipline to be a good husband. Mrs Akhaba was right she needed to focus on her. She had admitted a lot of her identity was tied to being married. It was as though the cloak of marriage was her crutch, something she was determined to hold on to regardless of the injury to her, her self-esteem and her livelihood.

"You also need to work through why you still give Soji free rein over the money you worked for despite his repeated bad behaviour. These are not questions you can answer today, but you should probably start doing the work to uncover the answers, so you do not continue to put yourself in financial jeopardy and compromise your job over your husband. I'm always here if you need to talk."

****

Tsola

As he walked through the lobby of The George Hotel, Tsola called Mr Lasisi to let him know he was done with his meeting and to drive to the entrance.

"Guy, how far?" a voice said from behind him. As he turned around, he saw Buchi, an acquaintance that worked in investment banking. They had done a few deals together in the past, but Tsola hated running into him because the guy did not know when to stop talking.

Oh no, not this guy, Tsola groaned in his head as he replied, "My guy, how far now? How's work? I heard you guys were working on the M and A for Aquatic and Doregos. Congrats!" He hoped that he could make enough small talk before his driver brought the car around.

"Yes, oh! It's about to be payday!"

"Good for you."

"Meanwhile, are you still dating that your babe, Zuri? The fine one that works in real estate."

"Yeah, of course."

"Oh, okay! I don't know why I assumed you guys had broken up. Strange!" Buchi looked like he would burst if he didn't share some dirt.

"Why would you think that?" Tsola was losing his patience and struggling to hide his irritation.

Buchi exploded. "No, *now*! It's nothing. I saw her with Olumide Sanni the other day having drinks at The Grill by Delis. And you know he's a player, so I assumed they were together."

"Right! It was probably just business. They are working on a new development."

"Ah! You are a better man than me, bro. If I were dating a girl like Zuri, I would never allow her to go anywhere alone with Olumide Sanni. The guy is a savage." He clapped Tsola on the shoulder.

As Mr Lasisi brought the car around. Tsola said his goodbyes and got in his car, fuming. Zuri hadn't mentioned drinks with her ex-boyfriend. The last conversation he'd had with her concerning Olumide, he had made it clear how he felt about her working with the man.
Vibrations from his phone interrupted his thoughts. It was a text from Zuri. She wanted to know if he was still up for dinner after work.

Tsola looked at his phone and ignored it. He wasn't ready to deal with her at this moment, and he didn't want to overreact. His anger was at boiling point. He couldn't help but feel like she had betrayed him by going behind his back. He would have preferred it if she had been stubborn and insisted she was doing the deal with Olumide because it was work. He could get with that; he would have been pissed, but he would have respected her honesty. However, going behind his back… that was different!

That was so sneaky, he thought. *This is the woman I wanted to marry. I can't accept lies from most people, and I won't accept it from her.*

****

Zuri

My stepbrother has put his mouth in the matter, my pops is looking like he wants to change his mind. Need additional incentive. Family meeting tomorrow morning. Call me, asap. Preferably tonight so we can have a game plan before the meeting tomorrow.

It was a text from Olumide. She looked at the clock on her phone. It was two in the morning.

What kind of wahala *is this now?* Zuri thought. They had been negotiating this deal for weeks. She had convinced Olumide to persuade his father to agree to the joint venture with Richmond. After several meetings with Mr Tunde and Zuri, Baba Sanni had conceded the idea of picking the construction company for the development. It turned out one of his sons dabbled in construction, and he wanted to throw him some business. Richmond had agreed to give an upfront payment of twenty million naira in addition to the units the Sannis would own after the development was complete. The agreements had been drawn up, and they were just waiting for final approvals after lawyers on each side had done their due diligence and vetted the documents.

She took a deep breath and quietly left Tsola's bedroom. She hadn't slept much because her mind was in turmoil. She had spent the better part of the day consoling Adesuwa and dealing with the aftermath of the Soji drama. She couldn't believe that he would do this! Adesuwa was the best wife to him, and he didn't deserve her. The worst part was her friend was still not considering divorce. She wanted to make her marriage work. Zuri wished she could show her that marriage did not equal suffering.

As she proceeded to the living room to call Olumide, she tried to close the door gently. Tsola hated it when his sleep was interrupted plus he had been in a foul mood when he came home from work. They were supposed to have dinner at R.S.V.P. after work, but when he hadn't responded to her texts or phone calls, she had decided to just meet him at home. He'd hardly said a word to her and had been unusually silent right up until bedtime. The last thing she wanted to do was to wake him up with her phone call. He would be cranky because it seemed work was taking its toll on him. She also felt guilty because she hadn't told him about working with Olumide. It never seemed to be the right time, and she had resolved to tell him when the deal closed. That way, he would know there was nothing to worry about.

"Hey, what's up?" she said as Olumide picked up the phone.

"Man! I'm tired of this your matter, oh," Olumide responded. "Seye had a meeting with Baba when I wasn't there and let's just say the outcome wasn't great. Pops came home and started ranting about how that small girl wants to use *oyinbo* to cheat me!"

"Cheat him how?"

"Seye told him that you guys have inflated the construction costs and that the profit you'll actually be yielding is way more," Olumide sighed. "Obviously, my brother is angling to still get the construction contract for the development, but the *koko* of the matter is Baba wants you to double your upfront payment."

"That's just ridiculous!" Zuri said. "I already moved mountains, getting the board to approve the twenty million naira! You know this. I really hoped we would close soon."

"Babe, don't shoot the messenger," Olumide said. "You know I'm on your side. This is a good deal for all of us, but the problem is family politics. I'll do my best to convince him but speak to Mr Tunde. see if there is anything they can do to sweeten the pot."

"This is a disaster! You've totally screwed me over," Zuri whispered furiously into the phone. "How am I going to explain this to him? He'll just think I'm playing games."

"Who will think you are playing games?"

She was startled as she turned around to see Tsola standing at the entrance to the living room.

How long had he been standing there?

"I'll call you back," she told Olumide, ending the call swiftly.

"Babe, you scared me," Zuri said, as she stood up from the sofa to walk towards him.

"Who were you talking to?" Tsola asked as he glanced at the clock in the hallway.

"It was work stuff," Zuri answered, avoiding the question. "I didn't want to wake you. Let's go back to bed."

"Work at almost three in the morning?" Tsola's voice was at a near shout by the time he finished. "Besides, you didn't answer my question. Who were you talking to, Zuri?"

Zuri was silent as she searched his face for answers. It wasn't in his nature to get angry over something as minor as taking a late phone call, but at this point, he was visibly upset, and she was worried that bringing Olumide up now would rile him further. Anxious, she wasn't quite sure how to answer.

Then, Tsola detonated. "Are you sleeping with him? Just tell me now! Zuri, have you been sleeping with him?"

Zuri recoiled in shock "Huh? Sleeping with whom? Are you okay?"

"You must think I'm stupid. I know that was Olumide on the phone."

"Yes, it was!" Zuri recovered herself and was beginning to feel offended. "But why would you think I'm sleeping with him?"

"Let me get this straight. First of all, I told you I wasn't comfortable with you working with him, and you said you would look for another location. That was months ago! Then I bump into Buchi, who tells me he saw you cosying up with Olumide at The Grill by Delis last week and was wondering if we were still dating. Do you know how humiliating that was for me? Now at this hour, you are sneaking out of our bed to have a conversation with the same Olumide! What do you expect me to think?"

"Babe, it's not like that." She reached for his arm.

"Please don't touch me!" Tsola jerked his arm away from her touch.

"Ah ah, chill now! You know nothing is going on between Olumide and me. I just didn't want to upset you by telling you I was going ahead with negotiating the joint venture for Richmond with the Sannis."

"How exactly do I know that nothing is going on between you?" Tsola spat. "You've been lying to me for weeks and sneaking behind my back to meet up with the man. If I hadn't heard from a third party or caught you tonight sneaking around in my house to talk to him, you would never have come clean."

"That's not true! I was going to tell you as soon as the agreement was signed so you could see there was nothing to worry about."

"Listen to yourself." His contempt for her was more than evident. "Zuri, you broke my trust, and you are standing there trying to justify it."

"Tsola, I'm sorry! Nothing happened between us. It was just work. I didn't want to jeopardise the deal. I was going to tell you, I promise." Her eyes were wet as she pleaded.

"You should have worried about risking our relationship and breaking my trust," his accusatory tone showed his mind was made up.

"Tsola, I'm sorry," Zuri repeated, trying to put her arms around him, but he pushed her away again.

"I'm sorry too. I can't do this anymore. I can't be with someone I can't trust."

"Tsola, don't do this!"

"I'm done." There was a finality to his voice. "You can sleep in the bedroom tonight. I'll sleep on the sofa." He stared at her for a full minute, and the pain in his gaze pierced her heart. Then he closed the door.

As Zuri stared at the closed door, tears rolled down her face. Then she heard the key turn. He had locked the door on her and their relationship.

What have I done? Zuri thought. *What have I done?*

****

Adesuwa

As Soji walked through the front door and saw Adesuwa sitting on the living room sofa staring listlessly into space, his heart sank. He had hoped she would be out or at least upstairs, so he would have time to pack a few things and make a clean escape.

After Sonia had told him about the text she sent to his wife, he had been angry at first, but he knew it was because she loved him and wanted to be with him by any means necessary. *It was kind of sweet*, he thought. She was young and naïve, so he couldn't blame her.

Admittedly, He hadn't wanted Adesuwa to find out like that. He knew it would be a double blow because apart from the infidelity, having a baby with another woman when Adesuwa was struggling with secondary infertility was just cold. Even for him.

He hadn't been home for a few days because he needed to avoid confrontation with Adesuwa. He thought he'd give her a few days to cool off before they had to have that difficult conversation, but to be honest, he still wasn't ready.

"Welcome back," Adesuwa said coldly, not turning around to look at him.

"Just came to pick up a few things." Soji glanced at her guiltily, then strode towards the staircase.

"So even after everything Soji, I don't deserve an explanation?" Adesuwa demanded as she stood up from the sofa and walked towards him.

"Listen, there is nothing to talk about," Soji said coldly. "She is pregnant, finish! What else do you want me to say? You already made your feelings clear from the hundred phone calls and messages you've sent me in the last few days."

"Really? This is how you are going to play this?"

"Play what?" Soji said defensively. "The cat is out of the bag already. She's having my baby. I didn't want you to find out the way you did, but facts are facts, and this baby is coming whether you like it or not."

"You are having a baby with another woman while you are still married to me, Soji? And you are saying it so casually as though this is normal? What did I ever do to you to make you treat me this way? All I have ever been is supportive and loving."

Soji slow clapped, derision seeping into his expression.

"Saint Adesuwa. I love how you want to pretend like none of this is your fault. Like you had no role to play in me finding comfort in the arms of another woman." His accusation hurt.

A tear leaked out. Then two, then a silent flood.

"Soji, so somehow I...I am to blame for you cheating on me... me again, and this time with a product of your infidelity on the way." Her breath caught every few words.

"You? Supportive and loving, *ke?*" Soji continued like he hadn't even heard her. "This marriage is a sham, and you know it. We've both been unhappy for years. This baby has just given us the clean break we all need. At least now you can finally be rid of me and live the life you've always wanted to live. Frankly, I'm tired of being Mr Adesuwa. I've finally found someone who respects me and doesn't put pressure on me to keep up with her friend's husbands."

"I don't even understand where all of this is coming from!" Adesuwa cried. "Put pressure on you? How? I've always respected you, and I've never compared you to any of my friend's husbands."

"Please save the piety for those who care. We both know that you are materialistic."

"Me? Materialistic? Soji, how?"

"Oh, Soji, we need a new kitchen! Oh, Soji, we need to put POP in the parlour," Soji derided, mimicking her voice when she'd asked about putting plaster of Paris accents in the major living areas. "I let you get your way because since day one you've been the man in this relationship and it only made things worse when my businesses started to struggle. You've used that as an avenue to disrespect me or tell me what Bode did for Ladun."

Adesuwa listened, aghast, as the poisonous resentment spilt from his lips. "I resent that because God knows I have never compared you to anyone not to talk of my friend's husband. Soji, what you forgot to add to your kitchen and POP story is that I was the one who paid for those things. I may have told you we needed them, but I never asked you for money to buy them. So how did I put pressure on you?"

"That's not the point, Adesuwa," He scoffed. "As usual, you miss the point completely. My point is, why did you need those things in the first place? I'll tell you why? Because you are spoilt. And trust you to try to make this about money. That's all it boils down to with you, isn't it? Naira and kobo, and you say you are not materialistic. So, you paid for the kitchen and POP now we won't hear word?"

"No, Soji. What I've been is financially responsible for this family since day one. You haven't paid house rent since the day we got married. I pay for everything from household expenses, school fees, travel expenses to your own personal debts! And the worst part is I do it all without complaint while pretending to the world that you are the breadwinner in this family. I have spent years lying to my friends about your contribution to our finances. I even give you money to go clubbing with your friends before you leave the house to help you save face. How can you now turn around and say that I am materialistic and compare you to my friend's husband?"

"Again, this is part of the problem," Soji said. "You always try to emasculate me and make me feel like less of a man when it's not my fault that you make poor financial decisions. For instance, why does SJ have to go to the most expensive primary school, if it's not because you are trying to keep up with the Joneses? Isn't that an example of you putting pressure on me?"

"Keep up with which Joneses?" Adesuwa's brittle laugh rang out as the conversation devolved into a farce. "SJ goes to that school because, A, its curriculum is one of the best in the country and, B, I want to give my son access to a high calibre network from the jump. The children in his class have a higher chance of becoming the business leaders and politicians in their generation. I don't know about you, but I've had to grow up in a world where that deal has gone to a family friend or the person they went to primary school or secondary school with because there's history and trust there."

"Madam, there are lots of people who didn't go to fancy schools that are successful today," Soji smirked.

"As a parent, my job is to work to give my child every advantage. The goal is for him to be more successful than his parents so if that means sacrificing flying upper-class or popping champagne in the club I'll do that because it all boils down to priorities."

It sounds like you are taking jabs at me."

"I'm not. If I wanted to do that I would say that the cost of your night out with the boys or upper-class ticket to London is the same as SJ's school fees for one term."

"*Abeg!*" Soji spat dismissively as he moved her out of the way and made his way up the stairs. "As usual, this conversation is exhausting. I just want to pack my things and go where I'm loved in peace. I didn't come here to argue with you. Thankfully, the Enyo Retail deal has come through, so I'll give you back what you claim I owe you."

"Despite all of your abuse, the only thing I've ever asked for in return is loyalty, not money," Adesuwa argued as she followed him up the stairs.

"Please get out of my way," Soji said as he reached for the handle of the bedroom door.

"And you still haven't given any kind of explanation for your mistress having your baby," Adesuwa said, attempting to block the entrance.

"Don't you get it, Adesuwa," Soji bellowed, holding both her shoulders and shaking her. "There is nothing to tell! I love her, and we are having a baby. Something you clearly cannot do anymore."

"Sojiiiii!" Adesuwa let out a guttural scream. It was all she could muster after that reprehensible blow. She couldn't believe he would throw her infertility in her face even after what he had done. The irony was she had completed her last round of IVF treatment at Olive Branch days before. Dr Emeka had asked her to stay positive, but after the failure of previous rounds, she had to admit to herself that she wasn't hopeful.

He shoved her aside and stormed into the room to grab a bag.

She was used to Soji being defensive, deflecting and making the argument about everything else aside from what he had actually done but this was vicious even for him.

I obviously married my enemy.

She sank slowly to the floor at the entrance to their bedroom, the room around her a blur through her tears.

SMART MONEY LESSON:
A FINANCIALLY INDEPENDENT
WOMAN IS AN ASSET, NOT A THREAT.

The Economics of African Feminism, Love and Money

In Africa, the word feminist has a negative connotation—in this part of the world when anyone calls you a feminist, it is not a compliment.

African women who declare themselves feminists and actively strive for financial independence are often viewed as women who want to make their own money so they can do away with the men in their lives. *Le sigh!* They are generally perceived as women who are too dominant, troublemakers, a threat to masculinity and a symbol of economic castration.

For clarity, in my opinion, a feminist isn't someone who hates men; a feminist is anyone who believes in equal access to opportunity for both men and women. In other words, if *I go school* and Femi *sef go school,* if we get the same grades, we should both have access to the same jobs and business opportunities.

We need to change the narrative, a woman who identifies as a feminist and actively seeks to become financially independent doesn't equate to "I don't need a man". When she chooses to be in a relationship, it just means she brings more to the table. Instead of being a financial burden, she becomes a value addition. Her success does not take away from his success. The pie they share just becomes bigger.

Sadly, the rules for financial success in this part of the world seem to be different for men and women. When a man is financially successful, society applauds him and tell him that there are no limits to his success. The more economically successful he becomes, the more access he has to the best women, the best entertainment, the best parties, the best social circles. Money openeth doors!

As women attempt to achieve financial success, it is not unusual for society to tell her to slow her roll because if she gets too successful, she won't get married. Make money but not so much you overshadow your man; don't buy property, rent, so you don't intimidate your future husband! Buy a car but not one that's so "big" that it scares off potential suitors.

If an African woman makes declarations like "I want a man who is ambitious, powerful and financially successful" she is usually met with statements like, "You are a gold digger", even though she makes her own money or "You are too proud!" and "You want to eat your cake and have it!" Expectations of wanting to be looked after by a man are viewed as greed.

Many successful men complain about the financial dependence of women and the rise of the gold digger in general but seem to punish women who are financially independent instead of rewarding them. Having her own money automatically means she wants to be a man and translates to being a woman incapable of submission. (Aunty! Please don't come and cause trouble in my house, oh!).

The irony is I have never met a successful African woman who doesn't want to be looked after by her man. I have also never met a successful African woman who wants to assert herself as the head of the household. Most African women who earn more than their husbands typically put on a charade, so their husbands look like the breadwinners to protect their ego.

The African millennial woman is evolving, most of us want to be Beyoncé's to our Jay-z and by that I mean the best versions of ourselves financially, physically, in our careers, on the home front, with our partners, children and we want men that won't force us to dim our lights but will help us shine brighter.

One of the most important lessons I learned from Mrs Ibukun Awosika, the chairman of First Bank in the last few years was this. Who you choose as your partner, husband or wife is one of the most important decisions that will have an impact in determining how successful you will be? Choosing the wrong partner is a costly mistake that can derail your success.

She argued that in Africa, we don't spend enough time encouraging girls to discover what their God-given purpose is first before they get married. The focus is on finding a husband as opposed to discovering who you are, who you want to be, and what kind of impact you want to have on the world. Your husband or wife should be your purpose partner on your journey through life. The goal is to help each other achieve success in your chosen endeavour. So if you don't know what your purpose is, it becomes difficult to know if the partner you've chosen is aligned with your purpose. I agree. The focus when it comes to marriage is mostly on emotions, spirituality, and societal norms; there's not enough conversation beforehand about purpose, values, and expectations when it comes to money decisions.

One of the most frequently asked questions during my book tour was "I'm asking for a friend, what do you do if you are the sole provider in your home because your husband can't seem to keep a job or do well in business but makes all the major financial decisions with money his wife earns?"

My answer is: I am not a marriage counsellor, and my first marriage did not work out, so I am not in a position to give marital or relationship advice. However, because I am so frequently asked questions about love and money, it made me think about how important it is to iron out these issues before taking the leap into marriage.

It is essential to have conversations about money in the dating stage. However, when these questions are raised, people tend to give what they think are the politically correct answers or what they think you want to hear.

It is essential to listen to the answers given and to even read between the lines; it is even more critical to watch patterns. How do they spend? How do they behave with money in a crisis? How forthcoming are they on their financial wins and losses? Pay attention to how people behave, and it might help with having a better financial picture.

EXERCISE:

Questions to ask your partner before you commit (note: you should be able to answer these too!):

On Earning

I find it hilarious that you can ask someone about the business or work their intended partner does, and they have little to zero knowledge about how they make a living. 'He's a businessman', or 'He works in oil and gas' may not be enough detail to truly understand your partner's source of income.

> What do they do for a living?
>
> What are their streams of income?

In A Financial Crisis

One of the most significant stress tests in any relationship is how people deal with financial problems.

> Who are they in a financial crisis: Do they sink or swim?
>
> What do they do first in times of crisis: Borrow money? Ask friends and family for help? Look for ways to leverage their skill sets to make extra money? Actively seek opportunities?

On Debt

> How much debt do they have?
>
> Are they honest and open with you about their debt?
>
> How do they behave when they owe?
>
> When creditors are knocking on the door, are they avoiders (avoiding phone calls, messages, pretending like it's not happening) or do they communicate and find creative solutions to the problem?

On Spending

A person's spending patterns are an indicator of what they value. In relationships, we tend to assume that what is important to us is vital to the other person, but people have different backgrounds, life experiences and money habits which can contribute to how they spend money, what they prioritise and their strategy for budgeting or achieving their financial goals. Different spending patterns do not always mean red flags because the difference might actually complement each other. However, sometimes, the seemingly trivial things that are not discussed beforehand are what breaks the camel's back.

On Core Bills

In some African countries where power outages are a regular occurrence (which means dependence on generators), diesel becomes a permanent feature in the monthly household budget. However, the frequency of use differs depending on the level of income and priorities. For example, if a man believes the generator should only be on for four hours and a woman believes it should be on until everyone is out of the house the next morning, there can be conflict. One person may see the other as extravagant, and the other sees their partner as withholding basic needs. It all boils down to what each person values and what each person is willing to compromise.

You want to do some scenario planning. If your partner was down to their last one hundred thousand naira and the car breaks down, utilities need to be paid, groceries need to be bought. What would be their scale of preference? What bill gets paid first?

On Lifestyle Spending

Again, this is even more subjective because, on the surface, we may look like we like all the same things, but we prioritise differently. Some scenario planning questions could be:

- What kind of education do we want to give our children? Boarding school or day school?
- Overseas education at a tertiary level or local university?
- Is travel an essential part of the budget?
- What comes first: a car or a house?
- Eating out regularly or eating in? Is eating at restaurants considered a luxury or a regular once or twice a month activity.
- What takes priority extended family financial needs or nuclear family financial needs? For example, if money has been allocated and put aside for your children's college fund and your partner's brother has a once in a lifetime business opportunity, what takes priority?

On Division of Labour
The expectations they have when it comes to gender roles and money.

- What are the expectations around being a stay-at-home parent or two-income household after the wedding?
- Do you expect a fifty-fifty split when it comes to bills? Which partner is expected to pay for the most expensive line items in the household budget, i.e. rent, mortgage, school fees, while the other takes care of food and household salaries?
- Is childcare (nanny, babysitter or day-care) considered a priority or a luxury?

On Career Choices
Nine-to five or entrepreneur? Does your partner require being with someone that has a steady income and structured work

environment that allows them to be back home by a certain time every day? Can they deal with the rigours and uncertainty of what it means when their partner is an entrepreneur?

- When one person decides to follow their dreams in a way that affects the household income, is your partner willing to shoulder the financial burden?
- Is your partner okay with you having a job that entails a significant amount of travel and being away from home?
- What is the plan of action when one person's job requires them to relocate to a different state or country? Is the decision made based on who earns more? Or who can provide the quality of life?

On Investing

When it comes to taking advantage of investment opportunities, we all have different risk appetites, and it is important to know if your own risk appetites complement each other when it comes to building your family's financial future.

- Is your partner a gambler that would bet all your savings on every business opportunity that comes along?
- Do they take calculated risks when it comes to making money or are they so conservative when it comes to money that they don't like to take any risks at all?

CHAPTER 8

DEBT, EQUITY & RESILIENCE

Tami

"I'm sorry that's the best I can offer," Mrs Faniro said.

"But these terms are not practical for the type of business I'm running," Tami said. "Isn't there a way around this?"

"I don't know what else to tell you," Mrs Faniro responded. "A bank is a business, my dear, not a charity. We do this to make money and we protect depositors' funds. Without any collateral or substantial cashflow, we can't afford to take the risk with a company like yours."

Tami could feel the anger boiling inside of her. She needed to get out of this office before she said something she would regret.

"Thank you for your time," she said as she rose from her seat and put her documents and other belongings together.

As she made her way out of Mrs Faniro's office, it was all she could do to stop herself from throwing a tantrum right there in the middle of the banking hall. This was the third bank she had been to, and she left each one with less enthusiasm for her business expansion than she had come with. With every rejection, she could feel her dreams slipping away.

As she settled into her car, she felt her phone vibrating through the pockets of her green ROCOCO jacket. She glanced at the screen of her phone. It was Zuri.

"How did it go? I tried to call you earlier, but when you didn't pick up, I figured you were still in the meeting."

"Zuri, I'm tired! I'm just tired," a frustrated Tami yelled.

A concerned Zuri went straight into soothing mode. "Babe, just breathe. What happened?"

"This system is rigged!" Tami complained bitterly. "It's as though it is set up for you to fail. I mean I'm looking for a twenty-million-naira loan, you are already offering it to me at a ridiculous twenty-six per cent interest rate. Are they crazy? Asking for collateral that's worth one hundred and fifty per cent of the loan. Tell me, Zuri, How? If I had collateral worth that much would I need a loan from them? It's ridiculous!"

"Take it easy, darling. Y—"
"Zuri, this woman actually had the nerve to ask me to ask my husband to put up the collateral," Tami cut her off. "I looked at my bare ring finger and said 'Ma, it clearly states on my application that I'm single.'"

"What an idiot! Even if you had a husband, what does he have to do with anything? Is he the one applying for the loan?" Zuri commiserated, shocked.
"I tire, oh," Tami sighed. "The witch then proceeded to ask if my father couldn't put up collateral. I didn't even know where to start with answering that one."

"Did you show them your bank statements?" Zuri asked. "Because that would show them that you've done more than twenty million in business in the last year, which shows healthy demand for your brand and supports the idea to expand production and go big on the ready to wear line."

"Sister! There's no English I didn't speak," Tami complained. "She said it wasn't enough. They all said variations of the same thing. I need collateral, and it's too high-risk for them without it."

"Tami, I know you are upset," Zuri said, "but we are going to work this out.

Let's meet up for drinks after office hours."

"Yes, please. After the day I've had, I could definitely use a drink." Tami let out a heavy sigh. "Where?"

"Circa. Lara says Chef Hadi and Hamada moved there, so you know that means we'll get free desserts and shots as well," Zuri laughed.

"OMG! That will definitely make me feel better," Tami sighed. "Chef Hadi makes the best food and Hamada makes the best cocktails in Lagos. I'm game, abeg. What time?"

"Seven o'clock," Zuri replied.

"Okay, great," Tami agreed.
"See you then, babe. In the meantime, please take it easy." Zuri reached out to hang up the phone when she heard—

"Zuri!"
She brought the phone back to her ear. "Yes, hun?"

"Do you think I'm going to make it? Is Irawo is going to make it?"

Tami's voice sounded hesitant, unsure.

"Of course it is. You've just had a few setbacks that's all! Listen, I'm incredibly proud of you and how you've transformed this brand in a relatively short time. *Irawo* is popular, we just need to figure out a way to turn that into money. I know you are overwhelmed. Go home, cry, take a nap, do yoga—whatever you need to clear your mind. Then come to Circa. We'll all brainstorm and figure it out."

"Will do. Thanks, babe." Tami seemed to breathe a sigh of relief. "You're right."

****

Lara

Lara stared out of the car window as her driver waded through Lagos traffic. She was worried. She had never been under more pressure to perform in her life. She had just left Abuja after a series of disappointing meetings with the regulators, and now she was on her way to meet up with the girls to catch up with even more drama.

For starters, Adesuwa seemed to still be in denial about Soji's girlfriend and soon-to-be baby mama.

Tami was going through a frustrating season, with all the doors closing in her face in her bid to raise capital for Irawo.

Zuri and Tsola had apparently broken up over some stupidity.

And Ironically, Ladun seemed to be the only one with her work life and marriage intact even after all the financial upheaval she and Bode were going through.

This adulting thing, it is a scam, Lara thought.

When exactly did any this get easier? Even though she had negotiated monthly payments to pay off her debts, her bills were still piling up. She had spent the last two months aggressively trying to close deals so she could get back in the black, all her efforts were yet to pan out. As tempting as it was to give in to the frustration. She knew that wasn't an option. She had to be resilient to the end.

Her phone rang, and she asked the driver to turn the volume down on the radio. This was not going to be a fun call.

"Lara, you are not serious," Deji barked as soon as she picked up the phone. "Good evening to you too, Mr Suleman," she replied in a breezy tone. After the day she just had, she wasn't ready to let him berate her.

"Why is Welch calling me to say that you are yet to submit the approval for the work programme?" Deji demanded, getting straight to the point. "Is there a problem?"

"Look, the work programme hasn't been approved by the regulators yet," she informed him.

She had anticipated this phone call, and she knew the deal could be in jeopardy, but she had hoped she would have better news for him after her meetings in Abuja. A month ago after several meetings with Deji's lawyers, she had gotten Pere to sign an agreement with Mayfield that they would get the contract to provide the pipelines and umbilicals for RM24 to bring the oil on stream, with the precondition that he facilitated the meeting with Welch in Qatar.

Deji had set up the meeting, and Lara had gone to Qatar to meet with Welch. She had shared their five-year work programme and budget. However, she had… fudged the truth a little, acting as though the regulators had approved the budget. She had thought it would be a minor obstacle to obtain the approval since she knew everyone that mattered in the towers, but she soon realised she had miscalculated.

"Lara, let me remind you that this is the reason I didn't want to vouch for Oasis because of issues like this. This situation here is exactly why I don't like working with small firms." His anger poured through the phone's earpiece.
"Deji, please calm down," Lara soothed. "You've spoken to Pere. You know we are good for it. There's just been a minor delay."

"Who is Pere?" Deji dismissed with an arrogance that annoyed Lara. However, she was the one that needed something from him. She needed to play nice.

"If I didn't have a thing for you, there's no scenario where I would be doing business with Pere and putting my reputation on the line with a company I've had a solid relationship with for at least ten years. This could mess up my credibility with them," Deji pointed out.

"Deji, I'm sorry for the delay. I'm going to sort it out," Lara promised. At this point, she knew it would infuriate him even more if she told him internal bureaucracy at Oasis was at fault.

"Fix it, Lara!" Deji's voice was hard and brooked no argument. He hung up without saying another a word.

Lara's irritated sigh echoed in the car as she sent Pere another text.

As she pulled up to the entrance of Circa, she saw a message from Ladun, telling the girls were seated upstairs. She walked up the winding staircase and could feel the toll of the last couple of weeks as she climbed the stairs. When she took off her carefully applied makeup at night, the dark circles underneath her eyes were like black holes. She wondered if Youtopia beauty had an eye cream that worked magic like all the other products in their beauty range. She made a note on her phone to call her beauty consultant Nnenna Okoye in the morning for a recommendation.

She got to the top of the staircase and scanned the room.

"Welcome, madam," Chef Hadi waved, stepping forward to give her a friendly hug. He was a Lebanese chef who had come to Nigeria to work and knew how to keep any restaurant's clientele coming because of his incredible hospitality. Plus, the guy made a mean steak.

"Your friends have all been waiting for you. Come, let me take you to their table." He took her hand and led her to the lively group of women.

"You look like you need a cocktail!" Hamada said jokingly, as she walked past the bar. "The usual?" He asked.

"Thanks, Hadi," Lara said before she took the empty seat next to Adesuwa. "What did I miss?" She asked as she put her left arm around Adesuwa's shoulders to give her a reassuring hug.

"Tami was just telling us about the ridiculous terms different banks have been giving her." Zuri brought her up to speed.

"*Pele*, don't worry," Lara commiserated. "You'll find something soon. You just need to keep at it."

"Man! This country is a scam," Tami said. "It's as though the system is set up for you to fail."

"Positive mindset, hun," Ladun said.

"This one is not about positive mindset," Tami said. "How can a bank be asking me for collateral worth one hundred and fifty per cent of the value of the loan?"

"I feel you, but remember that a bank is a business," Lara pointed out. "They are in it to make money. They hedge their risks with collateral because Nigerians have a habit of not paying back. You'd be surprised that even some rich people are on this table."

"So, I should suffer because some of my ancestors did not pay back their loans twenty years ago," Tami grumbled.

The girls laughed.

"No, but seriously, though it kind of bothers me that these days instead of being in the business of giving loans to businesses that can help to grow the economy, Nigerian banks seem to be more bothered about putting on their own fashion shows, concerts, and food fairs," Tami complained. "I mean, how do they justify having the money to spend millions of naira to fly in international celebrities into Nigeria and put on these elaborate shows but then turn around and say they can't afford to give loans to small businesses that need them without these ridiculous requirements?"

"Well I guess their justification is that they are providing a platform that helps to showcase these businesses," Lara replied.

"Oh, please! The last thing the fashion industry needs is more fashion shows. What we do need is financing for the other aspects of the value chain that are non-existent and keep us from expanding. I need them to fund someone's idea for pan-African distribution so my clothes can be accessible and sold to more people. I need them to fund businesses that want to create a production solution for fashion designers. They can keep their 'exposure.'"
Adesuwa laughed. "You have a point, *sha*. It's quite interesting that they don't focus on their core business of lending anymore. They take safe bets and put all their money in treasury bills, don't lend enough to SMEs and then seem to be copying each other with repeating the same entertainments."

"Have you tried one of those intervention loans the government is always announcing?" Adesuwa asked. "They are supposed to be single-digit interest rates and lower requirements than what banks offer traditionally."

"Actually, I heard those things are just PR," Lara laughed. "They make these announcements but how many people can you actually point to and say they got the loan?"

"I have one word for you," Tami added. "Bureaucracy! I've been trying to push for one of those loans for two months now, and the process is insane, and some of the requirements are frankly ridiculous."

"How so?" Ladun asked.

"First, I submitted my business plan. Then they wanted guarantors to basically underwrite the loan. *Then* they started asking for a notarised statement of net worth from each guarantor, which most people I approached weren't completely comfortable with. Because you know

Nigerians, nobody wants to declare their assets completely for any public record. After we semi crossed that hurdle, they said they would have to pay my suppliers directly, and my suppliers had to have a registered business name. You guys, my suppliers are market women, tailors, and Igbo traders. Most trade with their personal accounts." Tami said. "How exactly am I supposed to start explaining having a business name and requirements for opening a business account to *Iya* Basira?"

"It sounds frustrating, *sha*," Ladun sympathised.

"I was talking to Tsola about your difficulties, and he said the way debt is structured in Nigeria, it's too expensive for most small businesses," Zuri said. "He recommended looking into equity."

Tami expressed her misgivings with going that route. "I'm not sure I'm ready to give up control of my business to an investor. I know what Irawo is going to be as soon as I restructure it. I don't want anyone to claim part of my future money for giving me peanuts today."

"Girl! You can't be serious," Lara said. "Ten per cent of a hundred million is still a lot better than one hundred per cent of one million. And really, no one is going to ask you for ninety per cent of your business. When you are raising capital, you have to sacrifice something with debt, you are paying interest, with equity you are sacrificing control. You have to choose one. You can't be complaining about high interest and with the same mouth be saying you don't want to give up control."

"Whatever," Tami replied, rolling her eyes playfully.

"Have you set up your meeting with Tsola?" Zuri asked. "Let him help you figure this out."

"Yes. He told me to come by the office on Thursday with my business plan. I was surprised, *sef*! I thought he would hold your breakup against me, but he was super sweet and supportive."

"Breakup, *ke!*" Ladun said. "Are we calling it a breakup now? They are just having a misunderstanding."

Zuri's teasing expression faded as the conversation continued about her and Tsola. "You guys, He hasn't spoken to me in three weeks. I've called, I've emailed, I've sent texts. He hasn't responded. If he were at least responding, then I would know what to do next."

"But why were you meeting Olumide behind his back in the first place?" Adesuwa said, pointedly. "Obviously, I don't think you guys should break up over this nonsense, but I totally get Tsola's hurt. It was such a breach of trust. I can't imagine how he felt when that random asked him if you guys were still dating."

Lara was NOT having it. "*Abeg!* Yes, she shouldn't have hidden, but he should never have put her in that situation in the first place. She's not a baby. She should be able to conduct business with whomever she likes. Also, if he trusted her, he would know that that silly boy could never get in between them. Zuri is not like that."

"*Haba*, Lara," Ladun pushed back. "You know how men and their egos are. We have to support Zuri, but we also have to tell her the truth."

"Please let's move on, *abeg*! I don't want to talk about this anymore," Zuri interjected. "I've been so depressed the last couple of weeks, but the upside is that I've been super focused on work and the agreement has finally been signed by Baba Sanni. I even used that to negotiate a seven per cent commission for every unit I sell off-plan."

"I was going to ask you guys if you were interested in buying," Zuri probed, looking around the table to gauge the expressions on their faces.

"Everyone is looking for money right now," Tami replied. "There's no disposable income to invest."

Lara, on the other hand, jumped at the opportunity. "I'm actually interested, oh," Lara replied. "But first, let me close a few deals."

"It's not going to be ready for another twenty-four months, so we still have time," Zuri told her. "It's way cheaper to buy off-plan, plus there's an additional discount on each unit for employees."

"Hopefully, we'll all have gotten our acts together by then," Adesuwa said. "Actually, I was thinking we should register a company, all five of us," Zuri offered, "and open an investment account in the company's name. That way, we can all save towards it in the coming months."

"That's actually not a bad idea," Adesuwa said. "We can buy a few units together and share the rental income. My money is not exactly up right now, but in a few months, it might be feasible." The others all nodded in agreement.

Zuri was excited that everyone had agreed so readily. "Great! I already set up a meeting with Omosede to discuss my investment portfolio and talk about how to go about this joint real estate investment, but I wanted to run it by you first."

She began an animated run-through of her ideas of what they would be able to do together. As she chatted, Tami caught Lara sneaking a peek at her phone for the umpteenth time tonight.

"Madam, you keep checking your phone," Tami said suddenly, looking intently at Lara.

Conversation stopped, and three heads swivelled in Lara's direction. Tami continued, "I would have asked if it was that your sugar daddy, Deji, that you are texting with, but you are not smiling. Is everything okay?"

"You are not serious," Lara joked. "He's not my sugar daddy, please. It's strictly business."

"Na so!" Adesuwa laughed for the first time that evening. "The guy is obviously trying to get in your pants."

"Well, that's his business!" Lara wagged her index finger in rejection. "Seriously, I'm here dealing with work drama. These people at Oasis are getting on my nerves. I've been texting my financial controller all day."

"Ah! What happened again?" Ladun asked. "I thought you were about to close the deal."

"Long story short? I found out while I was in Abuja yesterday that my financial controller hadn't posted the performance bond, so an approval request from the regulators is a nonstarter."

"Which one is a performance bond again?" Tami said.

"Basically, a guarantee from the bank saying we have enough money to develop the asset based on the collateral we present to the bank. I was told today that the landed properties that we pledged to another onshore asset have not yet been released by the bank even though we have finished our work programme on that asset."

"And he let you just go to Abuja to set up meetings empty-handed?" Adesuwa gasped. "What a twat!"

"Tell me about it!" Lara sighed. "On top of everything else, I just found out that Pere went to tell that nitwit bootlicker, Festus, about the deal I cut for a commission if I bring the international partner in six months instead of twelve. Now he's cut the same deal and is apparently working another angle. If he signs before me, my commission on the deal automatically disappears."

"You'll sign before him, *jo!*" Zuri said, poking Lara in the arm playfully. "Plus, you are way ahead of him with your own IOC, and he still has to deal with the same hurdles you are facing now. Just keep your eye on the prize. Don't look left or right."

"Yeah, I know," Lara smiled. "But I still need plan B in case this doesn't work out. What hasn't changed in my life is the need for a significant increase in income."

"What did you have in mind?" Ladun asked.

"To be honest, nothing concrete," Lara responded. "I was thinking maybe I should cut a deal with the downstream traders because downstream is relatively easier. It's basically buying and selling, and they have a constant supply of the product, but it is *man know man*."

Tami chuckled because Lara was one of the most plugged-in people in the industry. "You know everyone, though! I'm sure you can hook something up if you really think about it."

"Well the real value would be to find a long-term off-take and land a five- or ten-year contract," Lara said. "If only I knew one minister of energy in one of these other African countries that I could convince to make Oasis their sole supplier. *Omo that one na hammer!* But my networking *no carry me reach there*."

"Actually, do you remember that my friend Mwamvita Makamba? She's very connected. I'm sure she knows a minister or two she could introduce you to," Adesuwa offered.

Lara thought for a second and then remembered. "Vaguely! The gorgeous Tanzanian that lives in South Africa."

"Yes, her! She works for Vodacom South Africa as their head of pan-African business development. She's kind of a celebrity in Tanzania because she's the scion of political royalty. Her father was a member of parliament, and her older brother January ran for president after being an MP himself, even holding positions like the minister of state. She knows a lot of people. I could make an introduction if you are interested."

"Ha! I'm interested for sure!" Lara said. "Please send an email tonight."
They finished their dinner with Ladun regaling them with stories from the
recently concluded influencer campaign she had spearheaded for the
Hargrave group. She had really started enjoying her work. Even going as far
as reading more, listening to podcasts and doing research on how to create
effective advertising campaigns. She had become Belema's star pupil in just
a matter of weeks.

****

Tami

As Tami got to the reception in Tsola's office, she was tempted to turn around.
It was one thing to be rejected by financial institutions; quite another to be
thought of as stupid by her best friend's boyfriend.

There's also the fact that Tsola and Zuri still weren't speaking and I don't want
to bear the brunt of his anger this morning. But he's is not like that, right? She
thought nervously.

"Hello, my name is Tami Davies," She said to the receptionist. "I have a
meeting with Tsola Preware. Please tell him I'm here."

"Yes, ma," The receptionist responded then dialled a number on her
intercom.

"He's ready to see you, ma." The receptionist stood and led her to his office.
"Thank you," Tami smiled.

Tsola's office décor had a simple but very sophisticated monochrome theme
with mixed textures in black and white. His trophies from sports and business
lined the backdrop behind his desk, alongside framed certificates from
several university courses including Harvard and Stanford. She loved the
design, but most of all, she loved that it mirrored his personality—simple and
sophisticated, but not ostentatious.

"Tami!" Tsola bussed both cheeks as he welcomed her into his private office. "I've missed you, oh."

"Story, story! It's you that has abandoned us, *now*. You don't call, you don't text. I'm just grateful that you made the time to let me pick your brain this morning."

"Anything for you Tam," He said, with a smile. "You know this. So, you want to raise capital? Tell me how I can help."

"Hmmm!" She settled into the chair across from Tsola. "This whole thing has been really tough with being rejected repeatedly, and I'm just about ready to give up. I've been thinking maybe my dad is right and I should just go and get a job because this passion is not feeding me."

Tsola grinned. "Do you know how many noes I got when I first started out? It's part of the game. The trick is to be resilient enough that your desire to succeed exceeds your fear of failing. Fail faster, learn, and move!"

"We'll see! Anyway, I wanted to show you my business plan." She whipped out the PowerPoint presentation she had printed.

Tsola folded his arms into his chest and said to her, "No. Don't show me, tell me. Give me a five-minute pitch that tells me where your business is now and where you would like it to be in the next five years."

Tami's pitch was stilted and full of business. Two minutes in, Tsola raised his hand to stop her.

"Tam! You are pitching your problems how you think I want to hear it, instead of from the perspective that no one knows your business better than you. Just tell me your story."

Tami hesitated, unsure what he was fishing for. "Uh… sure. What do you want to know about the business?"

"Everything. Why did you decide to become a fashion designer? Give me a quick run-through of your process. Things like production, marketing, customer acquisition strategy, financials. What are your revenue streams, main costs? How much did you bring in last year? How much did you take home in profits? Who are the key players in your team?"

Tami took a deep breath. "Well, I've always been interested in fashion. As a little girl, I was obsessed with colours and the feel of fabrics. I *lived* to go clothes shopping with my mum. As I got older and developed my own sense of style, it was difficult to find things that fit my vision. So I decided to create clothing for myself and for women like me. It was a hobby, but in the last two years, I've been trying to turn it into a viable business."

She continued, "As for the process, I illustrate my designs, procure fabric, draft patterns, before developing and correcting the samples, then finally the send the dresses for mass production."

"When you say mass-produce, what are your quantities like?"
"I produce about ten units per style for at least the first run. Then if there's excess demand, we produce more."

"Tell me, how much does it cost on average to produce one unit?"

Tsola questions were getting increasingly detailed, but Tami was well-prepared and didn't find it too difficult to come up with the answers he needed.

"It depends on the style and fabric, but between five and fifteen thousand naira," Tami said.

"And what's your pricing strategy?"

"If it costs five? I sell for twenty, and the more expensive fifteen k pieces are priced around fifty thousand. I mostly do a lot of custom-made items like wedding dresses, evening dresses, and *aso ebi*. The margins for those are a bit higher. I generally don't let my margins go below fifty-five per cent."

Tsola looked like he was doing some quick math in his head. "Okay, let's move on. What's your customer acquisition strategy?"

Tami looked puzzled. "What do you mean?"

Tsola was amused. "I mean, how do you find your customers?"

"Oh! Through social media. Mostly Instagram because people on the platform are more visual. I also try to go to exhibitions and fashion fairs to sell clothes."

"What would you say make up your highest costs?" Tsola asked.

"Payroll! My tailors' salaries, then probably fabrics. And I guess the costs of mistakes as well."

"Mistakes? Elaborate."

"One of the biggest issues I have is with tailors. It's hard to find and retain good ones. If they are skilled, they are expensive and hard to retain because they keep looking for better-paid jobs. If they are just average and the business can afford them, then they need a lot of direction, which usually means a lot of mistakes which costs me fabric, diesel, frustrates production and the customer experience and I usually need to give a discount to make up for the disappointment."

"I'm not surprised because human capital is one of biggest issues business in Nigeria have," Tsola said. "You can have a great idea but finding the talent to execute is tough and limits your capacity, so I can imagine it being frustrating with low skilled labour."

"Mmm-hmm, but also when big things like the generator breaking down or the machines developing faults occur, it affects my cost of production in a way that makes it slow to recover."

"Okay. Talk to me about your revenue and profits," Tsola asked, switching gears.

"To be honest, they are not great. I feel like there's all this demand for my clothes on social media, I'm always busy in the studio, we have regular clients, but the demand does not translate to cash. It always feels like we are waiting for the next payment just to catch up with bills."

"In a good month, how much revenue do you bring in?"

"I'd say about two million naira in a good month, but the truth is when I consider my overheads, that doesn't go very far. I have to stretch it so we can survive lean months. A bad month could mean we make as little as three hundred thousand, which can't even pay salaries."

Tsola seemed to be out of questions, so Tami sat back. She realised that this was the first time she had thought through her business so holistically. She watched, tense, as Tsola mulled their conversation over the last forty-five minutes.

Tsola took a few minutes to make notes.

"Right," he said as he sat back.

"I don't know much about fashion, but there are basically only two levers to manoeuvre to make a profit. You either increase revenue or find ways to reduce costs. Sounds simple, but the difficulty is in figuring out how."

Tami winced. "It feels like a never-ending saga of 'What am I doing wrong now?'"

"Without even looking at your books I can tell that you don't have a handle on your costs and you take a piecemeal approach to your production. It may seem cheaper, but it increases your costs in the medium to long-term. For example, you make ten units on average per style and per run, I assume to test out the market and see if there's a demand for the style. The thing is, that also means there's no economies of scale and its actually more expensive to produce the collection even if the demand is sustained."

Tami pushed back. "I get where you are coming from with economies of scale, but the reality is, ready to wear ties down capital. I produce ten to reduce my risk just in case I like the style, but the customers don't. I don't want to be stuck with stock I'm unable to sell."

Tsola laughed. "You must find ways to reduce your cost of production by planning better. Let's say you focused on planning only four production cycles a year. I'd imagine that buying fabric in larger quantities reduces your unit cost per garment, plus buying in bulk should give you bargaining power with your suppliers."

"But what if I mass-produce styles that no one wants." Tami feared that a poorly received line could be a death knell for her business.

"As an entrepreneur, you have to take on affordable steps, you can recover from," Tsola was not going to allow fear to push her into making bad decisions. "Tami, you've been doing this for a while so by now your gut or at least history should tell you what styles work."

"Sometimes it's hit and miss, but I think I know what my customers want," Tami replied.

"Great. My assessment is that you have something here, you just need a little help with structure. I suspect you are probably under-pricing because you don't have a holistic picture of your costs and are only factoring in the cost of goods sold, without including other indirect costs. Your lead time between a customer getting their goods and when payment is collected is too long, and you are paying suppliers too quickly. You may want to look at discussing credit terms with them, especially if you are buying in bulk. You should convince them to give you at least thirty days of supplier credit."

"Thanks, Tsola. I think I have a little more clarity now. But we haven't talked about this raising money issue. I just need you to point me in the right direction and a strategy to convert their noes into yeses."

"Man, there's no shield from noes, Tami! You just should figure out why, course correct, and try again. I close billion-naira deals, I have a proven track record, and I still get noes sometimes."

"Really?" She replied sceptically. "You are just trying to make me feel better."
"It's just the reality. Investors, banks, customers, it doesn't matter. They all want value! Investors want a return on their capital, banks want interest on their loan, and although value for customers is a harder thing to measure, ultimately, they want performance."

Tami tried not to show her simmering frustration. "I try to do that, but the money guys don't seem interested."

"It's your job to articulate the value proposition you are offering by creating a compelling story that they can buy into. They are assessing the level of risk they are taking on versus the value of returns they could get."

Tsola knew that it was important she changed the way she thought about the relationship between herself, her company, and financial backers for her to be genuinely comfortable with moving forward.

"When you don't close the deal with any of them, it's because you've not been able to convince them that the price is worth it," he told her matter-of-factly.

"It means I have to find better ways to communicate the value of my business." Tami nodded contemplatively. "In your experience, though, which one is easier to raise, debt or equity?"

"The easiest way is from your customers. Create something valuable and sell it. It all boils down to sales! Your job is to demonstrate that you can make sales whether you take on debt or equity," he answered.

Tsola came around the desk and sat on the corner, hands in his pockets as he pitched his business deal. "This is what I'm going to do. I'll invest two million naira of my personal money, not Zuma's, in an Irawo collection."

Tami sat stunned for a second at the generous offer before she replied, "Wow, are you serious? Thank you."

"Hold on, it comes with conditions. First, I want to see a one-pager that outlines your sales strategy to make sure the collection makes a profit. It must detail what you are going to spend the money on that will have a direct impact on the bottom line. Treasury bills are about thirteen per cent per annum, now, but I'll expect a higher return because I'm taking a higher risk. So, twenty-five per cent."

Tami did some quick math in her head. That was half a million naira.

"If your strategy document is convincing, I'll give you the money for ninety days. If you're able to deliver the return I've set, you'll have demonstrated your ability to extract value from your business," Tsola proposed.

"OMG! Thank you, Tsola. I haven't figured out the how yet, but I'm going to."
"No worries. If you can deliver, there will be proof-of-concept, and I'll host a cocktail party and put some investors together that I think might be interested in putting money into a fashion business. You can pitch them your expansion plan."

Tami couldn't hide her excitement. This was the best news she had gotten in months.

The phone rang, interrupting their conversation.
"Tami, my eleven o'clock is here," he told her as he dropped the phone. "I'm

glad we got to wrap this up."

"Thank you so much, Tsola, for taking a chance on me. I'll never forget this," She told him.

"It's all good Tami," Tsola smiled. "I love the passion you have for your business. You just need a structure that can help you monetise it properly, and I'm happy to help. Worst-case scenario, I lose two million naira," he joked.

"Haaaa! *Awon* big boys," Tami laughed, then sobered as she broached a sensitive subject.

"Tsola, I was hoping we could discuss this you and Zuri's matter," Tami said, slowly. "She puts on a brave face, but I know she's hurting. If only you would just talk to her, you guys can work this out."

Tsola smiled. "I knew it was only a matter of time before you brought it up, but thank goodness my next meeting was two minutes ago."

Tami shook her head. "*Na wah, oh.*"

"Don't worry. We'll talk about it another time," Tsola said as he stood up from behind his desk and began to politely usher her out.

SMART MONEY LESSON: UNDERSTAND YOUR CAPITAL STRUCTURE

Talk to nine out of ten entrepreneurs in Africa, and they'll tell you one of the biggest struggles they face is raising capital for their business. Debt (typically, taking a loan) is expensive because institutions' exorbitant double-digit interest rates often require collateral, which most small businesses do not have.

Equity seems elusive, and entrepreneurs often have limited information about where to find venture capitalists or private equity firms that are willing to invest in their industry and even when entrepreneurs do find out where investors are, they have limited access to the relevant parties. When they do have access, most entrepreneurs are scared of giving up control of their businesses in exchange for capital.

The bottom line is, debt is hard, equity is hard—you must choose your hard. What kind of financing do you have access to? And what type of funding is right for the business that you are in? The answer to these questions will be determined by your particular situation, but here are a few things to consider before you get in front of an investor or lender.

Whether you are seeking equity or debt, the core question for any external investor or bank's mind is—what is the return on their capital? If we give you this money, how much will I get back? It is not enough to say my idea is excellent and you will get your money back, you have to prove it by laying out a convincing argument backed by facts and tested assumptions that helps to rationalise their risk.

You need a business plan that explains what your idea is, how you intend to execute, how much money you need for how long, and the projected revenue that demonstrates that the business has the capacity to pay back the loan or provide an adequate return on equity. A business plan is crucial because it documents your intentions. However, I find that many people may have a business plan in writing but are unable to articulate said plan verbally if an opportunity presents itself. You have to have the facts and figures at the tip of your fingers to the point that you can have a conversation about it, whether you meet a potential investor at a party, run into a decision-maker at your bank in the lift, you should be able to say enough to pique their interest. So, practice, practice, practise your five-minute pitch in front of the mirror, with your friends, family, and colleagues.

EXERCISE:

Avoid Common Pitfalls When It Comes to Debt

1. Calculate your sales projections as accurately as possible. Overestimating your sales and the time frame it will take to make projected sales can put you in trouble with the lender because it puts you in a position where you are unable to pay at the specified time, which could trigger the sale of collateral and or affect your credit rating. Map out the middle ground between conservative projections of the worst scenario, and being overly excited about the idea that you don't factor in unforeseen circumstances.

2. Similarly, calculate your cost projections accurately. When taking a loan, it is essential to remember that your business can only afford to take the loan when your cashflows exceed your business expenses as well as the cost of the loan. Underestimating your costs and not looking at them holistically can lead to loss of control of cash flow which is the most common reason a business fails.

3. Create a document for your personal use that continually reminds you of what you need the funds for, so that you are not easily swayed by external factors that might crop up. Many entrepreneurs get into a bind when they start to spend the money on expenses that are not related to the business. It's vital that you put the debt to use in a way that improves your business's

bottom line. Many African entrepreneurs after going through the rigours of finding the capital may be tempted to justify spending on expenses that are outside of the business, for example, I need a new car for the look and feel of my business so I can attract more clients, or I need to attend family emergencies because they are essential.

4. Create alternative revenue-generating activities that can help you pay back the loan if your business idea is not successful or takes a longer period to succeed.

5. Formulate a negotiation strategy ahead of time. Don't be so afraid or intimidated by the institution you are approaching that you don't negotiate some of the finer points that may end up leaving money on the table. Negotiate reduced interest rates, ask for moratorium periods, that is, a holiday from paying interest. Sometimes the bank may be willing to give some breathing space when, for example, they see that your revenue is projected to start coming in the sixth month. This is not saying they will always acquiesce to your requests, but it's still worth trying because the answer is always 'no' when you don't ask.

EXERCISE:

HOW TO AVOID COMMON PITFALLS WHEN IT COMES TO EQUITY

1. Know your Investor

   Understanding that giving away shares in your company in exchange for capital is basically a marriage and you need to know who you are getting in bed with. And like any marriage the honeymoon period is sweet but in the event that there are issues in the medium- to long-term, you need to be able to answer specific questions to help you make the best decision. How do they make their own money? Who or what have they invested in in the past? How are they known to manage or resolve conflict? How are they under pressure? Are they the sort of person you can run to in times of crisis?

2. Know your Value

   Make a list of other qualities the potential investor may bring to the table. Capital is great, but it is always advisable to find investors that bring more than capital to the table. You want an investor that has technical know-how, expertise, and a network of relationships you can leverage on to scale and improve your business.

3. Protect Yourself

   Engage independent legal advice that ensures that the terms of the contract protect you and give clarity on ownership, dividends, and exit strategy. Sometimes, creative entrepreneurs are so carried away with the brilliance of their idea that they do not take the time to vet the terms of engagement before it is too late.

CHAPTER 9   MAKING MONEY MOVES

Lara

"I'll have the crispy baby salad with mango chutney to start," Lara selected off the menu.

"What would you like to have as your entrée?" The waiter asked as he jotted down her order.

"I'll try the lamb tenderloin with mashed potatoes," Lara responded, as she handed him the menu.

"Would you like to pair that with red wine. We have an excellent selection of—"

"I'll just have a glass of your house red." The prices at Nusr Et were already expensive enough, so she was not about to be bamboozled into spending extra on a fancy bottle. In fact, as much as she loved Dubai and everything the beautiful city had to offer, the prices were a completely different beast, and she had learnt to spend where she loved but cut expenses ruthlessly on the things that didn't matter that much to her.

She had decided to treat herself to a mini-holiday in Dubai to decompress before heading back to the madness that was her Lagos life.

It had been a gruelling few months trying to finalise the deal with Welch in Qatar, but she had made the final trip with Pere the previous week. They had flown into the Middle East on Deji's Bombardier Challenger 605. She had politely refused, saying she was travelling with her boss and it would be inappropriate, but to her surprise, Pere had called her an hour later to say they would be going to Qatar on said plane.

Lara and Pere were alone on the flight, giving Pere time to press Lara for the details of how she had overcome the performance bond obstacle as well as get the approval for their work programme from the towers in record time. Her response had been simple but less than forthcoming: "Pere, I'm sure you know by now that resilience is my superpower. Nobody that tried to act as an obstacle to me in this transaction stood a chance, especially when my six-month deadline was looming."

As they both laughed, she knew she sounded confident, but Lara remembered all the times she had cried real tears behind her office door. The bureaucracy at every point had threatened to frustrate her into quitting many, many times during the process. First of all, it seemed as though the financial controller at Oasis was on to her deal with Pere and was determined to sabotage it because there had been no logical reason for why he hadn't been motivated to make sure the bank released the asset they were to use as collateral. After several pointless meetings with him, she had gone to the bank herself to speed up the process. There, it should have been more straightforward, but alas, like everything else in Nigeria, it had not been. Thankfully once the performance bond had been posted, she had leveraged on her many relationships in the towers to make sure the approval process was swift.

They had signed the agreement in Qatar at the IOC's offices without incident; Welch had already visited their Lagos operations to carry out its due diligence after which both parties had spent weeks going back and forth on the terms of the agreement, so the final meeting was merely a formality. To celebrate, the Qataris had planned a two-day luxury experience for her and Pere. They had been wined and dined at five-star restaurants, then had been treated to the best seats in the house at a Cirque du Soleil show. All she could say was that the Qataris did luxury differently.

They were flying back to Lagos commercially and had to make a stop in Dubai, so Lara had taken advantage of Pere's good mood and asked if she could take a few days off there to reset. After all the hard work she had put in the last few months, she needed to rest and reflect. He had said yes, and he must have still been in a good mood when he landed in Lagos because she got an email notification with a credit alert from her bank. Oasis had paid her commission on the deal, no story, no argument.

She sat in the restaurant enjoying her version of self-care—relishing great food and wine by herself with her thoughts. She was contemplating her goals, what her next steps were, what she would do with her new windfall, and what she had learnt from all the obstacles and triumphs the last few months had brought. As she took a sip of wine, Lara noticed a group of black men on the other side of the restaurant. They were well dressed in their tailored designer suits. She could tell they were Nigerian or at least African because, besides their loud conversation which was littered with titbits from a transaction they had just closed, she could hear what was unmistakably pidgin English.

A good-looking guy in a navy-blue suit and white shirt seemed to be staring at her. He was light-skinned, with piercing light brown eyes and a mischievous smile. He looked familiar, but she averted her gaze, sipping her wine and picking up her phone, switching from WhatsApp to her Instagram feed.

She was engrossed with messages from her group chat, where the girls were congratulating her on closing the deal and proposing all sorts of ways to celebrate her win when she sensed a tall figure approaching her.

"I figured I would just come over to say hello and save you the trouble since you are stalking me," a voice said.

She looked up to see Mr light-skinned-with-brown-eyes standing in front of her with a naughty smile on his face.

Lara raised her brow. "Sorry? Are you talking to *me?*" *This one must not be well*, she thought. She dismissed him, deliberately returning her focus to the lamb on her plate.

He didn't budge. "Of course I'm talking to you. First of all, I saw you at the airport when I got to Dubai, I saw you again in my hotel lobby when I was checking in, and now I'm seeing you at a restaurant, just as I've finished my meeting. So yes, my suspicions that you are indeed following me have been confirmed."

Lara was stunned speechless by the boldness of this complete stranger and apparent lunatic, unable to decide whether to berate him or laugh at his audacity.

"But because you are such a beautiful woman I wanted to let you know, face to face, that I'm flattered," he continued with an amused look, clearly enjoying his own joke.

Lara took her time. She put her cutlery down, folded her arms in front of her, and pressed her lips together in a semblance of a smile before saying, "Clearly, you're the one following me because I've never seen you in my life until you rudely came to interrupt my alone time."

He raised his arms in mock surrender. "Okay, okay! Let's agree to disagree." He proceeded to plonk himself on the seat opposite her.

"My name is Zik. May I join you?"

"Well, seeing as you've already insinuated yourself into my lunch, you might as well," Lara said, sounding mildly sarcastic.

"Which one is insinuate again? You *dey speak plenty big English, oh*," Zik responded, laughing. "Are you a lawyer?"

Lara laughed at his good-natured humour, the smile on her face warming in genuine amusement. He was brazen in a way that was shocking but cute; his jovial nature didn't allow you to be offended. He spoke in a manner that indicated he was the beneficiary of a good education, but with a significant hint of an Igbo accent that told her he probably grew up in the east or that Igbo was his first language.

"No, I'm not a lawyer, I work in oil and gas. And my name is Lara, by the way."

"Beautiful name, for a beautiful woman," He said, as he signalled the waiter to refresh the drink he'd brought with him.

"Thank you." She had capitulated, but she wasn't going to let him have it that easy. "So, what do you do? For work, I mean. When you are not harassing unsuspecting women in restaurants."

Zik had the grace to look slightly sheepish. "We both know I did not harass you. You bewitched me with your eyes and willed me to come and talk to you. If you had said no, I would have promptly walked away, but I thought I should try my luck. I'm a farmer. I own a few pig farms across Nigeria, mostly concentrated in the east but we have a decent number in the south west as well. We are currently expanding, working on processing and packaging pork into cured meats like bacon and sausages. The goal is to become a pan-African brand in twenty-four months." However, I'm in Dubai thanks to a friend who brought and some other close friends in on an oil and gas deal.

"Hmmm. Pigs! I love a good pork chop. How did you get into it?"

For the next two hours, Zik and Lara drank wine, ate, and talked. She told him about her career at Oasis, her friends, and why she didn't think too deeply about being single.

He regaled her with stories from his youth, growing up in Enugu as the youngest of four. He had gone to University of Nsukka (UNN) and earned a degree in engineering, before gaining admission to MIT in Massachusetts, majoring in maths and computer science. He'd had a stint in investment banking in the States and the UK before deciding to move back home to build a business in agriculture, where he could create exportable value.

He lived primarily in Lagos but travelled to the east often to man that part of his business. He was thirty-six, never married but had been engaged for about a year four years ago. He was surprisingly easy to talk to, and they discussed everything from Nigerian politics and the global economy to his regular squash game at Ikoyi Club. As Zik paid the bill, he glanced at her and asked, "So, what next?"

"Next, ke?" Lara said. "I'm going back to the hotel to sleep. I've already spent way more time in this restaurant than I planned to."

"Lara, you can sleep when you get to Lagos." he cajoled.

"Ah! Okay, oh, Mr Nightlife! what did you have in mind?" Lara laughed.

"Let's go to the marina. We can walk for a while and then go to drinks and maybe dinner later if you are still hungry."

She was tired but she was enjoying his company, so she agreed.

****

Zuri

As she sat in Omosede's office waiting, Zuri perused her portfolio statements. She had been fifteen minutes early but just as they were to begin their discussion, Omosede's boss had called her into his office to have a word.

She had been apprehensive about having a progress meeting with Omosede for a while because she wasn't ready to confront what she imagined would be a considerable gap between where her investment portfolio was and the investment goals they had set a year ago. In fact, she had postponed the meeting at least four times, citing work emergencies and the fact that she had to focus on making money first before she could think about investing.

Omosede had obliged, but Zuri could tell she wasn't buying her excuses.

"Sorry about that, my boss needed me!" Omosede said as she waltzed back into the room, smoothed her skirt, and sat down on the swivel chair behind her desk.

Even though she worked in such a male-dominated industry, Omosede positively revelled in her femininity, amply demonstrated by her outfits and workspace. Today she was wearing a pink two-piece blouse and midi skirt that might have looked overly casual without the gold statement necklace and grey heels. Her office was primarily white, accented with silver and green, with a stunning silk flower arrangement of white lilies and green leaves that sat on the centre table in between two olive green wingback chairs in the corner of the office.

"In anticipation of our long-overdue meeting, I had prepared a few investment scenarios, that range from aggressive to conservative, depending on your current risk appetite," she said, tongue-in-cheek.

"First of all, that sounded like shade," Zuri laughed. "But it's fair enough because we both know that I've been putting this meeting off and generally avoiding you because I wasn't quite ready to face my money situation."

Omosede nodded. "Trust me, I get it more than you know because a fair number of my clients are like you. At first, they are excited to get on the investing horse, usually after a huge money event, like facing a financial struggle or even getting a large windfall, that they want to invest before they go on a spending spree. Of course, I prefer the latter because that is a healthy habit to have with money. However, many times, the thing those two types of clients have in common is that they become passive with their investments, not bothering to monitor investment portfolios or take meetings to assess or rebalance the portfolio periodically."

"Whew, so I'm not alone!" Zuri said. "I thought you were going to tell me off."
"It's not my job to scold you, honey. It's my job to help you reach your net

worth goals."

Omosede turned the computer to face Zuri.

"*Chai!* You've come, oh! All these graphs?" Zuri said, staring at the screen filled with numbers and pie charts that represented the different scenarios Omosede had mentioned.

Zuri didn't even know where to begin. "What am I looking at?"

"Don't worry. I'll walk you through it. First of all, let's look at where you are at the moment. I've tracked your cashflows in the last two years with regards to your investment portfolio. This statement reflects the amounts you transferred to us each time, the asset classes you invested in and the returns you've received in the two years we've worked together. You've mostly been good with your monthly payments of one hundred and twenty thousand a month. Probably because you automated it and set up a direct debit. Although you missed three or four payments, you were largely consistent. You should give yourself a pat on the back, most people set goals and don't follow through."

"Well, I try," Zuri giggled, flicking her hair with the back of her left hand for dramatic effect. "Seriously though, I was worried because I thought I had kind of fallen off, felt guilty."

"You also invested roughly six hundred k every quarter. Bonuses and commissions, I'm guessing?"

"Yup! I worked out a profit-sharing formula with my company where I could make more if I did more, so I did my best to invest a chunk of it before I spent. If I'm honest, it was mostly driven by the fear of blowing it all on fashion and travel as soon as it hit my account."

"You are hilarious. We shouldn't forget to include the roughly two million in cash gifts from Tsola, aka boyfriend of the year who transferred money to us directly to invest in stocks on your behalf. He was worried you were being too conservative with your portfolio and wanted you to take a little more risk."

"Lucky me," Zuri said, rolling her eyes. She didn't want to bring up the fact that they had broken up because she still hadn't come to terms with it herself. It had been a rough couple of months, but she had focused on work instead of the disastrous state of her relationship.

Tsola had the nerve to buy her stocks for Christmas and random 'I love you' presents. She often wondered why he couldn't just buy her Jimmy Choo and Chanel like a normal boyfriend. Even though she had whined at the time, the truth was that she secretly loved that he cared so much about investing in her future. Now, she wondered if he worried about her financial security because he knew he wouldn't be in her future. She shook the thought from her mind. She wasn't ready to go down that road again, and definitely not in the middle of this meeting.

"You have a healthy balance of about nine point two million naira, which is great, especially for someone who had no previous savings or investments," Omosede continued.

"At the moment you have an asset mix of sixty, twenty, twenty. You've put your money primarily in money market products that invest in treasury bills, which accounts for sixty per cent of your portfolio. There's twenty per cent invested in commercial paper, and the other twenty per cent is in equities. On average your portfolio has done well, even when you consider the dramatic fluctuations in the capital markets. You've made an average return of eighteen per cent in total which is great, considering about sixty per cent of your capital is protected. Our strategy at the time was to preserve your capital, dip your toe in the stock market pool, then add slightly more risk by adding the commercial paper."

"Sorry, but what exactly is commercial paper? I remember we discussed it, but I didn't really understand at the time."

"Well, commercial paper is an unsecured, short-term debt instrument issued by large companies typically to raise funds to meet short-term obligations. Basically, instead of borrowing the government money you are loaning it to a company for a higher interest rate because it is higher-risk."

Omosede shuffled the papers around and pulled a new document to the top of the pile. "Okay. Now that I've brought you up to speed with where you are let's talk about what you want to achieve in the next twelve months. As I said, I've prepared a few scenarios for you."

She proceeded to explain to Zuri the next two options she had drawn up to boost the portfolio.

"The mildly aggressive approach would be to rebalance the portfolio to include more stock. You are young, so I say go for it because you can afford to take the risk long-term. Say by about ten per cent? We can discuss which stocks to include in your portfolio. The ones you have now have generally appreciated in value and pay regular dividends. That would bring you to an asset allocation of fifty, twenty, thirty. The aggressive approach would be to increase it by thirty per cent and bring your asset mix to thirty, twenty, fifty which may seem overly risky because of the fluctuations in stock prices, but scared money don't make no money."

Omosede and Zuri pored over the options that lay before them. "You might want to consider increasing your monthly investment cashflow to reflect your promotion and new income so that you're building assets and growing your net worth in conjunction with your new earning capacity," Omosede suggested. "Any immediate plans to increase your earning potential?"

"I've recently spearheaded a project at work, building affordable housing in Yaba," Zuri responded. "And I've negotiated a seven per cent commission of every unit I sell. I've sold three so far, and I have a few other leads, but the truth is in this economy, it's tough. Many people just don't have the disposable income to invest in property. I initially planned to sell at least ten each month but hitting that goal is looking mighty rough."

"Have you ever heard that saying that people often romanticise their plans but dread the execution? The magic you are looking for is in the work you are avoiding," Omosede said.

"Yup! On Instagram. It's easier said than done because, trust me, I've been working," Zuri responded ruefully.

"I know you are, but you have to hustle harder if you want to hit those goals," Omosede replied. "The truth is, that as tough as this economy is, there are people that have the money you are looking for, you just have to find them. If you are trying to close on ten deals each month, you have to generate leads for at least a hundred."

"A hundred? The twenty I'm chasing are already giving me a headache. Where's the time? There are not enough hours in the day."

"Listen, with any kind of sales, it's a numbers game. The more quality leads you generate, the more likely you can convert them to sales and hit your target. What's your sales strategy?"

"Well, I have a few real estate agents in the area I'm working with. but I'm mostly tapping into my network of friends and family."

"Think about it like this—you've already created two sales funnels, real estate agents and your personal network. Let's say you target lead generation of twenty each for each category, now you have forty! You need to create three more with twenty each."

"Actually, my friend Ladun just started a side hustle managing influencers and she's become an evangelist for how effective influencer marketing is, so I was actually thinking about how I could use influencers to sell my property. I'm still looking at what it'll cost because the numbers need to make sense, but that could be one funnel, right?"

"Definitely! Also, a real estate developer friend of mine in Kenya, Solomon

Wangwe was telling me recently about how effective Facebook adverts have been for his business. He's the CEO of Goshen Acquisitions, and they are doing well out there. He said it has also helped to generate sales from Africans in the diaspora who want to invest in Africa but are looking for credible vehicles to do so. Obviously, they earn foreign exchange, so assets in Africa are relatively cheaper for them, and relatively higher-risk, but these investments also offer an excellent return on investment for those based abroad considering the capital outlay. So, you should definitely try Facebook too."

"interesting! I'll look into it," Zuri said. "Actually, you could also hook me up with some of your clients."

"Gladly! But for a fee, sha! I'll take a two per cent fee on every deal you close from clients I throw your way."

"Ah! *Na wa*, oh! You can't just help a sister out."

"You are hilarious! There's no sister in business. Do you think I got to where I am by accident? I take every opportunity I come across to make money. Besides, you'll still be making a healthy five per cent from high-net-worth individuals you probably wouldn't have access to previously."

"Ha! *Na me tell you, now*," Zuri said. "If I didn't tell you how much I was making now, would you know to ask me for two per cent? Anyways, it's a deal! Throw your clients my way."

"How much are the units?" Omosede asked.

"Between twenty-five and forty million each," Zuri responded. "Depends on which type of unit you are buying. There's a mix of two- and three-bedroom maisonettes, and four-bedroom townhouses. Also depends on what stage of the development you buy. There are two off-plan phases and a different price when it's finished and on the market."

"Send me a brochure, I might actually buy one for myself."
Zuri couldn't be more delighted. "Sure!"

****

Zuri

"I can't believe I let you drag me here." A reluctant Zuri said as she made her way to Tsola's apartment with Tami. *Things we do for a bestie.*

"He's going to think I came here to stalk him since he has not been taking my calls and has barely been responding to my texts," she whispered in consternation. They were in the parking space outside Tsola's house to attend the cocktail event he had set up for Tami to meet potential investors.

"No, he's not. He'll understand that you are here to give me moral support. However, I don't care. You guys need to talk so you can squash this nonsense. It's been months! This whole thing is getting ridiculous."

"Uhm, I've been trying to talk to him, but he's being pig-headed. How do you go from loving someone to ghosting them like they are some random girl you met in the club a month ago?"

"Man! To be honest, I don't know, oh. The *thing weak me.* I've tried to talk to him a couple of times during this fundraising and restructuring process, but he always politely shuts it down and redirects the conversation to business."
Zuri changed the tack of the conversation, refusing to dwell on the effed-up limbo that was her relationship status with Tsola. "Let's go inside and get this over with. How are you feeling? Prepared? Nervous? Don't worry, it's normal." She rubbed Tami's forearm reassuringly then reached out to ring the doorbell.

Tami took a deep breath. "Well, I'm as ready as I'll ever be. Let's go in."

Ernest opened the door to greet them.

"Ah, madam Zuri, long time!" Ernest said excitedly, as he led them to the terrace upstairs where the rest of the guests were. "*I never see you since. We dey miss you for this house, oh!*"

"Ah, I *dey* miss *una* too," Zuri smiled uncomfortably. She wondered if he knew they had broken up or if he had helped Tsola entertain other women in this house over the last two months.

Deep breath Zuri, deep breath. She was here to support Tami, but she was also here to make her ex see precisely what he was missing. Besides going hard at work, she had also been a fiend at the gym. To avoid bumping into Tsola on the Lekki-Ikoyi bridge, she had joined the brand-new CrossfitterNG gym in Lekki. Her body was killer at the moment, and tonight, her perfect-size-ten figure fit snugly into a black custom tulle dress from Irawo that Tami had made especially for this evening. In truth, she was acting as cheerleader slash model for Tami tonight.

As they reached the top of the stairs, Tsola stood waiting, looking magnificent. He was wearing a white shirt, with the sleeves rolled up to his elbows and the buttons undone to reveal just a hint of chest, matched with a pair of grey khakis. He was looking directly at her, and as tempted as she was to avert her gaze, she looked right back at him.

"Hello Tsola, how have you been?" Her smile was gracious and only juuuust a little fake.

"I'm good, you look well." He replied curtly as he gently clasped Tami's elbow to lead them to the other guests.

Tami had lingered a few steps behind, hoping that as soon as Tsola and Zuri saw each other things would thaw a bit but from the way they spoke—not making eye contact with each other after their initial hellos—she deduced that the two of them were not yet close to patching things up. *This is going to be a long night.*

"How are you feeling?" Tsola asked Tami. "Ready to wow them?"

"I don't know about wow," Tami responded. "But I'm ready to knock it out of the park."

"You'll be fine. Just stay calm and do it the way we rehearsed in my office," Tsola said. "Remember, Irawo is your business, nobody understands it better than you. You have a handle on your figures now, so just share some of the highlights and explain your vision for the next five years."

"I'll do my best." She had presented her business plan to Tsola the previous week, and he'd given her an outline for how to prepare her deck, whittling most of the information down to the essential points. He had told her to focus on images of her designs and bullet points and to explain the rest verbally. The last few months had been a steep learning curve, but the sacrifices and hard work had been worth it.

"I've invited about fifteen people," Tsola said. "They all have varied backgrounds, some of them are venture capitalists, some are in private equity but are interested in investing in early-stage businesses like yours, and some of them are private investors that have a higher risk appetite. I've already had preliminary conversations with each of them, and I think you'll definitely find the right fit with at least two of them."

"You think?" Tami sounded unsure.

"I know," Tsola responded. "We'll have cocktails on the terrace first, so I can make introductions, and you can meet everyone. Then Ernest has set up a projector in the living room with your slides and everything, so they'll listen to your pitch there, then questions and answers will follow, and hopefully you'll end the night with a few investors that are ready to take the plunge."

Zuri followed their conversation silently, slightly hurt that she was still getting the cold shoulder from Tsola. A random person in the room could look at them and not know that they had dated for two years and until a handful of weeks ago, were happy and in love. He wasn't rude, in fact, he was very cordial but treated her like a guest, a friend that had tagged along with Tami, that he had met for the first time. She cast a sidelong glance at Tsola and wondered how he could be so aloof, but It was Tami's night, and she wanted her to succeed, so she put her feelings aside.

The terrace was beautiful. There were fairy lights everywhere that lit the and tiny tea light candles in beautiful ceramic bowls arranged at the centre of each cocktail table. There was a champagne bar on the right end of the terrace and a cocktail bar on the left. Waiters moved around offering guests cocktails and canapes. Everything looked lovely. She wondered if the hors d'oeuvres were catered or if Ernest had made them.

"Tami before you make your presentation, I'd like you to meet Nisha Kanabar, a friend of mine that's in town for a few days from Tanzania," Tsola said.

"Hi, Tami," Nisha greeted her with a wide smile. "It's nice to finally meet you. I've heard good things about Irawo."

Nisha was a stunning Indian woman with lush, long black hair. She was wearing what was unmistakably a Lisa Folawiyo two-piece from the Autumn/Winter '19 line that flattered her petite frame. Tami admired the way she had styled it with simple white Common Projects sneakers and an oversized Chloé clutch. She was one of the most fashionable people Tami had ever met.

"Love your outfit," Tami told her appreciatively.

"Nisha works in fashion and I thought you two would get along, so I begged her to join us," Tsola said as he rounded up the introductions. "She just launched Industrie Africa, a space that tells the stories of the best of African fashion to an international audience. She's had stints working at Vogue Magazine in New York and India but recently moved back to Tanzania to help shape the fashion landscape in Africa. I sent her your pitch the other day. "

"'I see a few opportunities for us to collaborate," Nisha said, "but let's chat later—I know what it's like at these things. There'll still be a pit in your stomach until after the presentation."

"Tell me about it," Tami agreed. "Thank you so much. We should definitely talk after my pitch. I would love to collaborate."

Tsola had ushered everyone into the living room to hear the spiel. A nervous Tami surreptitiously took several deep breaths, then launched into her pitch.

"I've been passionate about fashion since I was a child," Tami said. "I would repurpose my mother's old clothes to make outfits that were more my own style. As a teenager, while my friends got excited about shopping for clothes, I was more interested in learning how to sew, so that I could create the kind of clothes I wanted to wear. It started out as a hobby then developed into a business. I admit that I had zero business experience, and I've made a lot of mistakes, but it's been a steep learning curve. It's taken a while to recover from mistakes like not keeping proper financial records, which led to mixing my personal finances with my business finances, not tracking my costs, recycling cashflows without realising I wasn't really making a real profit, even though there seemed to be a high demand for my brand."

Tami talked them through the Nigerian fashion landscape, showed them pictures of a few pieces from her next collection and her plans. She talked them through the aspects of her business that Tsola had taught her investors cared about—her turn over, her profit margins, year-on-year growth, cost-to-income ratio, et cetera.

"Tami, your efforts are commendable but can you give us specific examples of how changes you've made improved your bottom line?" A gentleman who Tsola had introduced as a private investor looking to branch out into other industries probed. "It's all well and good to know what changes you *think* you need to make, but this is already a risky investment prospect. I'd like to see proof-of-concept."

"Thank you, sir, that's a great question. A few months ago, Tsola was kind enough to review my business and show me what was clearly not working and show me possible ways to fix them. He was also kind enough to fund a mini Irawo collection to test out my theories. The fact that we were able to turn around two-million-naira investment in sixty days, implementing those changes on a small scale. That stands as my proof-of-concept. You see, two of the biggest takeaways from my strategy meeting with Tsola was that I was pricing emotionally, instead of taking all my costs into account for each garment, I would conjure up a price I thought the customer could afford to pay. I simply wasn't accounting for the total cost of production per unit, percentage of marketing and distribution costs, etc., that went into each garment. I also realised that I was primarily applying capital to aspects of my business that focused on how things would look such as on cosmetic changes, instead of focusing on the aspects that would impact the bottom line directly and turn the most profits."

Tami delved into the nitty-gritty of the two gruelling months she'd spent turning the business around with the plan she and Tsola had formulated.

"For example, with the capsule collection Tsola invested in, I decided to launch the collection by tying it to an event that I knew would have a lot of fashion it-girls and celebrities in attendance. Instead of creating brand-new designs from scratch, we went back to look at our best sellers in the last few years and revamped them by making small adjustments and new colours. We also partnered with BellaNaija Style to display the pieces on Instagram and do mini articles on each fashion girl that wore the pieces. This was a hit with our target audience and translated to bank for Irawo. In the past we would design the collection, gift them to influencers but only make limited pieces, so even though the strategy would lead to an increase in demand, we did not have the ready supply to fulfil the demand."

She even went into detail about adjusting her production to take better advantage of economies of scale. "Customers would call to order the pieces only to learn they were sold out, meanwhile we had only made five or ten of each style to hedge our bets. And although we would tell the customers we could still make the pieces and deliver in seven to ten days, it frustrated the customer experience and led to lost sales. This time was different because we were confident that these styles would sell because they had sold before. We made fifty pieces per style in historically popular sizes for our customer base, and when the inevitable demand came from our social media campaign, we had the supply to match. We sold three hundred pieces in less than sixty days, which brought in six million naira in revenue."

"Excellent, Tami," Mensah, a venture capitalist from Ghana, praised. "How much are you asking for? And how do you intend to employ the additional capital raised?"

Tami explained that she wanted fifty million and planned to invest in increasing her production capacity by one hundred and fifty per cent. In addition to buying additional machines, she would bring in trained tailors from Togo and get them to retrain her staff so that they had enough capacity to not only produce four collections a year for Irawo, they would also create the capacity to produce for other fashion designers.

Her strategy would also involve co-creating collections with talented up and coming designers who had complementary brands to hers but couldn't produce at scale. Tami explained that she intended to take on fifty per cent of the cost of production, leverage on her social media following (which had grown to about half a million) to market their brands and distribute the collections in her store in exchange for sixty per cent of their profits.

Down the line, she also wanted to create an accessory label, starting with leather bags. The leather would be sourced from northern Nigeria and other parts of Africa. She had already begun recruiting two artisans who made bags from Senegal. She had done her research and bags could bring in substantial additional revenue, with profit margins of at least sixty per cent, a turnaround production time of three to five days and without the hassle of the sizing issues that came clothes.

****

Zuri

As Zuri watched Tami reel off numbers by heart from her financials and answer the investors' questions with confidence, she felt a sense of pride for her friend. Tami had been working extremely hard the past few months to restructure her business and make Irawo truly profitable and she admired her tenacity because there had been many obstacles and you had to admire the girl's growth and her newfound resilience because Tami of before would have given up *tey tey* when things got hard.

She saw Tsola leave the room and walk to the terrace, so she followed him. She hadn't wanted to distract from Tami's presentation, but now that she was rounding up and things seemed to be going favourably, it was time she and Tsola had a chat about the state of their relationship.

As she walked into the terrace to approach him, he had his back to her and was giving a waiter instruction. "Tsola," she said softly as she placed her hand on his elbow to get his attention. He turned around and looked at her. "Hi, everything okay?" His attitude was distant, cold.

Zuri plunged ahead. "I'm good. I just wanted us to talk. Thank you for helping Tami with this. It's very magnanimous of you, given the state of our relationship. I'm sorry about everything that happened, but you have to know that I didn't mean to hurt you and I'm committed to—"

"Time and place Zuri, time and place," Tsola interrupted, before turning around and walked back into the living room, leaving her standing there. Shock.

That and the hot tears welling up were all that Zuri could feel as she stood there watching his back retreat. Humiliation soon followed.

This. THIS is how the man who said he loved me treats me? Over what? At last, her anger came through.

Enough. She had been begging and pleading with him for months to forgive her, but clearly, he was ready to throw away the relationship.

****

Tami

"That was fantastic, Tami." Nisha walked up to Tami to congratulate her, beaming. "I was particularly fascinated by your detailed understanding of the fashion industry on the continent and your financials. You'd be surprised how many established African fashion houses don't have this insight into their businesses and frankly don't bring in these numbers. It's tough, but keep at it."

"I appreciate the vote of approval! The response so far has been awesome. I just hope I've convinced a few of them to invest," a clearly relieved Tami responded.

"Trust me, you definitely have," Nisha replied enthusiastically. "I overheard a few conversations about how much to invest and how to structure it, so there's valid interest."

"I hope so. Anyway, you wanted to talk to me earlier about a project we could collaborate on? I'm really excited to hear more."

"Yes, I'm putting together a big showcase during London Fashion Week for the continent's most promising talent in fashion—featuring some mainstays as well as next-gen up-and-comers. Each designer will need to create a capsule collection for the event, inspired by a specific theme, that will be shown at an exclusive presentation attended by top buyers and press. We'll cover the cost of your travel and accommodation, but the core criterium requires that designers have the production capacity to produce the collection at scale. In the past—and like you pointed out in your presentation—I've found that even though international buyers take an interest in a look they've seen on the runway, African designers aren't able to replicate them in the quantities and quality that is expected of these establishments. Ultimately, I'm toying with the idea of a long-term partnership with these designers where Industrie Africa co-funds production for special capsules or pieces created exclusively for us and supporting that with online retail on IndustrieAfrica.com."

"Oh my God! Tami squealed in excitement, "that sounds like an amazing opportunity. I'd love to be a part of it. Please let's exchange deets, so we can work out the details but first what's your Instagram page, so I can stalk your fashion. I absolutely love your style."

****

Zuri

The room was almost empty. Most of the investors and guests had left, and Ernest was supervising the waiters, as they cleared out the space and restored Tsola's house to its original condition. Zuri was slumped in an armchair on one end of the room and sulking at her phone. Tami could tell she was upset. She wondered what had happened as Zuri and Tsola had obviously not found a way to sort out their differences at this event. She had hoped they would.

"Babe, are you okay? Tami asked gently. "Did you guys talk?"

"There's nothing to talk about, I'm done!" Zuri said angrily as she looked up from her phone.
"Don't be like that. You
guys need to talk about this," Tami tried to calm her. "This matter has been dragging for too long. You love each other, you need to figure it out. She said as she took Zuri's hand and dragged her to the other end of the room where Tsola was standing."

"I already tried, and he was incredibly rude."

"Try again." Tami laughed. "I know he's stubborn, but just try again. You must fight for your relationship. You were wrong, so it doesn't matter the amount of grovelling you have to do to sort it out."

"Nah! Today is the last day I'm going to grovel," Zuri said. "I've tried my best. It is not by force."

Tsola walked up behind Zuri.

"Hi Tsola," Tami said, sounding excited. "Thank you sooo much for tonight. I don't know how I'll ever repay this kindness. Putting this whole thing together for me, the prep, inviting the investors. I have no words, but thank you," she said as she gave him a hug.

"It's not a problem at all," Tsola responded. "In fact, you made me look good. I had a few proud daddy moments during your presentation. You told your brand story, didn't flinch when they asked you about numbers and answered the questions they threw at you like you had done this a million times. You did great. Spoke to a few of them after your presentation, you'll get at least three formal offers by tomorrow. Let's schedule a meeting next week to decide the structure of the financing and which investors would be the best fit."

"That's amazing, thank you so much!" Tami was smiling from ear to ear. She couldn't have gotten better feedback. Her whole night was made.

"Okay, I'll leave you two to talk." Her eyes darted nervously from Zuri to Tsola. "Zuri, I'll be in the car."

Tsola stared at Zuri. He had so much to say, but he was afraid if he said the words, his hurt would be evident, and he had already given her too much power over him. She had broken his trust, and until their fight, he hadn't realised how vulnerable he had allowed himself to be with her in their relationship.

He wasn't used to letting people in, but he trusted Zuri completely and her actions had broken his trust. His friends had said he was overreacting, but as much as he hated to admit it, she had hurt him. He knew the way he had bottled up his feelings in the last couple of months was unhealthy, but it was less painful to say nothing than to say something.

"Tsola, you've made it clear that you are not interested in communicating with me," Zuri said. "And that's fine! At this moment I would rather your silence, so you can hear me."

Zuri's voice radiated hurt and anger, but she was resolute. "I messed up. I agree. I shouldn't have met up with Olumide behind your back, but I didn't cheat on you, Tsola. It was for work, and because I know how you feel about him, I wanted to spare your feelings and tell you about it when the deal had closed. You made your position clear, but the mistake I made was that I didn't make mine clear to you. I should have stood my ground and told you that you had to trust that any communication I had with my ex was only about work. I should have made it clear that working with Olumide wasn't up for debate because work is work and I don't interfere with your work so even if, as my boyfriend, it's great that you voice your opinions and make your feelings clear, you shouldn't have the power to interfere with mine. I accept that even though my intentions were pure, my methods were underhanded and if I'm honest I'm ashamed of myself and I apologise for handling it the way I did."

Tsola tried to interrupt.

"Please." She raised the palm of her hand to stop him from speaking. "Let me finish."

"I'm sorry for my part in it, but I'm done. This is the last time I will beg, apologise, or cry over this. My actions may have been hurtful but the way you have handled this whole thing is the real betrayal and frankly, tonight was the final straw. You said you loved me, but you've treated me with total disrespect, as though I don't matter to you. It was so easy for you to cut me off like I meant nothing. Like, the bond we built over the last two years meant nothing. I honestly thought you were the one, that I had found my partner in life, but I'm grateful that I got to see this side of you now before we committed to a life together because I'm far from perfect. I'll make bigger mistakes, and if you find it so hard to forgive something like this, I don't want to find out what you would do if I made an even bigger mistake. I need to be with someone who realises that love is about forgiving your partner every day, for the trivial things and the big things."

Her breath hitched several times as she inhaled.

"I've been broken without you the last few months but I'm done. I hope you find what you are looking for." She turned to leave.

"Zuri!" Tsola reached for her elbow, but she evaded his grasp and disappeared down the stairs leaving him standing there, stunned. He wanted to go after her and say something. He wanted to tell her he was sorry. He wanted to tell her he had missed her so badly the last couple of months. He wanted to hug her and explain his hurt, but he just stood there in silence.

"Shit!" the expletive burst out of him. It was as though all the stubbornness, ego and self-righteousness that had clearly been clouding his judgement were slowly melting away and what was left was the pain and fear of losing the woman he wanted to spend the rest of his life with.

SMART MONEY LESSON:
MAKE MORE

Focus on Earning

You want to be rich? The reality is there are only two levers that control wealth—earn more or spend less. It's essential to learn how to spend less than you earn and how to apply your limited resources most efficiently. However, let's be clear: no one ever got rich via a savings account. Your goal is to focus on making sure the engine that generates your income is as productive as it can be. You must focus on revenue-generating activities and how you can maximise them. For example, if you are an employee, is it possible to negotiate performance-based bonuses? Can you take on new tasks within your organisation that are outside of your regular assigned duties but put you in a position to earn more? If you are an entrepreneur, which products and services are your cash cows and bring in the most income? Which products and services have growth potential but need additional investment in terms of time and money to increase earnings? What products or services need to be cut out because they absorb time and money but don't yield substantial income? Can these be eliminated so that the time or money put there can be reinvested in more lucrative revenue-generating activities?

Create Multiple Streams of Income

You can't depend on a single income, especially not in this economy. You should have several fires burning at the same time to make sure you cover both your long-term and your short-term game. And you can do this in several ways: invest in a side hustle or a business run by someone else, leverage your social media to sell other people's products, sell your knowledge by writing a book, creating an online course or providing consulting services. Make your money work for you by investing in an asset that generates a regular passive income.

Be Active, Not Passive with Your Investments

Most people buy land or stocks then forget about it. Investing becomes an event as opposed to a lifestyle. The result is years go by, and you don't know the value of the land you have invested in; you don't check on your stocks to see if it's time to sell and invest in another stock. To maximise your earnings from your investments, you have to check on them regularly, so you can assess and rebalance your portfolio.

Set Profit Goals

In business, we set targets for the company so that we have a clear understanding of where we are and where we want to go in terms of profits. If you treated yourself as a business, what would your profit be? When you subtract expenses from revenue what is left? If you set a profit goal for a million naira a month, what skills, products or services can you offer to reach that goal. Setting profit goals help us to stay on track and ensure that we are productive and not just running around in circles "forming busy" but not being productive.

Negotiate

Negotiate everything! Negotiate your salary, credit with your suppliers, the value of that contract with your client. You leave money on the table when you don't negotiate.

Invest in Your Skills

We all have genius-level talent. There is at least one thing that you do better than other people, and you need to figure out what that is. However, to earn more from that skill, you have to invest in mastering it because your ability to make more increases when you are in at least the top 10 percentile.

EXERCISE:

· What value do you create better than others, and how can you monetise it?

· Set regular monthly or quarterly meetings with your investment adviser to check on your investment portfolio.

· Do one thing every month to improve your skills—read a book, take a course.

CHAPTER 10

COLLABORATING TO COMPETE

Zuri

"Are you busy?" Zuri asked.

"No, what's up?" Lara groaned with exhaustion on the other end of the phone. "We just finished a three-hour strategy session with Pere. My brain is fried."

"*Pele*," Zuri commiserated. "Listen, I just wanted to run something by you. I know I had brought up the idea of us investing as a group in this Yaba development project. Everyone seemed a bit hesitant, and I didn't want to push it, but I just had a conversation with my mentor Mrs Abafo-Williams, that really made me think."

"I guess I hesitated a bit because mixing money and friendship can be very tricky sometimes and we could all do without the drama," Lara mused, "but what did you have in mind?"

"I know, babe, but I think if we do it properly it could really work," Zuri enthused. "I was trying to convince Mrs Abafo-Williams to buy some units in, and she asked how many units I was buying because I offered her my staff discount. I started laughing because I thought she was teasing when she said 'units', plural, but she wasn't. She said it would be silly of me not to take advantage of this opportunity. I told her I had thought about it, but I wasn't sure I had enough disposable income to buy spend up to forty million right now, not to talk of multiple units."

"For a two- or three-bedroom?" Lara asked.

"A three-bedroom. And it'll probably be cheaper when you factor in the staff discount and if the property is purchased in the first phase of the project," Zuri replied.

"That sounds reasonable."

"Anyway, when I said I wasn't sure I could afford it right now, she asked me why I couldn't buy the property with my friends. She then proceeded to share a story about how she's been investing with some women in her close friendship circle for the last ten years, pooling funds together to invest in everything from land, property in estates, stocks to even property abroad. Apparently, they've made a lot of money together. Lara they each put at least two million in the pool every single month. Please just calculate that over ten years! I was blown."

"Wow! That sounds awesome. How many women? Because that's a long time to do something like that together. Did you ask her if they ever fought or had any disagreements?"

"Ha! I did, oh," Zuri laughed. "I think there's about eight or ten of them. She said that in the first couple of years, there were disagreements because they had varied risk appetites. One friend was a huge risk-taker and wanted to put money in things she had heard would double their money quickly, while a few of them were overly conservative and didn't want to hear any stories. She said it was tough at first to find alignment and they lost money a few times, but overall made more than they lost. As they progressed, they found alignment and drew up contracts and bylaws that dictated how the group would choose investments or exit strategies. That way the procedures they put in place guided them when there was any disagreement and the bylaws trumped any one person's opinion or personality."

"Man! That is so dope, I can't lie." Lara sounded pumped. "The idea of owning assets together definitely sounds interesting."

"That's what I thought too," Zuri sounded just as excited. "I was like, that could be us. We plan holidays together, we go shopping together, we are there to support each other in times of trouble, why can't we also make money together? I was so inspired."

"Listen, it's a great idea on paper, Zuri, but the reality is as a friendship circle, we are all in different places in our lives and besides that, we have very different money personalities."

"Girl, we have wildly different personalities, period! We've found a way to make this friendship work over the years, though."

"Fair point! Me, I'm game, *sha*. It's the rest you have to convince. Actually, Adesuwa is always ready to put her money in investments, but with her whole Soji situation, I imagine that her assets are tied up and she may not have as much disposable income."

"She's my next phone call!"

"I'd love to see is how you'll convince Tami and Ladun," Lara laughed. "The drama with getting them to put money down monthly in that Diamond and Pearls Travel *ajo* thing for our upcoming Cape Town trip was hard enough, and that was for something that they enjoy doing."

"To be fair, Tami has been struggling with her business for some time. And whether Ladun admits it or not, her financial situation had changed, so things like holidays are difficult to justify," Zuri reminded Lara.

"I agree. I'm just saying it's not going to be an easy conversation to have," Lara clarified. "We are all earning differently, with different amounts of levels of disposable income, and sometimes people are uncomfortable sharing. Plus, I imagine Ladun especially will be particularly sensitive because she doesn't seem to want to talk much about her challenges."

"I hear you, but I'm going to try anyway because I honestly believe that our friendship is not based on material things. We've come a long way, Lara. If we invest in assets that increase in value, in the long run, it will put money in everybody's pocket. My goal is for all of us to win."

"You are right," Lara agreed. "In fact, men do it all the time with minimal drama, and they don't even have to be that friendly to invest in property or do deals together. When that Zik guy I met in Dubai was telling me about all the opportunities he and his friends take advantage of as a unit, I was honestly a little jealous."

"Exactly! Something Mrs Abafo-Williams said really struck me. She said African women don't really understand the levels their collaborative power can have if they get organised because we can never really have power or a seat at the table without economic power. She explained that if there was land that cost five million and I only had one million naira, I should be able to get my friends to bring a percentage each to invest and sell at a profit. You all make money. She said, 'If you don't have friends that you can make money with, how valuable is your friendship circle, really?'"

Lara was all in. "Listen, I'm glad you are bringing this up when all my debts are paid, and the money from that deal is still fresh. I had actually been thinking about where to put the money before I spend it."
"Cash-money Lara!" Zuri laughed as she got off the phone.

****
Zuri

"These look good," Omosede said as she perused the contract Adesuwa had drawn up for the group's investment club, a document that would bind the five women in their first commercial venture as a group.

"I think it reflects everything we discussed in the last meeting," Omosede continued, nodding as she turned each page.

It was a Thursday afternoon. The five friends had taken time off work to have this meeting with Omosede at Circa Non-Pareil, their fave upscale restaurant in Lekki Phase One, to discuss the structure of the investment club and look through the contracts.

"I tried to be as thorough as possible," Adesuwa said. "However, I think we should still have one last conversation about the structure of the partnership and discuss any loopholes or misgivings anyone might have before we sign the agreement."

Her lawyer hat had kicked in during this process because as much as she loved her besties, she knew many things could go wrong doing business with friends, and she needed to be objective and prepare for all scenarios.

After many weeks of back and forth, they had decided to combine their resources to invest in the Yaba development Zuri was spearheading for Richmond. Still, each had their individual worries about potential downsides. Ladun and Tami worried that they didn't have enough disposable income to contribute to an equal share of the asset. Lara worried about how it would affect their friendship if things went badly as many investments do. Adesuwa worried that all had different personalities and different goals and how they wanted to invest their money and the risk that each person was willing to take may not be in sync.

Zuri had suggested that they have a meeting with Omosede to see if this was a good idea and how they should structure it. Omosede had told them to start by laying out clear objectives as well as policies that would take effect in the event of a conflict. They had plotted out several scenarios and arrived at ways to handle them rationally putting all the information together in a document that acted as their bylaws.

"Can I ask a question? I'm still confused about the structure of ownership. I understand the importance of us investing, by registering a company that we all own equally so that we can buy the property under one name, but how do we split the returns given that we all have different amounts to invest. For example, twenty per cent of Lara's salary is very different from twenty per cent of my salary." Ladun was still slightly nervous and she wanted to make sure all the bases were covered.

"That's a fair question," Omosede replied. "Let me put it like this. You all own the new company, Tribe Ventures, equally. However, each individual transaction will pay out returns differently. If the Yaba property is worth forty million and Lara brings eight million, and you bring four million, it means Lara owns twenty per cent of the investment, and you own ten, and those proportions apply to any profit from sales or rental income you have. The beauty of this is that on another transaction, proportionate ownership can change with you giving more and Lara giving less, with the percentage rewards changing accordingly."

All the women nodded in understanding and agreement. They all felt a mix of relief and excitement that all of this was coming together.

Omosede continued, "However, technically if you all own the company equally, it could be argued in court—if it ever got to that—that you all owned the assets equally, but of course that's not the intention here. Omosede said. I know you all trust each other but just to do everything by the book. I've asked Adesuwa to put in an additional clause. The articles will say that this is set up as a joint investment vehicle between partners and it will further clarify that each investment is subject to a capital call with equity to be allocated by contribution and documented as a sub-agreement."

"Okay, that's fair. It gives us an opportunity to do more when we have more and still keeps us individually protected," Ladun said.

"Yes." Omosede agreed. "Alternatively, you could decide to set up and individual company for each transaction you do together. That way, you set up the rules depending on the transaction. It's up to you, really."

"My question is, does the document cover issues like how we choose investments?" Tami probed. "Because with this transaction it was clear Zuri spearheaded the whole thing, and even though we all looked at it to make sure it made sense as an investment, there was a level of trust. I suspect the next one might not be so clear cut. What if tomorrow Adesuwa wants to invest in an internet company and Zuri wants to invest in a fish farm? How do we decide?"

"Yeah, I put that in, that's why Omosede created that checklist," Adesuwa responded. "It gives us some criteria that a majority of us have to agree on before we choose any investment. It covers issues like what level of risk we are prepared to take, minimum acceptable profit margins, duration of the investment, exit strategy, if the capital required fits in the pre-existing bands that Omosede prescribed that we work within when investing as a group. For example, is it above one hundred million naira or below five million?"

"Those bands are not cast in stone by the way," Omosede chipped in. "I just wanted you to work within certain parameters because I assume you'll each be investing individually alongside this group investments and I don't want any one person's income to be solely concentrated in the group's investments. That way, it reduces each individual's overall risk. You can make changes to the band as you begin to earn more, whatever you are comfortable with."

"That's fine," Zuri said. "You mentioned something about designating roles as well?"

"Yes. You should appoint a chairman, treasurer, secretary and probably a working committee that helps to decide the investment strategy for the group. It just helps to give the group structure. The treasurer is working on the financials, gives reports on how well each investment is doing, what it's costing, if there are any maintenance fees, things like that and the secretary is keeping records of the operational stuff, and then you can have regular periodic meetings to decide as a group."

"Wait, oh!" Ladun said. "How do we decide the exit strategy? That could be tricky. What if one person wants to divest and the others want to hold? How do we decide?"

"That's why you have the voting procedures in the contract," Omosede replied.

"Now I get the point of the voting procedures in the contract," Lara laughed. "In the event of conflict and we can't agree on something, the document spells out how we must handle it. Almost always by voting."

"Exactly!" Omosede beamed. "I see it all the time friends come into a partnership like this with the best intentions, but when issues arise it can bring out the worst in them. To avoid emotional decision-making, the voting procedures help to mitigate the breakdown of the relationship or any fallout."

They chatted together for a few minutes, making sure that everyone was satisfied and on the same page.

"Okay, girls. I think we have it covered." Omosede stood up and gathered her things. "Wish I could stay for lunch, but I have another meeting in twenty minutes."

"Thank you so much for giving us your time," Zuri told her. "I'll let you know if we have any other questions."

The rest of the girls murmured their thanks as Zuri walked her to the entrance of the restaurant.

"Let's order, *abeg*," Lara laughed, as she signalled to the waiter to bring the menu. "I've been looking forward to this meal all week."

"Ah! No need for menu," Ladun grinned cheekily. "I already know what I want. The pork ribs."

"You and food, *ehn*," Tami teased. "I think I'll have a salad."

Adesuwa was quiet. Her thoughts were all over the place. In the last few months, the trouble in her marriage had threatened to wreck her. She had been focusing on work, but she hadn't been eating or sleeping since she got the text message from Soji's mistress informing her she was pregnant. Her confrontation with Soji and his attitude to the situation infuriated her even more. As much as her friends had been there to support her through it, she was reluctant to talk about the situation. More than anything, she felt an overwhelming sense of shame. The shame of a woman in this society who had failed in marriage. There were so many questions she had no answers to. Where had she gone wrong as a wife? Would she survive the stigma of divorce? Would she survive being a single mother?

"Adesuwa!" Zuri's voice startled her back to the present. "Babe, are you okay? You seem so far away."

"I'm fine, I just have a lot on my mind," Adesuwa said solemnly. "I'm fine," she repeated.

"You are not fine, Adesuwa," Lara said sternly. "Frankly, I'm tired of tiptoeing around this Soji situation. We need to deal with it. Burying your head in the sand is not going to make a baby magically go away."

"Lara calm down, it's a delicate situation," Ladun said, kicking her under the table and simultaneously giving her a stern glance to indicate that she needed to stop.

"What?!" Lara glanced at the others with a look of stubborn confusion. "I'm only telling her the truth! Bottling it up like this is not healthy. You need a plan, and we are here to talk it through with you, babe, that's all I'm saying." She rubbed Adesuwa's forearm reassuringly even as she gave her harsh opinion.

"Lara is right. You need to talk to us, babe," Tami gently pressed. "What are you going to do?"

"I've asked him for a divorce," Adesuwa's face crumpled as she admitted to her friends her marriage was over.

Silence reigned in their cosy corner of the restaurant. All you could hear was the quiet hum of the air conditioners and the well-modulated background music.

"This is the first time, I'm actually saying it out loud," She sighed. "I'm getting a divorce. I'm going to be a divorcee. Me, Adesuwa, whose parents have been married for thirty years. I'm going to be a single mother. Guys I don't know if I'll survive this, but I'm tired."

"Babe, to be honest, I didn't think you would get here so quickly, but I'm just glad that you are here. Divorce is definitely the way forward at this point. Soji is scum! Soji is a scam!" Lara slammed the table dramatically several times as she made her proclamations.

Some of them started to giggle.

"Lara, please don't make me laugh, *abeg*. This is a serious situation," Tami tried to look serious.

"No, I'm serious," Lara insisted. "Adesuwa, you've always been too good for him. I don't understand why you've never been able to see it."

"Then you are definitely not going to like what I'm about to tell you," Adesuwa announced, as she looked around the table at all their concerned faces.

"What? OMG, he gave you an STD?" Zuri looked horrified at the possibility. "What? No! God forbid!" Her horrified reply set all the other women sighing with relief

"Ah, see you! Which one is God forbid?" Lara scoffed. "The same way he got someone pregnant by not using protection, is the same way he can give you an STD."

"Anyways." Adesuwa rolled her eyes at all the histrionics. "I was going to say after I confronted him about his whore's pregnancy, he told me it was my fault. That I forced him into the arms of another woman because he doesn't feel supported by me and that I don't support his dreams and I haven't trusted him since the whole Chinasa fiasco."

"The nerve of this man," Ladun said, shaking her head. "This is the part I can't condone. You finish cheating with the product of your infidelity on its way, and instead of taking responsibility for your actions, you turn around and try to make it the woman's fault. Let Bode try this one first!" She hissed.

"That's not even the worst part," Adesuwa continued. "He told me all of this, and at first I was angry, but the next morning I responded by getting on my knees and begging him."

"You what?!" Lara cried in shock. "You were begging a man that has not only financially abused you for at least the last five years, put your finances in jeopardy by making you pay off the debt his stupidity created, has been unfaithful multiple times and now has a baby on the way. You are telling me you begged that man?"

"Yes, oh. I begged him. And that was not the worst of it," Adesuwa laughed ruefully.

"There's more?" Tami gaped with disbelief.

"I told him I knew things were bad, but I was willing to forget about everything and start afresh if he was willing to put in the effort to make our marriage work. You know what he said to me? He would think about it," Adesuwa shook her head in self-disgust.

The girls looked at each other in shock.

"And the worst part is, I let him. I actually sat there for one week waiting for him to get back to me with his answer. It's definitely not how it is in the movies where if you find out your husband is cheating, he begs you."

"Honestly, a part of me still wants to slap you for begging him. But I'm just glad you've come to the only logical conclusion yourself. Marriage can be difficult, but it shouldn't be this much of a burden, *abeg*. Even Mother Theresa would have bailed a long time ago. I don't know how you let it get this far," Lara commiserated.

"He wasn't always like this, Lara," Adesuwa said. "Remember when we met at university? I was nineteen, and he was twenty. He worshipped the ground I walked on and would do absolutely anything for me. He had so much potential that I didn't care that he didn't have money."

"Potential!" Ladun dismissed the word with an eye roll. "A word that has led many unsuspecting women into a life of mediocrity, with men they now have to feed."

"Facts!" Zuri said. "I'm starting to think this whole potential thing is a scam. I definitely want to marry for love but is it too much to ask for a man that is also financially secure not because I want his money because I make mine but because I'm not cut out to be financially responsible for any man, *abeg*."

"Preach!" Lara yelled like she was in church, complete with a hands-in-the-air gesture. "I just find it funny how if a man opens his mouth to say, 'I only date yellow girls with big bums', no one will bat an eyelid because that's what he likes, but if a woman says 'I only date men with money, I need a man that is financially secure', she's a gold digger."

"Well to be fair those are not exactly the same thing," Adesuwa said. "On the one hand, the man is talking about physical attributes, on the other hand, the woman is talking about money. Apples and oranges."

"You are just speaking English," Ladun interjected. "Men and women want different things in a relationship. Actually, I take that back! In my opinion, in Africa men and women want different things. Men are visual and are looking for a trophy, women just want someone that will provide and protect her and her children."

"Exactly!" Lara said. "African women want different things. Frankly, I don't think there's anything wrong with a grown woman who makes her own money to say 'Hey, I want to be with a man that has money because I don't want to be with a man that brings nothing to the table. I'm not a gold digger I'm just not interested in being anyone's mummy.'"

"The thing that gets me is how hypocritical our society is," Tami complained. "With one mouth they will vilify gold diggers but in reality, they reward them because they still get everything they set out to get. Cars, designer clothes, all of that. So, why do the same men complain so bitterly?"

"You know what bothers me?" Adesuwa said. "This false notion that Nigerian society actually wants women to be financially independent. It's a lie! People say it because it sounds nice, but they don't actually mean it. I find that there are two types of guys that say they want a woman to be financially independent. The ones that don't want to ever spend their own money on you and want to split the bills fifty-fifty, and the ones who are looking for a sugar mommy to take care of them."

"That's a generalisation, but I tend to agree," Zuri said. "Some men genuinely like women who are ambitious and bring value to the table, though and honestly, that's my kind of relationship."

"Of course it is," Lara teased, "because that's exactly the kind of guy Tsola is. What's going on with that anyway? Have you guys finally sat down to talk?"

"Are you minding this one? He told me he's been trying to get you to have dinner with him and you've been blowing him off." Tami looked at Zuri pointedly.

"So what?" Zuri retorted. "Please, how did this conversation become about Tsola and me?" Besides, he shouldn't be complaining about anyone blowing him off. I begged him for two months after that Olumide debacle, and he wouldn't even talk to me. Sending flowers and bombarding me with requests to meet up for dinner for a week don't even compare to his two-month silence. It's so funny how men can't take it when the tables turn. *Abeg*, he should be happy I'm even returning his calls."

"Don't push it, oh," Lara said. "I definitely think you should play hard to get small but don't overdo it, babe. I think you've made your point."

"Tell her!" Tami warned.

"Please, be quiet!" Zuri laughed. "Since Tsola raised capital for you we won't hear word. In your eyes, he can do no wrong. Angel Tsola, *abi?*"

"Yup! I'm definitely a Tsola advocate." Tami admitted, unashamed. "But the truth is, you guys are perfect for each other. You are both just stubborn."

"Relax." Zuri she swiped the screen of her phone. "We are having dinner this week," she shrugged.

****

Tsola

Tsola had never been so nervous to go on a date before, especially not with his girlfriend—if he could still call her that. Zuri was already about twenty minutes late, and he worried that she might not show up at all. It had been two weeks of grovelling. After their heated conversation at his apartment. He had come to his senses and called her the next day to apologise for his part in their fight, but she refused to take his calls and left his messages unread, with no response. Even sending a bouquet of lilies to her office every day for a week hadn't helped, but she'd eventually caved and was meeting him for dinner tonight.

"Hi, Tsola," Zuri said coolly, glancing at her watch. "Sorry I'm late. The traffic was terrible."

"It's fine," Tsola said hesitantly as he helped her into the chair, "I'm happy to wait. I'm just glad that you came. I thought you had changed your mind about dinner."

"Well, I'm here."

She beckoned to a waiter to take their order.

"Listen, I'm sorry, babe," Tsola said, sounding remorseful. "I was upset but I shouldn't have taken it this far. I deserve the silent treatment, but I need this to be over. I don't want to lose our relationship because I was being pig-headed."

"You really were," Zuri said, with an amused smile. "Thank you for the flowers. It was sweet of you."

"I was beginning to think you didn't receive them since you still weren't responding to any of my messages."

"Well, I wanted to give you a taste of your own medicine. Your silent treatment hurt and I needed to show you just how it felt to be disregarded after just one mistake."

"I am sorry," Tsola's sounded honestly upset with himself for his behaviour. "It just triggered my trust issues, and it was easier to ignore you than communicate that I was hurt."

"I'm sorry too," Zuri said sheepishly. "I should not have met with Olumide behind your back. It was stupid, and it won't happen again."

Does this mean we can put this behind us?" Tsola said, placing his hand on hers. "I've missed you."

"I've missed you too," Zuri smiled. "It's been a rough couple of months, but I guess we had to have this sort of blow out to learn how to treat each other when we have conflict. Just promise me that you'll always communicate with me. I honestly can't deal with your silence again. I can't."

"I promise," Tsola smiled.

They spent the rest of the evening catching up on what they had each missed. Tsola told her about the new deals they were assessing and their plans for the entertainment fund. She told him about the Yaba development and how the girls were going to take a stab at investing together.

****

Ladun

"Bode, I know you are busy working on your proposal, but can we talk?" Ladun said as she made her way to the sofa where he was working on his laptop.

"Am I safe?" Bode laughed as he raised an eyebrow but patted the sofa next to him for her to sit.

"Why would you not be safe?" Ladun said with mock irritation. "Can't I talk to my husband again?"

"You can, oh," Bode laughed. "Just remember that I am poor right now. Because I know the combination of that face and that little girl sing-song voice only means one thing. You are either about to ask me for money, or you have already done some damage."

"I'm low key hoping it's the former because we don't have the cash to splurge right now," Bode said.

"Ok, I actually want to ask you for money," Ladun said, looking at her husband sceptically. "But it's not what you think."

Bode laughed. "Ladun I don't have! Please, let's be serious. I'm barely back on my feet, and it's going to be a while before I can get this family back to where it was. Trust me, I can't wait to spoil you with Chanel and Gucci again but not now. Just pray that these investors for the Fintech app come through and we can finalise our partnerships with the banks."

"I'm not asking for money for Chanel, Bode," Ladun said. "That's the least of my worries right now. My friends are coming together to invest in a property, and I can't afford it on my own. I was hoping you would help me."

Bode looked at her with surprise. "A property? My wife wants to invest in property? Wow, this is new. In all the years we've been married this is actually the first time you've asked me for money for something reasonable Ladun." "Oh, whatever!" Ladun said, eyeing him.

"Seriously! I just wish you asked me for money for things like this when we were rich. We would have probably been better off because there would be assets in your name that were not tied to the Ashoni family fortune and we would have been better off."

"You are not making this easy," Ladun said. "Please, can you stop teasing me and focus on the matter at hand? Let me know if you can help me or not." "Okay, okay! Bode laughed as he sat upright. "How much is this property?"

"Well, it's thirty million naira. Divided by the five of us that's six mill each."

Bode looked at her.
"Bode, I only have about two million saved. I'm not sure how to come up with the rest, but I was hoping you could help me."

"Babe, it's a tough time," Bode said. "I'm not sure I can raise the balance either, but I have to say I'm proud of you for wanting to do this and for saving this much. The Ladun I married would never be interested in investing not to talk of saving towards it."

Ladun felt hurt. "Please stop saying that, babe. It's like you are rubbing my past decisions in my face and I don't like it. Especially since I'm trying."

Bode sobered. "I'm not trying to make you feel bad, I was just trying to get you to see how far you've come. I'm proud of you, babe. But honestly, I can probably only scrape one million together, but it's going to be tough. I'll get you the money next week but how are you going to raise the rest?"

"I'm not sure, but I'll figure it out. I really appreciate you helping me. I'm grateful, honestly!"

"It's okay, my love," Bode said as he reached out to hold her hand. "I wish I could do more. Now let me finish this proposal, so I can go back to making enough money to lavishly spend on my beautiful wife."

****

Tami

"Tam Tam!" Zuri said. "How far?"
"I'm good! Just out here hustling but mostly preparing for my Industrie Africa showcase in London this summer. I still can't believe it's happening."

"Of course it's happening. I'm so proud of you, boo. This is just the beginning!"

"OMG! Did I tell you about my last conversation with my dad?" Tami laughed. "Nigerian parents, *sha!*"

"No!" Zuri said in disbelief. "What did he say this time? Is he still advocating for you to quit fashion and get an engineering job?"

"Babe, on the contrary," Tami said. "Last week over breakfast, he told me he was so proud of me, he's so glad I found my calling, and he knew I would succeed in this business. I was in shock until my mother told me that after that profile BusinessDay did of me in the newspaper, his friends have been calling him to congratulate him."

"*Chai*, Otunba!" Zuri laughed. "Nigerian parents are the real MVPs, *sha*. But I've always told you to just keep at it. Success has many fathers, *failure na bastard*."

"You can say that again," Tami laughed. "Meanwhile, that Bidemi Zakariyau girl is a PR beast! Since Tsola introduced me to her after we closed the first round of funding, she's been executing a strategy that I have to say is working. I've been on so many television and radio shows, the press I'm getting is attracting new kinds of clients and new types of partnerships. It's so exciting."

"I can imagine," Zuri said. "Anyway, I'm calling to ask how far with your own contribution to the Yaba property? Your money don complete?"

"No, but I have a plan."

"Tell me."

"I can't take any of the money from the funds I raised from investors because it's solely for my business, so I thought about the upcoming WIMBIZ conference in November. It's just a couple of months away, and I had a conversation with one of my clients who had this brilliant idea that I could dress some of the women on the council for the two-day conference. I decided to make an exclusive WIMBIZ collection and run a PR and social media campaign around it to sell to the women who are attending this year and want to stand out in an Irawo piece.

"That's brilliant," Zuri said. "You know almost two thousand women attend every year. Your conversion will be out the roof! In fact, please let me just place my own order now."

"Exactly! Two thousand women," Tami exclaimed. "If I can convert even two hundred women into customers at an average price of thirty thousand naira apiece. That's six mill in revenue. I plan to invest a proportion of the profits in the property. And I have some savings. Even if I don't hit my goal, I'll make up the rest."

"Tam Tam!" Zuri laughed in delight. "I'm loving the way your brain is working these days, oh. Good luck!"

****

Adesuwa

"How far?" Lara greeted. "Has Zuri called you about your contribution to the Yaba property yet?"

"Yup! She's been hounding me all week," Adesuwa groaned.

"The girl's blood is hot," Lara laughed. "I guess we are getting a glimpse of her sales strategy with her clients."

"Abi!" Adesuwa laughed. "I've told her to calm down, though. I'm not very liquid right now, and I'm trying to sell the last asset I own jointly with Soji, a piece of land in Ibeju-Lekki. And I have to deal with it delicately if I want Soji to cooperate. If I'm too pushy he will smell that something is up. Right now, he's on board with selling because he believes fifty per cent of it is coming to him and he needs the money."

"The bastard! Did he contribute any money to buy the land that he wants to collect half? Adesuwa I'm so triggered right now! If he weren't SJ's father I promise, I would have him arrested," Lara ranted.

"*Abeg*, calm down! He's not getting a dime. I just need him to sign all the documents first. I'm taking every single naira. He's entitled to take me to court, but I don't even care. He can explain to the court how he contributed to the purchase of the property. I'll cross that bridge when I get there. He and his new family are not getting a dime of my money."

****

Ladun

"Madam, any luck with your contribution?" Zuri said.

"No," Ladun said as she fidgeted with her hair on the other side of the phone. "I'm not sure I can be part of this, to be honest. There's just a lot going on right now."

"Ladunnnnnn!" Zuri laughed. "If it was fashion we were saving for now, you will find the money. Babe, please be serious, I really want all of us to do this. Lara predicted this. She said you were going to be the toughest to convince." Ladun exploded. "What the hell do you mean by that, Zuri?! Do you know my financial situation? Do you know how I'm paying my bills?"

"Ladun, please calm down. I was just teasing you, didn't realise you would take it so personally. I'm sorry."

"No, Zuri!" Ladun yelled. "Sorry doesn't cut it. You are acting like I wouldn't have done it if I was still in the financial position I was in two years ago. I get it! Ladun likes material things! Ladun is obsessed with designers, but things have changed dramatically since Bode's dad passed away. And you know this. I feel like this is just a roundabout way to rub me and Bode's situation in my face."

"How can you say that, babe," Zuri said, sounding distraught. "I honestly thought you guys were okay now. Obviously not back to where you were before but back on track. I am truly sorry."

"Wait! Let me understand this." Ladun said. "You and Lara were gossiping about my financial situation before you both decided to come to this conclusion, *abi*? I really don't blame you."

"I'm sorry, Ladun," Zuri repeated. At this point, she realised that Ladun was hearing her but not listening. She couldn't see past her anger.

All I can do is apologise, Zuri thought. *I should have never brought up Lara's name.*

"For your information, I actually tried," Ladun said. I even asked my husband to give me some of it even if I already know how tight things are for our family. He offered to scrape together one million naira, but I knew I wouldn't be able to complete the required amount even though I add the savings I managed to put aside."

"Listen maybe I took the wrong approach to this," Zuri sighed. "I could have said it better but Ladun, you are one of my best friends and neither Lara nor I would ever gossip about your financial situation."

"Anyway, I'm done with this conversation," Ladun said. "I only wish I hadn't been saving towards the South African trip in the travel ajo thing. I don't want to go on holiday with people who look down on me because I can't afford things. Can you call Diamond and Pearls travels? Is it refundable?"

"*Haba*, Ladun!" Zuri said. "You are taking this too far. I know you are upset but please don't go down this road."

"No! I will, oh! I will. In fact, I'm clearly too poor to be you people's friend."

"Ladunnnn." Zuri chastised. "I can't believe you are saying this!"

"Goodnight." Ladun hung up abruptly.

****

Lara

"What kind of trouble has Zuri put me in now," Lara thought. After an hour-long conversation with Zuri explaining what had gone down with Ladun, she was mentally exhausted.

She texted Ladun. *Please let's meet for lunch today so I can explain. I don't want to do this over the phone.*

SMART MONEY LESSON:
COLLABORATE TO COMPETE

Women have been fighting for a seat at the table for many years, but to indeed have a place, we need a powerful voice and the economic means to truly effect change. It is possible for us to achieve those things faster when we pool resources, even as we negotiate some of the most prominent places that collaboration can help—closing the income gap between men and women.

There's a global conversation about closing the pay gap between men and women, and like most global conversations, I often think about how it applies in Africa. In Africa, men are more likely to be wealthier than women. But I've frequently asked myself why and I have a few theories.

Women Save to Spend, Men Save to Build

There's something culturally ingrained in us that makes men and women think about money differently. From an early age, men are raised to be providers and told they are going to be responsible for the family's financial future, so they are more likely to be aggressive with growing their earnings and investments. They tend to take more risks with their careers and investments to attain financial security.

On the other hand, women are raised to be nurturers. So, even though more women have become entrepreneurial and make up a considerable chunk of the workforce they don't automatically think about how to keep and grow money. Even though women are better savers we tend to save to spend as opposed to saving to build. Women's incomes tend to translate to how to make a house a home, a better quality of life for our children, which are important things but are not assets that protect our financial future.

Our society is comfortable talking to women about saving and budgeting, but not about making money and investing.

Women Don't Have the Same Conversations About Money That Men Do

African society is generally secretive when it comes to talking about money; people don't really like to share how they make their money. When the conversation is had, though, men have a much different conversation.

I hate the stereotype that all women do when they come together is talk about men, fashion, and frivolity, but I find that when I'm in a room with intelligent, accomplished women the conversations are ultimately different from when I'm in a place with smart, accomplished men.

We may talk about our goals and our businesses and being bosses, but I find that the conversations women have about money tend to be more cosmetic. A woman is likely to talk about her business idea, maybe her marketing strategy, and the rigours of balancing a career and life, but will seldom broach the topics around investment opportunities, the financials of her business, the details of her distribution network, capital structure or how to scale the business.

It's not that the men don't gossip, talk about women or sports but they also talk about the deals their making, share investment opportunities, compare the returns on the investments they are making, what the stocks they've invested in are doing that week in the capital markets.

There are definitely cultural biases that come to play in the workplace that keep women from earning less than men. For example, in a case where an employer can tell a single woman with a straight face that they can't make as much as their male counterpart because they don't have a family, and so do not need to make as much as men—whether or not those men have families.

However, without discounting the role of cultural biases, and obvious issues when it comes to women taking a break from work to focus more on raising their kids, I often wonder what role women play in limiting themselves in terms of making more. Sometimes a man and woman could have similar educational backgrounds, similar exposure, access to the same opportunities, but at some point, there's a divergence when it comes to how much they earn.

It's not that we don't work hard or hustle as much as the men, but sometimes while you are both putting in the same amount of work, he's targeting a hundred-million-naira deal while you are targeting a five-million-naira deal. The same level of work but different results.

EXERCISE:

· Is your friendship circle your money circle? Do you have friends in your inner circle you can talk about money with?

· Assess the conversations you are having with your friends. Do you have conversations about:
  i. How much you earn?
  ii. How to negotiate salaries?
  iii. How to grow turnover in your business?
  iv. How to improve cost efficiencies?
  v. How to scale up distribution?
  vi. Which investment opportunities are you assessing and why?
  vii. When it comes to their finances, do you have a culture within the friendship of being able to ask each other for advice?

Make it a habit to put each other on and help each other level up by having richer (pun-intended) conversations about your money. Nothing grows when shrouded in secrecy. You earn more when you share more. Have conversations with your friends about money because peer to peer learning can be very effective in growing your net worth. African women need to be more intentional about having conversations about money.

CHAPTER 11

INVEST IN
YOUR CIRCLE

Lara

Lara twirled her favourite black pen between her fingers as she gazed out the window of Maison Kayser. It was a beautiful Saturday morning, but the Lagos sun felt like it was going to pierce one's brain, it was so hot. She was glad to be in the airconditioned confines of the restaurant's beautiful space while she waited for Ladun, who was already twenty minutes late.

Lateness was usually a pet peeve for her but being friends with Ladun for so many years had taught her to find something useful to occupy her time if she had solo plans with her. It was more productive because getting upset with her for coming late was a waste of time. She always meant well but, somehow, she'd still be late. If it wasn't so annoying it would be hilarious. Besides, she was more concerned with making sure she cleared up the misunderstanding with Ladun before it got out of hand. Their friendship was too important.

She scribbled into her notebook, prepping for the Pan-African Oil and Gas conference she had been asked to speak at in Cape Town. It was a prestigious event and she planned to knock it out the park her first time out. She was sketching out her speech, listing the points she wanted to make on the panel she was speaking on and a list of people she wanted to meet at the conference. It was going to be filled with the who's who of oil and gas across the continent.

This was the type of event people attended to close deals, get a meeting with an oil and gas minister, or meet a central bank governor. Getting to speak on stage was an opportunity to highlight your knowledge because you never knew who was watching. In her career, she had learnt that it wasn't enough to just be good at what you do but you had to continuously build your access if you wanted to get to the next level, and to do this you had to be intentional.

"Hi, Lara," Ladun greeted cheerily as she placed her bag on a chair before she took a seat. She wasn't as upset as she was a few days ago but she was still apprehensive about having this conversation. She felt entitled to her anger but her feelings on the matter were too complicated to explain.

"Hello, love," Lara smiled, as she closed her notepad. "Would you like to order? I ordered a coffee and croissant already."

"Yeah, I'll have the same," Ladun replied as she signalled to the waiter and placed her order.

"You look lovely," Lara said admiringly. Ladun was outfitted in an orange Kaftan Lara suspected was from Virgioli fashion, but her compliment was more about softening the tension before the conversation got intense.

"Thank you," Ladun replied cooly. She took a sip of her cappuccino.

"So, first of all, I'm sorry if you took what I said the wrong way," Lara began. "You have to know that neither Zuri nor I meant any harm. We really were just teasing."

"I see. Two of my best friends were having a conversation about my family's finances behind my back and mocking me because I can no longer afford to do the things I could once upon a time." Ladun replied coldly.

"And that wasn't meant to be negative?" She continued calmly.

"Why are you being like this," Lara said, sounding frustrated. She had planned to lead this conversation with love and understanding, no matter how upset Ladun got but she didn't understand this upside-down thinking.

"Being like what, Lara?" Ladun asked in a measured tone. "I'm simply asking why me and my finances became a topic of conversation behind my back."

"Ladun, we were not talking about your finances," Lara said. "We were talking about the Yaba property and the possibility of us all investing together, and I made a comment to Zuri that you and Tami would be the hardest to convince. It had nothing to do with who could afford what but more to do with the fact that, A, its typically difficult to plan anything as a group, case in point our impending holiday to South Africa, and B, you and Tami are historically the least likely in the group to want to invest in anything that's not fashion."

Ladun rolled her eyes.

"And before you say anything else," Lara continued. "I would have said that whether you were still in the financial position you were in three years ago or not. It had nothing to do with money, Ladun. I'm actually quite disappointed that you would even think that. When has our friendship ever been based on money or who can afford what? You are one of my best friends and I love you."

"Fair enough!" Ladun said, tears welling up in her eyes. "I guess when you say it like that, I do sound a bit paranoid. However, I think you and Zuri should have been a bit more sensitive. Just because I don't talk about all the financial changes to our lives regularly doesn't mean it's not a sore subject."

"I understand," Lara said, reaching across the table to touch Ladun's hand reassuringly.

"Every time I think about the amount—just six million! —I get upset." Ladun sighed. "That was money I would spend easily on a bag or watch without flinching. Now I can't even raise it for something as significant as owning property."

"So, I have a proposition," Lara said. "Don't get offended, just listen first, okay? I really want you in on this. Zuri told me Bode offered one million and you have about two million, yes?"

"Yes, but that's barely half and I have no idea where to get the rest from."

"I'll loan you the rest. You'll pay me back an agreed amount every month with interest. It doesn't matter how long it will take, but you also have the option to pay lump sums when you get bulk money."

Ladun was stunned. "You can't be serious, Lara. I know I'm not in the greatest financial position right now, but I'm not a charity case either. Besides I'm not trying to go into debt doing things I can't afford."

"Laduuunn. Charity case, *ke*?" Lara laughed. "Was I a charity case six years ago when you contributed to helping me pay my mum's rent because I had too many bills?"

Ladun looked at her blankly. "I don't know what you are talking about. When did I do that?"

"You see, you have always been very materialistic," Lara said with a teasing grin, "but you've also always been very generous Ladun. You've sown so many seeds in this relationship and you have goodwill with each of us in this group. You've bailed all of us out in one way or another."

"That's such a nice thing for you to say, Lara, but I'm still not accepting your money."

"Listen, it's not for *dash*!" Lara said. "I'm not Otedola's daughter, oh! You are paying me back. Second of all, you are taking on affordable long-term debt to buy an asset. That's good debt, not bad debt. I really want to do this for you. Let's make it happen, Ladun."

Ladun smiled. There were tears running down her cheeks.

"It's decided," Lara grinned back. "I'm not giving you the option of saying no!"

****

"What do you have to drink, babe?" Ladun said to Zuri. "Can I have a glass of wine?"

It had been weeks since their little tiff and she was glad they were all back to normal. The girls had planned to meet at Zuri's for brunch on Sunday but Adesuwa had to work on a brief for a new client and Lara had a date with her new *bobo* who had only just gotten back into town.

"Actually, Tsola dropped off a case of Veuve Clicquot last night when he heard we were doing brunch," Zuri smiled. "Do you want champagne instead?"

"Of course!" Ladun and Tami said in unison.

"Tsola needs a medal for best boyfriend of the year, *abeg*," Ladun said. "He just gets it. It's the little things."

"And this one wanted to break up with him," Tami hissed. "Let me just tell you, Zuri, I would have broken up with you."

"Sometimes, I wonder whether he has bribed you guys behind my back," Zuri laughed. "These days, it doesn't matter what he does wrong, all of you side with him. I can't lie, *sha*. He's been great the last couple of months. Super attentive."

"Girl, don't get it twisted, we still have your back," Ladun smiled. "We love him because he loves you."

"Plus, he looks after all of us," Tami said. "I feel like he's my older brother."
"*Abeg*, rest!" Zuri replied. "Anyway, how are things going with Irawo?"

Tami looked absolutely joyous as she replied, "Stressful, but great! I'm working on building my team because I want to scale up the company. I've been trying to hire a business-development-slash-salesperson and it's been a nightmare. Everyone I interviewed was either too expensive or too fresh, but I think I've found the right candidate. She's starting on Monday."

"That's awesome!" Zuri enthused. "How did you find her?"

"OMG! I met this awesome girl at a Facebook event I went to last month, Chika Uwazie. She's a tech entrepreneur that focuses on providing human resource solutions for SMEs."

"Oh, I've heard of her!" Zuri said. "'The Career Queen,' *abi?*"

"Yup, that's her," Tami said. "After our initial consultation, she sent me a bunch of CVs with awesome candidates that were within my price range."

"Please send me her details," Zuri said. "We've been trying to hire for a number of positions at Richmond, but my HR department hasn't been able to find any decent candidates. I was just telling Mr Tunde that we may need to outsource."

"Definitely, I'm sending the details to you now." Tami picked up her phone and began typing.

"I really envy you guys and how you are able to establish these relationships when you go to networking events. Belema has been sending me to all these workshops and networking events but I find them so tedious and annoying. It's like the people there are already successful and already know each other, so they don't bother to mix with the likes of us," Ladun complained.

"That's the wrong attitude to have, babe, but I get it," Tami said. "That used to be me until I realised it was my insecurities talking. Networking is really about building organic relationships with people and you can only do that when you know the value you bring to the table and are able to articulate it."

"How?" Ladun said. "I don't get it. I always introduce myself, give them my business card and explain that I work at an advertising agency."

"That's a start, but it's more than that," Zuri said. "You have to change your mindset. If you walk into a room thinking you offer nothing, others can smell it and they'll think it too. You have to really think about what your value is, whether it's in your expertise or how you can support them in their own endeavours."

"Very true, I also find that it helps to set clear goals," Tami said. "When you're clear about what you need or the pieces you are looking for to help your project or business come together then people know how they can contribute."

"Preacchhh, Tam!" Zuri enthused. "Without clarity, people don't know how to help you. You have to be vocal about the aspects of your business you need help without being overbearing. You never know who can help with distribution, PR, or entry into a new market. I'm always clear about the specific problems I'm looking for solutions for."

Tami laughed. "I listen to other people's stories because honestly there's a lot to learn there. But I also keep in mind what skills or opportunities I have because we are all human beings we gravitate towards helpful people."
"I'll try that," Ladun smiled.

"You know what's funny," Tami smiled. "These days I don't really bother with business cards. If I meet someone at an event I find interesting, I'll take their number and send them a WhatsApp message. More importantly, I'll go and find them on Instagram."

"This girl! You are not okay," Zuri laughed. "Really?"

Ladun laughed.

"I wish I was joking," Tami laughed. "These days people lose business cards all the time. Being connected on Instagram makes it easier to really get to know a person's interests, what their passionate about, job changes—you know, the works. Even if I don't see them every day, interacting on their posts almost always means we stay connected, so when they are thinking of an opportunity that I could be eligible for I don't seem far away."

"You know what? That's actually smart," Zuri said. "I could see how that would work because these days, people are busy and it's easier to keep in touch via social media."

"I guess my challenge is I haven't really found my purpose like you guys," Ladun confided. "I like my job a bit better now but I'm not sure if this is what I'm supposed to be doing for the rest of my life and I don't earn enough."
"Listen, sometimes I'm not even sure if working in real estate is what I'm supposed to be doing with my life either," Zuri said. "I know I'm really good at it, so while I'm very conscious of finding purpose I'm also focused on building my skills and finding ways to monetise my passion."

"Maybe I'm lucky because I've always been passionate about fashion," Tami added. "But to be honest I only started feeling like it was my purpose when I focused on building my business. In fact, I've started developing a workshop for new fashion entrepreneurs to teach them what I've learnt about raising capital in Nigeria. I was afraid to charge because I thought I am no expert. However, talking to some of the designers that are stocking in my showroom, I realised that going through the process myself, I've learnt so much and I can share. It's also extra income stream for Irawo."

"That's such an amazing idea, Tami," Zuri said. "There are designers who are more established than you that are still trying to figure that out. Trust me, they will pay you for the knowledge, because it's not about being at the pinnacle of your career or about being perfect. There's something to teach at every level."

"Well done Tam," Ladun smiled. "I'm so proud of you."

"Thanks, guys," Tami demurred. "I guess what I was trying to say is you need to figure out what your strengths are and identify where you can apply them."

Ladun hesitated. "I'm not quite sure what my strengths are? All I did for ten years was buy clothes and throw parties. Not sure they qualify as strengths."
"Look at this girl!" Zuri laughed. "When it comes to spending on fashion and lifestyle, I would definitely say you are a tastemaker. You understand what people like or aspire to have so much so that, every time you bought a bag or found a new designer, all the yummy mummies immediately dubbed your style. Besides throwing all those lush parties just means you have contacts to leverage on when we pinpoint exactly what you want to be doing."

"Actually, I think you may have a career managing influencers," Tami suggested.

"Managing influencers, ke?" Ladun was taken aback. "You are such a joker!"

"No, I'm actually serious," Tami said earnestly. "Remember when I had that social media debacle? You helped me close two deals with lifestyle brands I hadn't even thought of when one of the brands I had already signed with refused to move forward with our contract."

"Yeah but that was because of my job," Ladun said, brushing off the point. "It was a one-off. It worked because we handle their advertising, their brand managers had mentioned that they were looking for influencers to work with, and you are the only one I had a personal relationship with."

"Listen, Tami might be on to something here, Ladun," Zuri said. "You work at an advertising agency, so you have direct access to brands a lot of people don't have, which means you are uniquely placed to offer this service."

"And I know so many of these influencers are always looking for ways to monetise their brands," Tami added. "Ladun, it wasn't just about knowing these brand managers were looking for influencers. It was about how you were able to sell my market, write proposals, and convince them I was the right fit for their campaign despite the negative press I had received."

"I quite enjoyed that actually." Ladun seemed pleased with herself. "Plus the fifteen per cent you gave me from each deal we closed was sweet, *sha*, I can't lie."

"You see this could definitely turn into a side hustle for you," Zuri encouraged. "You just need to find more influencers to work with consistently."

"I guess so," Ladun said. "Actually, I became friendly with some of the influencers we used for that South African hotel's campaign. Maybe I should start there."

"Also, how do you think Belema would feel about you starting a side business managing influencers?" Zuri asked.

"Hmm. when I was doing it for Tami she didn't seem to mind," Ladun said. "She even congratulated me when we closed each deal. She said it was very entrepreneurial. Anyway, if I decide to do this there's no conflict of interest because we don't manage influencers and in fact, if I can build a portfolio of influencers I work with, it could act as a funnel for the company's clients. Belema is very into this influencer marketing strategy at the moment, but I'll run it by her just in case."

"I'm messaging people I know that have over fifty thousand followers now to see who might be interested," Tami tapped away into her phone. "You'll have some contacts by the end of the week."

"I think we've birthed a business, guys!" Zuri said as she clinked her glass in celebration.

****

Zuri

Zuri sat back on the multi-coloured pin-striped cushions that were framed by wicker. She was having coffee with her mentor Mrs Abafo-Williams on the patio that faced her beautiful garden. It was a serene scene, filled with exotic potted plants that made it seem worlds away from Lagos. Zuri's favourite feature was the swing that hung from a large tree. Every time she sat in it and heard the birds in a cage nearby chirping, she felt like a kid again. There was something so old-world and romantic about the garden, but it also oddly reminded her of her childhood, even though her parents never had a garden. "So now that you've succeeded in making me buy two of these Yaba development units, madam, what do you want?" Mrs A said, her smile reaching her eyes.

"Ah ah, Mrs A," Zuri said as she shot her a playful look. "You say that as though I only come here when I want something. I was just here the other day, just to hang out with you."

"I'm just teasing," Mrs A laughed. "To be fair you also brought the strategy document you prepared for my new jewellery line. Thank you for that. It was very useful. My team are absolutely obsessed with you."

It was a pleasure, ma."

"We both know you didn't come down here to just sign the documents for the property," Mrs A said. "What's on your mind?"

"Actually, I need your help with something," Zuri said. "I've done fairly well selling these units, but I think I need to expand my network. I've spent so much time calling all the successful people I've networked with, but they are not biting. They just tell me they'll call me back and I never hear from them again."

"I see," Mrs A smiled. "So how do you plan on getting around that dear?"

"I have no idea," Zuri said. "I just need a new strategy to get in front of more high-net-worth individuals and celebrities, expand my network. As they say, your network is your net worth, right?"

"Darling, I hate to break it to you, but your network is only your net worth if you can use it to create opportunities or remove obstacles. Those people are not calling you back because they hardly know you. You met them at a conference, collected their business cards but they are not invested in your progress and they are not inclined to give you their business when they have no knowledge of your track record or ability to perform."

"But they've met me, now. And I told them I worked in real estate," Zuri said. "I definitely articulated the value I offer like you taught me."

"It's not magic, honey," Mrs A laughed. "If I met you at a conference and gave you my business card and the next time you called me was to tell me about property you were selling, chances are I wouldn't buy from you because at that point I have no real idea who you are or if you are credible."

"Ouch!" Zuri laughed. "What can I do then?"

I've told you many times, love. Two things," Mrs A advised. "Build organic relationships and highlight your performance. When people know you are excellent at what you do, they gravitate towards you, naturally. Besides, I've already referred you to quite a few of my friends, so you should be expecting some phone calls pretty soon."

"Just don't disgrace me," she teased.

"Aww! Thank you so much, ma," Zuri smiled. "I'll do my best to incorporate what you've said. I guess I was just a little impatient."

"That's the problem with your generation, impatience," Mrs A said. "These things take time, and quality relationships don't happen overnight. one of my favourite examples of someone who invests in their relationships in your generation is Adebola Williams."

"You are always saying this," Zuri laughed rolling her eyes.

"I'm serious! The young man wasn't born with a silver spoon, but he's built an impressive network of people who would do almost anything for him," Mrs A said. "I mean you don't win three presidential campaigns in multiple African countries without working with people."

"Actually, I've watched that man at several networking events and it's an art," Zuri mused. "The way he even introduces people to each other is definitely something to learn. 'ABC, have you met XYZ? She is a financial whiz kid and our generation's answer to Bizmark Rewane. XYZ, have you met ABC? He is revolutionising digital distribution in Africa.' Honestly, the first time I witnessed it, I laughed. However, when I thought about it later on, I realised that it's genius. Even in saying nothing about himself at that moment, he's made two individuals feel really important and valuable and it endears him to them."

It's a little more than that," Mrs A agreed. "It's about the way he's constantly seeking opportunities for others, he's not afraid to share his platform. I've known Adebola for years and even when he didn't have any money or any platform, his currency was acts of service."

As Mr Kofi came to the patio to clear the table Zuri knew it was time to start heading home. "Thank you so much, ma, for all your advice. I don't take it for granted. You are truly a woman that supports other women."

Mrs A started laughing.

"Let me make your head explode," Mrs A said. "I hate that phrase. I loved it at first because I truly believe in its premise, but since it became a popular Instagram hashtag, I find that it has bred entitlement in your generation, and eye-service in mine."

Zuri's rueful laugh was in total agreement.

"Seriously, many women in your generation seem to think that they should be supported just because they are women and it doesn't work like that. People are inclined to support you when you are a woman who has created something valuable. They walk up to me at events and ask me to mentor them, but they have no idea what they need mentorship for? They haven't articulated what it is they actually need help with. Mentorship has become a fad, an Instagram symbol of letting people know who you know and think you have access to."

"Aunty, oh!" Zuri screamed with laughter and said in pidgin, "*Please don't kill me with laugh.*"

Seriously, it's ridiculous," Mrs A said. "The answers you are looking for lie in the work you refuse to do. If I find you interesting and I think we have a connection we can build on, great! This idea that all women must support all women is unrealistic. Not everyone will be interested in what you do or what you have to offer."

"Fair enough," Zuri replied as she contemplated her mentor's words.

"It's actually, the *agbayas* in my generation that irritate me the most," Mrs A continued. "They'll be saying women supporting women and while some of them genuinely mean it, a few of them are secretly competing with girls that are young enough to be their daughters. It's ridiculous."

Actually, I've heard that a lot," Zuri said. "But I don't even concern myself with them because I am a product of women who have supported me unreservedly."

"If you truly want to support another woman, give without expectation," Mrs A said. "Bring her accomplishments into a discussion when she's not in the room. Share your connections and your resources."

"I totally agree," Zuri said. "One of my favourite things about you is that you don't just share your accomplishments, you share your setbacks. For me, it's important to have a mentor that not only knows how to make millions but also knows what it's like to lose millions, rebuild and share those lessons. That's one thing I'm super grateful for, that you share your highs and lows with me."

"Well, my darling, that comes with learning to bury my ego and insecurities," Mrs A said. "And understanding that there's no shame in failure. There are enough opportunities and money out here for all of us."

SMART MONEY LESSON:
BUILD A VALUABLE NETWORK

People constantly throw around the phrase, 'Your network is your net worth,' but I've come to realise that the premise only holds true if you can leverage it to create opportunities or remove obstacles. What do I mean? Take a look at the people you say are in your network—that *egbon* that sits on the board of a consumer goods company, that bank MD you met at a conference that gave you his card or that rich relative. If you were looking for a job or a business opportunity, are you in a position to call any of these people to help? And when you do, will they leverage their resources to help you or send your call to voice mail?

The only relationships that matter are the ones where meaningful bonds exist.

For your network to truly be your net worth you need access to a community of people that will go to bat for you even when you are not in the room—you know, the friends, mentors, and colleagues that think of you when they find new opportunities. Will that person pick up the phone and call that bank manager to consider your business for a loan, or call their friend who has a large distribution network to stock your products? Or are they available to give valuable advice based on their experience?

Leveraging Access
In my opinion, talent is distributed evenly but opportunity is not. When we talk about the importance of networking what we are really saying is we are looking for access—to markets, funding, information, opportunities. The more valuable your network is

the more access you have.

For instance, if two people are seeking capital for a project, it stands to reason that the quality of access the to an entry-level analyst at the bank will often be very different from the person who has access to the managing director.

For example, I'd imagine that when Dangote is looking for capital to build a new refinery, he has access to some of the biggest financiers in the world. Bank managing directors, chief executive officers of private equity firms, and generally, people who are ready and willing to give him capital that will most certainly be cheaper than what is available to the average Joe. This is mostly because he has a proven track record. The more successful you are the more quality access you have.

Rotimi from Ilupeju may have a killer idea that can revolutionise an entire industry, but with no proven track record, limited access to funding, no access to markets or additional research, his idea will most likely be dead in the water.

Bottom line: the quality of the rooms you have access to improves as you climb the ladder of success. The conversations in the rooms that rich people are in are very different.

Focus on Being Valuable
When it comes to networking at conferences and such, I often hear millennials complaining that successful people prefer to socialise with each other, have no interest in helping and generally do not engage. In my opinion, this is an incredibly negative mindset to go into a networking situation with.

First of all, nobody owes you anything, so you can't walk into any networking interaction feeling entitled to anyone's time, attention, or help. Building quality relationships take time, it's a process and it's ultimately about an exchange of value, so what do you bring to the table? Is an association with you valuable? There are examples in this chapter where Adebola Williams is said to volunteer acts of service even when he didn't have any money or hadn't come this far in his career. Zuri volunteered to create a strategy document to help with her mentor's new jewellery line.

If you don't believe that you are valuable or that you create value, others won't either. However, you must be honest with yourself because value is not entitlement. Value is not deceiving yourself. You need to figure out what value you bring to an interaction and know how to articulate it.

Network Horizontally

As important as it is to network upwards, looking for mentors who have been successful in their industries and can help provide guidance because of their wealth of experience, its equally as important to network across. Instead of constantly looking for the Mrs Awosikas and the Tara Fela Durotoyes, we need to start looking at who is with us in the trenches, the soldiers that are beside us who are just as hungry as we are and explore ways we can help each other grow, so that we too can be the next set of leading women of our generation.

Studies have shown that building a large network is important in becoming successful but I think it's also important for women to have a small tribe of women within they friendship circle that they can turn to and count on for a wide range of things, pulling resources, testing the validity of your ideas, give valuable advice, strategy, PR and opportunities. I call this your 'Money Tribe'. Within your friendship circle, you are not going to be able to do business or take advice from everyone; some friends are just friends, but your money tribe are friends who act as the board of advisers for your financial life. Each one should bring a mix of experience and skills for different aspects of how you make money, directly or indirectly.

Collaborate to compete
There is power in numbers. My East African book tour was one of the most illuminating experiences when it came to watching women collaborate to create wealth. In Kenya, I was blown by how financially literate and aware the average woman was. Kenyan women are increasing their ownership of property through Savings and Credit Co-operative Organizations (SACCOs). They come together as a collective to save towards the goal of buying land and investing in other instruments. A woman I know told me she and her friends came together to form a group of twenty-five women who were contributing money. Over a few years, they ended up collectively investing in land and had cash in the bank of about $1,500,000.

What I loved about this was they could all leverage the cash in the bank to raise capital individually for their businesses. In Nigeria, we have a version of this in the form of *ajo* and cooperatives but it is still in small pockets, in Kenya it's a whole wave. Plus, I find that Kenyans tend to be more patient when it comes to saving for the long term, while Nigerians are generally more short term in their thinking when it comes to money, they want it *now now,* which is why we are prone to falling for get-rich-quick scams.

This is not to say that saving and investing in groups doesn't have its drawbacks because like any good thing there can pitfalls and it depends on how you choose to use it. To invest successfully as a group, you have to be united in the quest to achieve a common goal. For example, if the purpose of the group is to build assets for the long term, Ronke cannot come and say after six months that she has to withdraw some of the money because I want to pay rent. The goal of the fund and Ronke's goals are clearly not aligned. One of the major problems with *ajo* is that when its person A's turn to collect money from the group she might put it in treasury bills which are relatively safe, then when its person C's turn they put it in Lagbaja's fish farm and unfortunately, the fish die or don't sell and the money is stuck. The problem in this scenario is that the risk appetites of the individuals in the group differ. When investing in a group it is important to have some sort of constitution that dictates how money is administrated, via a legal document that communicates clearly the goal, how money will be invested, the agreed risk, how people can exit etc.

Building a Money Tribe

These are five types of friends you want to have in your money tribe:

Zuri: The Plug

This person is an opportunity bringer. They are always trying to put all their friends "on", and are the ones that sell your market even while they are looking for opportunities for themselves. They are an active connection to revenue-generating possibilities. This is the type of friend that will come to you with propositions like "Hey, I met the CEO of Walmart and they are looking to push more African brands through their distribution network. I told them about your Madam Ori products and you need to send a proposal this week", or "I heard XYZ bank is giving low interest loans and you should apply".

Lara: The Strategist

This person is an idea machine and tends to have very sophisticated analytic capabilities. They are the ones in the group you are most likely to go to when you have an idea and need to brainstorm to flesh it out, create structure and figure out how to monetise it. They are the ones you call when you have a pitch meeting and need to practise your presentation or to discuss the numbers of your business.

Adesuwa: Mrs Make-It-Happen

This person is a doer. They are very organised and pay attention to detail. They are the ones you want in the trenches with you when you are executing an idea. They like executing on a project and they like to be where the action is. I find that they are usually in the event planning space or the ones who are most likely to organise church events.

Ladun: The PR

This person toots your horn whether you are in the room or not. They are constantly "selling your market" and are most likely the friend who knows all the products and services you offer, what their benefits are and how to market your strengths. They are the most likely to repost on Instagram when you launch a new product or have a new accomplishment. They are always proud of your wins and not afraid to show it.

Tami: The Connector

This person is a social butterfly with purpose, not only do they know everyone worth knowing they are always eager to introduce you. For them networking is an art form but they don't just enjoy meeting people they are strategic about pairing people to create synergy.

EXERCISE:

1. Do you have a valuable network and within that network are you considered valuable yourself? Is an association with you profitable?

2. Do you have a money tribe? How many of the types of members do you have in your money tribe?

CHAPTER 12

SOCIAL MEDIA:
A GIFT AND A CURSE

Adesuwa

Adesuwa reversed into one of the parking spots in front of SJ's school, ignoring the incessant messaging pings emanating from her phone. She turned off the car, rummaged through her bag to find her school ID before finally picking up the handset to see who or what was spamming her inbox.

It was their Instagram direct messaging group. Tami had sent a photo from Soji's page to the group chat. She felt lightheaded for a split second. She couldn't believe he would do this. They had been separated for six weeks and had started divorce proceedings, but damn!

She stared at the picture—Soji and his pregnant mistress. The girl, who looked all of twenty-two, was wearing a white dress and rested one hand on what looked like a five-month bump, with the other caressing Soji's head as he kissed the bump.

Her chest tightened; it wasn't so much the picture but the caption underneath it.

Sometimes we find love in unexpected places! Can't wait to meet you, princess... we've waited for you for so long.

As the first tear rolled down her cheek, Adesuwa wondered if this man was referring to the fact that he never loved her or the fact that she had been trying for years to give him a second child and failed. Either way, it hurt.

She shook herself, swiped away any traces of her tears, put on her shades, then got out of the car and walked towards the school gates. She knew she had to put her frustration aside because her six-year-old could always sense when his mum was in low spirits, which had been pretty much every day in the last couple of months.

At two o'clock on the dot, the school bell rung and Adesuwa gave quick thanks—she could be in and out quickly. Then she heard a familiar, grating voice.

"SJ's mummy!" The lady shouted.

Adesuwa was tempted to keep walking and pretend she couldn't hear the familiar voice of Tobi's mum, aka the woman that could never mind her business. She didn't even know her actual name, but this lady was super annoying. She had gleaned from several mundane conversations they'd had that Tobi's mum was a stay-at-home mum married to a wealthy man. Unfortunately, it meant she spent an inordinate amount of her not insubstantial spare time judging everyone else's parenting style.

On a normal day she would allow the woman and her rant *to waka pass* then roll her eyes behind her back, but after Soji's shenanigans today, she was not in the mood, and she was worried that she would go off on her.

"SJ's mummy I've been calling you, didn't you hear me," Tobi's mum asked as she tapped Adesuwa's left shoulder.

Adesuwa took a deep breath and turned around with a thin smile plastered on.

"Hello, Tobi's mum."

"Ah. You are doing pick up today?" she said trying to sound innocent, but Adesuwa knew better—this was yummy mummy code for, 'You are a bad mummy. You don't do pick up every day'.

She shaped her lips in the appearance of a smile and made some non-committal noises as she let her eyes sweep the grounds for SJ.

She had never understood this unspoken rivalry between the stay-at-home mums and the working mums. Yes, she couldn't pick SJ up from school every day, but she had gotten over feeling inadequate about that a long time ago. She had picked two days each week when she could make the time, and besides, spending an hour gossiping with other parents while her kid watched was not the best use of her time.

Sometimes, she actually preferred the nanny and driver pick SJ up and bring him to her office to say hello before he went home. That way, he got a glimpse of what she did all day and understood that she was working so they could have a good life.

SJ had a basic understanding of the relationship between the value of money and hard work. A lot of these Lagos Academy mums were of the stay-at-home variety, and she respected their choice because frankly, she couldn't do it. It was a lot of work but what she didn't get was the need to "mummy shame" other mothers who had made the choice to work. She didn't criticise their own parenting choices, and so she didn't understand why they thought criticising hers would make them feel better.

Adesuwa wanted to remind her that the reason she could do drop-offs, pickups and hang around the school for all hours of the day was that she didn't actually work for a living, so she had time on her hands. She was already in a foul mood and had an appropriate retort, but as SJ ran towards her with his open arms and a big smile, she looked at Tobi's mum and decided that silence was probably best because this woman was probably battling more significant insecurities.

SJ greeted her with a beaming smile and hug.

"Hello, mummy. You look beautiful!" He said happily, looking at her like she was the eighth wonder of the world. Adesuwa grinned back in delight because she knew she looked haggard.

She settled back into the car after securing SJ in the back seat then grabbed her phone to see if there were any updates, only to see two missed calls from Zuri and Ladun. There were a slew of messages asking if she was okay, followed by a tirade of insults calling Soji names that ranged from 'ungrateful bastard' to 'useless man'. And, there was a link.

The post had landed on a gossip blog. The humiliation had begun. Her heart sank, and tears began to roll down her face.

The headline read:
Lagos Big Boy Announces Crash of His Marriage to Entertainment Lawyer with Photo of His Pregnant Girlfriend!

****

Lara

As she walked off the stage after speaking on the panel 'Finding a Gender Balance in the Oil and Gas industry in Africa', Lara felt a burst of pride. She was wearing a yellow midi dress by Tolu Bally, paired with grey Prada heels. She knew she looked amazing, but this was the first time she was speaking at an international conference, so she had been very nervous. The sheer size of the crowd and the industry leaders present had felt daunting initially. However, she knew she hit a home run with her points and ideas because of the audience's reaction and applause.

They were about to break for lunch, and the hall was buzzing. There were at least a thousand oil and gas practitioners from all over Africa present. As she walked past different groups of men huddled together, she overheard snippets of conversation, people closing deals, enquiring about how they could work on certain projects together and generally making valuable connections.

"Hello, Lara," She heard a voice say as she walked into the lunchroom. She turned around to see Mariah Lucciano-Gabriel. She was a tall, dark-skinned woman with the cutest dimple Lara had ever seen, second only to Tami's. She was the head of commercial and business development at the largest indigenous oil and gas company in Nigeria. They had both been on the panel.

"It was lovely speaking alongside you on stage," Mariah said. "You made some very valid points about the gender inequalities in energy access."
"Thank you so much. I loved the work you're doing—you are actually out there doing the work to close the gender gap. Well done!"

Mariah had started an initiative to make STEM subjects in secondary schools more inclusive for Nigerian girls. She believed some of the inequality in energy education, came from the fact that girls mostly saw careers that required science, technology, engineering, and maths as better suited for men, which led to very few women being able to take on certain oil and gas jobs because they didn't have the skills required.

She had spearheaded an initiative to solve the problem by creating workshops and mentorship programmes for young girls. She convinced women who worked in high-level oil and gas positions to not just give talks at these workshops, but to allow some of the most promising students shadow them once a quarter. In under a year, they had reached over a thousand girls. "Thank you so much," Mariah smiled. "It's tough balancing it with work because the programme has become so much bigger than my company or me but it's very fulfilling to know that we are making an impact."

"You really are," Lara responded. It's very impressive. "Can I ask how you created awareness for it so quickly? These sorts of initiatives usually take several years to gain momentum."

"I know, right?" Mariah replied. "But I have to credit social media. As soon as I started talking about it on Instagram, telling people about the work and our process for choosing the schools to partner with, and promoting the events with media partners like BellaNaija and BusinessDay, the donations and participation from individuals and institutions started rolling in."

"Wow, that's amazing. There's definitely something to be said for how social media can help to build your profile."

They were walking through the buffet line as they chatted, picking up nibbles and discussing the challenges and rewards of being present on the internet.

"I'm telling you," Mariah replied. "I used to be one of those people that thought that all I needed to do was put my head down and do the work, and my profile would grow organically. Then I met this PR lady Bidemi Zakariyau, who volunteered her services because she liked the work we were doing and wanted to help us increase awareness."

"LSFPR? I've heard of her," Lara nodded as they found seats. "She did some work with my friend, Tami, recently and I've heard nothing but good things."

"She's brilliant. Her work on this initiative made me realise that times have changed. People don't depend on logos to build their brand. These days consumers want to buy into people's stories. That way, they connect with the individual promoting the brand and connect to why they do what they do. Even as an intrapreneur, how accessible your profile is could determine the next job you get. I was at a Bloom Africa event recently, and I heard one of the speakers, Bozoma Saint John, who's completely amazing. Her personal brand has helped catapult her to the top."

"That makes sense," Lara replied. "Tami is always going on about how we all leave a digital footprint intentionally or otherwise, and that's the way most people find about who you are and what you do."

"Very true," Mariah laughed. "When I meet someone for the first time, the first thing I do is search for them on Google and Instagram."

"Hey ladies, may I join you?" Modele Idiahi said. "We seem to be the only

Nigerian women our age here."

Both Mariah and Lara cheerfully agreed, making room for her at their table. Modele was a tall, dark-skinned beauty who had also spoken alongside them on the panel earlier. She was wearing a two-piece grey outfit that accentuated her tiny waist and enviable hips. She looked like she had just stepped off a runway which was a heavy contrast when compared to her accomplishments in the boardroom.

The definition of beauty and brains, Modele was the youngest female founder and CEO of a gas-to-power project development company in Nigeria. She had just successfully structured project finance, with a mix of debt and equity to the tune of several million dollars.

"I'm actually glad I ran into you guys," Modele said as she placed her plate on the table and put her Chanel bag on the seat next to Mariah.

"Yeah, I was definitely hoping to connect after," Lara said. "You were amazing on the panel."

"You really were," Mariah agreed.

"Thank you so much," Modele smiled. "So, you know my company is a gas-to-power project development company that specialises in domestic gas commercialisation, right?"

Lara and Mariah nodded.

"Besides the speaking opportunity, I also wanted to come to this conference to identify companies that might be willing to partner with my company, Eleva, to commercialise their flared gas. And, I was wondering if any of your companies were working on any projects we might be able to plug into."

"That's a great idea! We are producing from one of our assets in the Niger Delta, and we flare our gas. It would be great to do something about it to avoid flaring penalties and make a bit of money as well." Lara looked extremely pleased.

"Exactly. It's a win-win," Modele agreed.

"Let's sign an NDA when we are back in Lagos," Lara said. "Then we can take it from there."

As Mariah began to talk to Modele about how they could work together too, Lara couldn't help but marvel at her peers and the amazing things they were accomplishing. She loved being in rooms like this, surrounded by African women sharing ideas, making an impact, and changing the world. It was genuinely inspiring it made her want to do more and be more.

She realised she had been ignoring her phone all morning as she swiped to view her messages.

Lara froze. Tami had sent a post from an Instagram gossip blog to the group. There were over 600 comments already. She looked again at the picture of Soji and his little tart and swore.

"Bastard!" She muttered, made her excuses and walked out of the hall to call Adesuwa.

****

Tami

"One of the most difficult things we have to deal with trying to build a fashion brand in Africa is distribution and logistics," Tami expounded. "There are so many like me who do great work and are good at creating the demand they need to sustain their brands, but constantly run into problems when it comes to getting our products to consumers."

Tami was speaking at the Industrie Africa showcase in London, England. They were in a newly converted warehouse in Shoreditch which was hard to believe, given the combination of high ceilings, the magnificent floral installation and the models clad in African designs, standing on platforms. The entire space was completely transformed.

"What key factors would you say contribute to this?" Helen Jennings asked. She was the editor-in-chief of Nataal, an international fashion media publication, and the moderator of the panel.

"First of all, there are not many options in terms of retail outlets," Tami responded. "Then there are the typical African problems with the lack of infrastructure, inadequate or non-existent road networks, and finally the fragmentation of the consumer base. Although there is strong market from other countries in Africa and the diaspora community, the logistics of shipping clothes from Nigeria to Los Angeles is easier than that to ship to Botswana. Potential customers see your clothes on Instagram, love it, want to buy it, but when the cost of shipping is more than the retail price of the actual clothing item, they get turned off."

As Helen asked the other African designers on the panel how they managed to navigate these challenges and wrapped the panel, Tami's mind drifted. Although she had known for a while that she was going to be part of the fashion presentation and participate in the fashion conversations, it still felt like an out of body experience.

It was all so surreal speaking in front of a global audience. In the front row, there were representatives from Grazia, Harper's Bazaar, Refinery29, Glamour, and Vogue.com.

Nisha had really pulled out all the stops. Tami spotted Isoken Ogiemwonyi, the editor-at-large for BellaNaija Style, who had flown in from Toronto to review the collection—excellent not only because there would be international press, but also because the BellaNaija team would provide full coverage back in Nigeria.

After the panel, she headed to the pop-up souq scheduled for after the fashion presentations to maximise sales for the designers. There was a mix of buyers for huge retailers who had stayed on to take orders, fashion influencers, and members of the public.

As Tami mingled with her guests and answered questions about her inspiration for the collection and individual pieces, she was impressed by the number of Africans in the diaspora who had come out to show their support. "Hi!" Fisayo Longe squealed as she gave Tami a hug. "I love, love, love your collection! You made me so proud. In fact, I want one of each."

She was a fashion influencer with her own brand, Kai Collective, had successfully worked with international brands like Nike and Malibu Rum and had also been featured in international press like Elle UK.

"Listen! You know we are trying to be like you and Kai collective," Tami grinned. "We should have lunch after, so you can give me tips on production and how to navigate the international market."

"Sure thing," Fisayo agreed. "Just let me know when."

Tami thought for a second then asked, "Actually, are you doing the zazaii.com showcase as well?"

"Thinking about it," Fisayo replied.

"Me? I can't wait, it's so exciting. I feel that everything is happening all at once, but I'm definitely taking the Zazaii opportunity because I want to capitalise on the buzz Irawo has right now," Tami enthused.

The two women chatted for a few more minutes about upcoming shows and opportunities before Tami said goodbye.

As she walked across the room trying to find Nisha so she could say thank you, her phone started to chime insistently and without looking she already knew it was about the Soji drama on social media that had begun that morning. Tami had tried to block it out so she could focus on work, but it was time to catch up with the girls to find out how Adesuwa was doing.

****

Ladun

"Essentially, I would be your first client?" Doshima asked, her immaculate bob framing her delicate face.

Doshima was an investment banker turned private chef who had abandoned her six-figure-dollar salary to pursue her passion for food and travel. She had trained at the cordon bleu, worked at some high-end restaurants in Europe before she moved back to Nigeria. Her reputation for creating exquisite meals fusing African food with European and Asian techniques and cuisines had put her on the map.

She had gained a following because she started a food and travel blog documenting her experience. She had about forty thousand followers on Instagram and Ladun wanted to land her as a client, so she had invited her to a late lunch at the Lighthouse, a lovely outdoor restaurant situated at the bottom of the Lekki-Ikoyi link bridge overlooking the water.

In the last couple of weeks, Tami had set up meetings with her other influencer friends, so that Ladun could pitch them her idea of managing their brands. So far they hadn't panned out—some of them already had representation, some of them didn't believe they needed a manager because they'd had terrible experiences in the past and had decided to go it alone, and the rest were just horrible, self-involved individuals Ladun had no interest in working with.

At first, she had contemplated quitting but Zuri had convinced her that all the pitches were just practise for the client she really wanted. And maybe she was right because Doshima was the type client she really wanted—passionate about her work, smart, sassy, and seemed to know exactly what she wanted. The deeper they got in conversation, the faster the wheels in Ladun's head began to turn, as she envisioned many opportunities for monetising Doshima's brand.

"Yes, technically, you would be my first client other than Tami. And Tami doesn't count because she's one of my best friends. However, that's good news for you because it means you have first dibs on the corporate brands I work with at the firm and you also have my full attention."

"Fair enough," Doshima agreed as she took a sip of her freshly squeezed orange and mango juice. "Listen, Ladun. You seem lovely! But let me be one hundred with you. I'm still sceptical about your ability to help monetise my brand. I've gotten similar offers before but let's just say they give a good presentation but have zero follow-through. And after six months I'd have been paying someone a monthly retainer, no value adds, no understanding of my brand and where I want it to go. It always ends up being just a waste of money."

Ladun completely understood the woman's misgivings. "Thank you for being honest, it saves everyone time. I understand your misgivings, and I'm not going to sit here and say I'm different because I'm more professional or have more expertise than the other people you've tried out in the past because I don't."

"You are not?" Doshima raised her eyebrow. "That would certainly be a first."

"In fact, I'll be equally honest and say that I'm probably the most inexperienced manager you have worked with because up until eighteen months ago, I was a rich housewife whose idea of work was planning dinner parties, shopping, and travelling all over the world."

Doshima's face was blank, but Ladun could almost see the thoughts rotating in her head.

"My life changed when my father-in-law died and well, let's just say our financial realities became a living nightmare when he passed. I was forced to get a job to help provide for my family."

"I'm so sorry about that," Doshima commiserated. "That must have been tough."

"Don't be sorry, honey. I like to think it was the push I needed to be more intentional about my life. At first, I hated my job and was tempted to quit every single day, but the more I focused on what I actually liked about it the more I found I was good at it. I work hard for my clients. I'm very creative, and I've become very passionate about influencer marketing because I've seen how effective it can be in helping convert an audience into customers."

"Why do you want to work with me, though?" Doshima asked.

Ladun didn't think twice before she answered, "Well, it's simple, I'm a huge fan. I've followed you for years, used quite a few of your recipes to wow my husband and children. You share your content in a very unique way, telling relatable stories about your travel experiences and the interesting ways you share your food. However, content is only as valuable as the distribution strategy that's used to deploy it. What you've done so far is great, but visibility is a currency, and I want to help you get both."

"I agree with everything you've said," Doshima replied. "My biggest question is, what makes you the best person for the job?"

"I'm inexperienced, but I'm hungry," Ladun said earnestly. "What I lack in professional experience, I have in practical know-how. My years of party planning and hosting dinner parties for my husband, his rich friends and their wives mean that I have a Rolodex of high net worth individuals who have first-hand experience of my good taste and could be your potential clients."

Doshima chuckled. "That would be lovely. I'm always looking for rich people to cook for,"

"Besides, my working at one of the biggest advertising companies in the country means I have direct access to over fifty corporate brands, some of which would be a good fit for your brand," Ladun continued.

"This wouldn't be a conflict of interest?" Doshima asked.

"No, it won't," Ladun replied. "Initially, I was worried it would because many Nigerian companies don't encourage a side hustle but my new boss Belema is very forward-thinking and saw the advantages of having a roster of influencers on hand without the stress of managing them. She has also insisted the firm takes a ten per cent fee for every campaign they actively bring to the influencers. Which might look like less money for you in the short term because of the combined fees but in the medium to long term this association will lead to more."

"Anyway, if you are going to manage my brand, one of the things I struggle with is how to charge," Doshima said. "Obviously, at first, I didn't start this to make money from social media. My primary income stream was from my work as a private chef. However, as time went on, I began to see that Instagram was a business for some of my international contemporaries, one that had a very real revenue stream attached to it."

"Are you telling me?" Ladun laughed. "Look at Chiara Ferragni, for instance. She's a fashion influencer that's raking in a lot of cash. She started her blog 'The Blonde Salad' in two thousand and nine, and since then she's had collaborations with everyone from Guess, Pantene, and Tod's."

She began to give a quick rundown of Chiara's history as an influencer.

"I've followed her for years," Ladun explained, "but I knew it was real when she started gracing the covers of magazines and getting invited to sit in the front rows of major fashion shows. However, what I've found the most fascinating is her growth as a businesswoman. She went from collaborating with Steve Madden and co-creating a nine-shoe collection which did extremely well, to creating her own Chiara Ferragni shoe collection."

"But is the shoe collection doing well though?" Doshima asked. "Because it's such a risk to create your own products. What if people don't buy?"

"Well! Harvard Business School did a case study on it," Ladun informed her. "So, probably!"

"I also hear she commands like twenty thousand dollars per sponsored post," Doshima said. "They are in a developed market, that could never work here. I mean corporate brands want to work with me, but they want to do it for free or in exchange for goods or services they offer, not cash."

"I actually think it's getting better," Ladun responded. "African brands are starting to understand the power of influencer marketing because it has a higher conversion rate and better feedback mechanisms than the more traditional mediums. Think about it! As great as it is to be on a billboard or in a newspaper, it's a one-way dialogue. You can't actually say what you think or feel about the product or service, so you see it, but you can't leave a comment or start a conversation. With Instagram or Twitter, it's the opposite. Your target audience can connect directly with what you are selling, especially if it's been experienced through the voice or story of an actual human being they follow and trust. The recommendations just mean more."
"Exactly! That's what I'm always trying to explain to brands that approach me," Doshima agreed. "The way we consume information has evolved. We get our news from Twitter, not the newspaper because it's more instant. We make our purchasing decisions on Instagram. Even when I'm in traffic these days, I'm too busy on my phone to notice billboards. And even when we watch actual TV, we don't pause to watch the commercials anymore, we are on Instagram and Twitter talking about what we are watching. It's changed!"
"Yup! Social media is the most effective advertising platform, and influencers are its digital referral medium. These days many influencers have more reach than the newspapers or magazines have circulation."

"Again, how do we get them to understand it and value it in this part of the world?" Doshima said.

Ladun laughed. "Listen, have you heard of Kefilwe Mabote? She's a South African digital influencer with over six hundred thousand followers."

"Yeah, I follow her," Doshima said excitedly. "She takes such great pictures. Her entire page looks like an editorial in a magazine."

"Yes, but you see it's not just pretty pictures," Ladun explained. "It's a business! The woman is very strategic about what she posts, she understands her audience. She gets that her brand is aspirational, and she focuses solely on luxury brands and gets paid for it! She's not trying to attract mass-market brands.

"Are you serious?" Doshima said in amusement. "She just looks like a wealthy woman living her best life."

"Yes, living her best life and making bank doing it! She's worked with international brands like Dolce and Gabbana, Dior, Grey Goose and Prada. She's even been flown to fashion shows in Milan and Paris!"

"No wonder she won Glamour magazine's digital influencer of the year!" Doshima said.

Ladun wanted to stay positive without making unrealistic promises, so she told Doshima, "It will take time, but the key thing is to build your audience and build your voice. When brands see that you have a decent following and strong engagement, they'll come to you. Brands are essentially looking for value. They want to work with influencers that can convert their audiences to customers. I know influencers that command millions of naira even in Nigeria to be part of campaigns or post on social media. You just have to have an intentional content strategy and understand your audience, that way you know what brands you even want to work with. The ones that are the right fit."

"Millions, *ke?*" Doshima said with disbelief. "A hundred thousand naira maybe but millions? I'm sceptical."

"Trust me, I just closed a deal for Tami the other week that involved a few million naira," Ladun lowered her voice and explained. "It's a lot of people's reality, you just have to hire someone that can find you the right brands to work with."

"Okay! Okay!" Doshima laughed. "I'm sold! Where do I sign? How much is this going to cost me?"

Ladun smiled. "Just fifteen per cent of any deals I close for you. After six months if you are happy, I want a two hundred thousand naira a month retainer in addition to the fifteen per cent."

Doshima mulled over the offer for a few seconds, then came to a decision. "That sounds steep, but I'm in."

"Don't worry with the amount of business I have lined up for you, you will be able to afford it," Ladun promised with a quick grin.

She glanced at her phone. It was a message from Zuri.

Adesuwa needs us NOW! Meet me at her house.

****
Zuri

"Where is she?" Zuri asked Olivia as she strode through the door of Adesuwa's house.

"Upstairs, ma! *She dey cry since she return from work,*" Olivia said. "where is SJ?" she asked.

"Sleeping, ma," Olivia responded, reaching for Zuri's Gucci bag to help her carry it up the stairs.

"Don't worry," Zuri said, waving her hand away. "Aunty Ladun is coming.

She's just parking her car. Bring her upstairs when she comes, okay?"

"Okay, ma!" Olivia nodded in response.

As Zuri reached the top of the stairs. She took a few seconds to take a deep breath. This was going to be a tough conversation, but she knew she needed to be strong for her friend.

"Adesuwa!" Zuri said softly as she knocked on the door to the bedroom. She opened the door slightly. The lights were off, but she could hear sobbing.

"Is she okay?" Ladun said as she reached the top of the stairs, slightly out of breath.

"I don't know," Zuri said solemnly. "Let's find out."

It was dark, but Zuri could see that Adesuwa was underneath the covers, still wearing her work clothes, shoes included. She was holding her phone and scrolling through with one hand.

"Put on the light," Zuri whispered to Ladun as she made her way to the bed and sat next to Adesuwa.

"Babe, are you alright?" Zuri said as she rubbed Adesuwa's back to comfort her.

"Do I look fine?" Adesuwa responded.

"You don't, babe!" Zuri agreed softly. "But you will be. I know this is humiliating, but it's going to pass, I promise."

"This is worse than humiliating," Adesuwa said as she sat up on the bed. "It's bad enough that my husband has left me for a younger woman and gotten her pregnant when I've struggled to have a second baby all these years, now strangers who know nothing about my life are tearing me down in the comment sections of these gossip blogs. Saying that my over-independence is what caused my marriage to fail! Imagine that, Zuri! After everything I've endured in this nightmare of a marriage to Soji."

"Don't listen to them," Ladun soothed. "Most of these people are low lives that have nothing going on in their own lives and frankly have no real-world perspectives because they are trapped in their own mental prisons."

"Exactly! You know in this country a marriage breaks up, and it's the woman's fault. Men will say it and women will also chime in with their own crooked mouths and contribute to it."

"I even saw a comment that said it's because I'll be doing big madam lawyer instead of focusing on my husband and child," Adesuwa said as she scrolled through the comments. "All I ever wanted to do was build with that man. I didn't even care that I had to provide for him, all I asked for was fidelity. Was that too much to ask?" She wept.

"Adesuwa, you have to stop crying," Ladun said. "You can't listen to randoms that know nothing. I definitely couldn't put up with half the nonsense you put up with babe. We expect women to work like they don't have children and raise children as if they don't work. Same applies to marriage and the expectations society places on African wives."

"Preach!" Zuri said. "You are not a rehabilitation centre for a badly raised man. It was not your job to fix Soji. No matter what you did, he would never really grow up, never recognise his mistakes, never acknowledge his faults, and definitely never admit he was wrong."

"Hmmm!" Adesuwa's chest heaved as she struggled to stop sobbing. "What did I do to deserve this sort of treatment? I was even ready to walk away and wipe the slate clean and all that, but did he have to humiliate me like this? I know it's because he's angry about not receiving any proceeds from the sale of the land. But I honestly thought he was going to come back and at least apologise."

"You'll never receive an apology from him, Adesuwa," Ladun said. "And you have to make your peace with that. You took him back even after the whole mess with Chinasa only because he ran out of money and he missed 'Bank of Adesuwa'. It's time to face facts."

"Would you believe that Banke liked the post of Soji and his pregnant girlfriend," Adesuwa said in disbelief. "She even went as far as commenting, 'I'm super happy for you!' with heart emojis. What kind of friend does that? She knew me before she ever knew Soji! She hasn't even called or texted to ask how I am."

"Honestly, you know that one is not a friend," Ladun said. "She's a frenemy! I don't know why you are surprised."

Zuri picked up her phone and began to scroll through the comment section of the post.

"Ah! This one is finished," Zuri said.

"What?" Ladun asked.

"It's a vendor that does some interior work for Richmond," Zuri replied angrily. "She commented saying, 'Ghen ghen! All these women that can't keep their homes'. I honestly don't understand people that use their business pages to comment on rubbish that doesn't concern them. As of tomorrow, her contract with Richmond is terminated."

"You guys, maybe they are right?" Adesuwa wrestled with herself and her insecurities. "Maybe I didn't try hard enough. Maybe I didn't focus on being a good enough woman to him."

"Stop that!" Zuri walked up to her and shook her gently, trying to knock some sense into her. "Listen to me! Being a good woman is not about how much nonsense you can take. That's what this sick society wants you to believe because it benefits only two types of people. The men who do the shit, Soji does and expect you to close your mouth and endure and the women who take it and are stuck in bad marriages they can't leave so they want everyone else to be miserable with them."

"I don't care how attractive Soji is," Ladun added forcefully, "because that's all he ever brought to the bloody table. There's nothing sexy about long term struggle, lack of commitment or no vision for the future."

"Exactly, my sister! Zuri exclaimed. "Don't worry about his new girlfriend. She has entered one chance. She just doesn't realise it yet. You gave this broke, unambitious man access to you for so long and you were his gift, whether he saw it or not. It's time to focus on you and SJ now."

"I always felt like I was begging for his love," Adesuwa stared at the ceiling as she felt the tears start to well. "I don't ever want to feel like that again."

"And you shouldn't ever feel like that," Zuri replied, hugging her friend. "Adesuwa, you deserve to be with someone who invests in you too. Finding a life partner is more than being Mrs somebody. It's about finding someone compatible with your life's goals."

"How will I ever find someone?" Adesuwa lamented. "With this sort of disgusting scandal attached to my name. With all these lies on the internet."

"See, something about God that I am sure of," Ladun consoled with a reassuring smile. "If he makes you live through their lies, he will make them live through your blessings."

****

Adesuwa

A bleary-eyed Adesuwa looked at her bedside clock as she stumbled to the bathroom. It was two seventeen in the morning. After hours of talking, plotting, and trying to figure out her next steps with her friends, she had fallen asleep, not even realising when Ladun and Zuri left.

As she sat on the loo to pee, she mindlessly reached for the pregnancy test in the top drawer of the bathroom cabinet. It was an action she had become accustomed to in the last few months as she attempted to complete IVF treatments to have a baby with Soji. This would probably be her last attempt for a while. She tossed it on the counter by the sink. Done, she flushed then washed her hands, and as she reached for a towel to dry her hands, she glanced at the stick.

It was positive!

She felt a wave of conflicting emotions. She didn't know what to do first cry or laugh. It was such an impossible time. This was something she had wanted for such a long time, but this felt like such an inopportune time for it to come. God certainly had a sense of humour.

Adesuwa turned out the light and went back to bed.

For the first time in months, things were beginning to look up.

SMART MONEY LESSON:
SOCIAL MEDIA HAS DEMOCRATISED
OUR ACCESS TO OPPORTUNITY

Social media might look like it is all about selfies, banter, display of wealth, jokes, gossip, and all that is superficial but, darlings, it is NOT a game. It has quickly become a marketplace and a platform for people to start businesses, get jobs, and build brands.

Lots of people like to focus on how fake it all is and the frivolities that it showcases that unfortunately drives people to compare their lives with others. Like everything in life, social media comes with both advantages and disadvantages, and we must understand that it is a tool; it all depends on how you choose to use it.

I choose to focus on the fact that it has made the world so much smaller, which has, in turn, increased our access to a larger market. In the last chapter we discussed networking and how networking gives us access to opportunities. People often complain about the fact that Africa is a 'man know man' place where only the connected get anything done. They complain about not having access to customers with disposable income to buy their products or to celebrities to endorse their products and create visibility for their brands.

Social media has created a free platform that has democratised access to opportunity in many areas. For example, a talented but obscure artist from Nigeria can do a portrait of Kevin Hart and put it on Twitter or Instagram, it goes viral, Kevin Hart sees it and offers to make a purchase.

Ten years ago, if I wanted to do business in Kenya. I would probably have to make several trips to the country, meet people, see how things are done there before venturing to carry out any business activities there. In 2016, I launched a book 'The Smart Money Woman' on Instagram, and it gained traction across several African countries. I was able to go on a book tour to Tanzania, Kenya, South Africa, Uganda, and Ghana to name a few countries. Complete strangers, women who I had only met via social media, took control of planning book events as well as television and radio interviews to help me promote my book without ever meeting me until I arrived in their country. It became a movement, and it's still one of the most amazing things I have ever experienced.

There is always someone watching you that has the power to bless you, but the question is, what are they watching you do? Who are they watching you be? How you show up on social media is important. If you are always liking negative posts and having ridiculous arguments about celebrities on gossip blogs, you might think it's all fun and games because its "just" social media but think about what those comments say about you. If you saw the person you were talking smack about on the street could you walk up to them and say what you said in the comment section of a blog? If the person who was about to bless you with a business, or job opportunity was watching you, how are they watching you interact? And most importantly how is it moving you forward?

We need to use social media to gossip less and start putting out what we want to get out.

EXERCISE:

· Audit your social media pages. When you look at your bio, your posts, the things you comment about, and the conversations you engage in, do they represent who are and how you would like to show up?

· Find people who do what you do in other parts of the world and take a look at what they do that is similar to you and what they do differently. Pick out three things you have learned from their pages that could make your work better.

· Find people or brands who complement the work you do, try to connect, and find ways to collaborate.

· Follow pages that inspire you to grow, be the best version of yourself and unfollow pages that exacerbate your toxic traits.

CHAPTER 13

A TRIBE CALLED
SCHMONEY

Zuri

As they walked through the usual chaos at Murtala Mohammed International airport, Zuri could feel the excitement of travellers eager to get out of the country. She was certainly one of them. They had been planning and saving towards this girl's trip for at least ten months and there had been many reasons to cancel—marriage palaver, job woes, project deadlines, the responsibility of children, but the drama in the last few months alone had intensified their need to take a break from the Lagos madness.

"Adesuwa, how are you feeling about leaving SJ for one week," Zuri asked, as they approached the South African airline queue to check in. She knew her friend had been wary of taking off and leaving her six-year-old to go on holiday with her girls, but they had all convinced her that a break would be ideal right now given all the drama she had been facing with the collapse of her marriage.

"Hmm, honestly? A little guilty," Adesuwa sighed. "And my mum didn't make it any easier. She made it very clear that she thought this was a frivolous trip when I have a toddler to look after, a baby on the way, and a marriage to fight for, according to her. Thankfully, my doctor cleared me to fly, so I'm not worried about the baby. I can't lie, though, saying goodbye to SJ pulled my heartstrings, and my mummy guilt kicked in. I know it is irrational because I know in my heart that I need this and it's just a week, but it feels a little irresponsible."

"I honestly never understand when mums say this," Ladun laughed. "I love my children with every fibre of my being, but I never feel any sort of guilt, leaving them to go on holiday once in a while. I'm a mother, but I'm also a person, and a Ladun that's well-rested and mentally balanced is a better mummy."

"Ladun! I love it, I swear!" Lara laughed. "That is certainly going to be my philosophy when I have my own kids. I want to be a great parent, but that shouldn't include sacrificing my own personal goals all of the time. Adesuwa, you are an excellent mother. You've looked after SJ for six years and the kid is awesome. Taking seven days to rest and recalibrate is not going to change that. Besides, you've been through a lot and self-care is important."

"Preach!" Ladun laughed. "A mother in school actually had the nerve to ask me who I was going to leave the children with when I travel. I promptly told her their father! The person I had them with who has equal responsibility to care for them, alongside me. I've never understood that thing, *sha*. When a man is travelling, no one asks him these sorts of silly questions. I guess I'm just lucky Bode and I are on the same page when it comes to this. Plus, my mother-in-law is actually excited to help look after the kids when I'm away. In fact, she encourages it because she welcomes any opportunity to spend uninterrupted time with her grandkids."

"I think my mum is definitely going to be like mama Ashoni when I start having children," Tami joked. "The pressure she is putting on me to find a husband is largely tied to wanting grandchildren she can dote on."

The girls laughed.

"Would you be interested in an upgrade, ma?" The lady at the check-in desk for South African Airways asked.

"Uhm, no thanks," Zuri said with a small laugh. "No money for an upgrade, madam."

"We are doing a promo, ma," The lady insisted. "It's just five hundred dollars to upgrade to business class. It's usually about one thousand, ma."

"Well, there are five of us so that would be twenty-five hundred dollars?" Zuri said. "I don't think we can swing that, oh! It's not in the budget."

Lara was getting restless about the delay and asked, "What's going on, babe? Check in let's go, *now!*"

"Calm down, sis," Zuri said, rolling her eyes playfully. "The babe was just telling me they are doing a promo and we can upgrade for five hundred dollars each."

Immediately, Lara knew what was up, and her eyes lit up as she began to make the calculations. "Oh, nice. But madam, we both know that's travel industry speak for your plane is empty, so you are trying to maximise your profits last-minute. Reduce it to two hundred and fifty each. That way, five of us can upgrade."

"Ha! I can't do that, ma! My supervisor will never agree," The lady said. "Do you want them to sack me?"

Zuri could see Lara was in negotiation mode. This poor woman didn't stand a chance.

"Okay, Janet?" Lara said, glancing at the lady's nametag. "Please call your supervisor for me, let me speak to him or her."

"Allow this thing, *jo*, let's check in," Zuri said under her breath as Janet summoned her supervisor. "You know they'll never agree to that price. And even if, I can just bet at least one person is going to complain." She glanced at the rest of the girls weighing their luggage in the queue.

"Ah ah! One step at a time, love," Lara whispered. "Let's first of all find out if they agree then we can worry about convincing the others."

"This man's face looks strong, *abeg*! I doubt he'll agree," Zuri whispered back as Janet's supervisor walked towards the counter.

"Listen, the worst he can say is no! And *no no dey kill.*"

The stern-looking supervisor approached the counter and introduced himself. "My name is Ezekiel. How can I help you, ladies?"

"Hello, Ezekiel!" Lara responded. "My friends and I are travelling with you today, and Janet just told us you are running a promo. We really want to take advantage of it, but there's five of us, and that's way above our budget. I was trying to negotiate with Janet here, but she wasn't budging."

Lara leaned in for the kill laying on the flattery thick as she negotiated, telling him the price she wanted. "You look like the boss man around here, so I'm sure you can make it happen."

"I'm afraid that amount per upgrade is not possible, ma," Ezekiel replied.

"Okay, what can you do for us, sir?" Lara said. "This plane is about to leave. I doubt there'll be many people buying last-minute business-class tickets. Wouldn't you rather have one thousand two hundred and fifty dollars instead of zero?"

Zuri rolled her eyes. This girl was not okay. But she loved that Lara was always a shameless negotiator. The girl was so secure in herself that she never cared who was watching, as long as she got what she wanted.

"Ma, I really want to help you out, but the amount won't be possible," Ezekiel said. "You know what I can do? Pay for three people, and I can upgrade two people for free."

"Really?" Zuri said in amazement. "Thank you, sir."

Lara smiled at her knowingly as she beckoned for the other girls to join them at the counter.

"What's going on?" Tami said as she rolled up with her suitcase.

"This fine gentleman has just agreed to upgrade us to business class," Lara informed the rest of the girls.

"Really? For free?" Tami squealed in excitement.

"Uhm, no, but for a small fee," Zuri replied.

"What's a small fee?" Ladun asked sceptically.

"About three hundred dollars per person," Lara answered as she did a quick mental calculation, confirming the amount on her Samsung phone.

"Ha! That's not in my budget," Ladun said, looking crestfallen.

"Don't worry, I *gatchu*," Zuri said. "The rest of you can settle me later. I'll pay with my card."

It's a good deal," Adesuwa said as she opened her wallet and handed Zuri her share. "Trust me, I've done this before at the airport, and it cost me over a grand. Lara, *abeg*, lend me the sugar in your mouth."

The group burst into laughter as they completed their check-in and headed towards immigration.

As they boarded the South African Airways flight and settled into the spacious business-class seats, Zuri could feel the girls' excitement. It had been such a long, trying year for all of them, but they had each made it through and most importantly, they had made it through together.

Zuri had decided to sit by herself, giving herself a little time to think on the six-hour flight. Lara was paired with Tami, and Adesuwa and Ladun sat next to each other. As she watched them chat away over complimentary champagne and nuts, she couldn't help but feel grateful that they had decided to come on this trip to Cape Town ten months ago.

Everybody's money had been tight for one reason or the other, but the idea to put down a deposit with Diamond and Pearls travels and contribute monthly to their travel *ajo* package had been stellar. It made the cost of the trip quite manageable. Instead of paying in one large chunk, they got the opportunity to save *small small*.

December was always a busy time in Cape Town because it was summer in South Africa. All the excellent hotels and villas were usually fully booked months before. However, the fact that they had booked in advance and Ladun was doing some work for the Sun International group of hotels had helped them get a reasonable rate.

It was nice to get out of Lagos for a few days and escape the December-in-Lagos madness which was always a good time with the non-stop, back-to-back Christmas parties, concerts and all sorts of events. It could be exhausting, even for a seasoned Lagosian. You needed stamina to survive the enjoyment, and it was nice to do something different for a change.

They were all taking time out to think, recalibrate, and plan for the new year ahead and she was excited to be spending quality time with her girls, but she missed Tsola. Zuri soon fell asleep on the flight.

****

Ladun

As the car approached the front entrance, Ladun couldn't help thinking how grand everything seemed.

"Good morning. Welcome to the Table Bay Hotel," The porter greeted as he pushed the trolley to the trunk of the car to get their bags. "Please go in. We'll bring your bag to the check-in desk."

The five women strolled through into the lobby of the hotel and were greeted with glasses of champagne.

"It's so beautiful," Zuri said. "It's giving me old world glamour but with a very modern vibe."

"I'm telling you," Lara agreed, with a squeal of delight. "I love it already!"

"I can't wait to get to our suite so I can put my feet up," Adesuwa said. "I'm exhausted, I forgot about the joys of the second trimester. At least I don't have morning sickness like when I was carrying SJ. I'm just constantly tired, and that flight kicked my ass."

"Aww, Ade!" Tami said as she rubbed Adesuwa's belly. "I still can't believe you are pregnant. I'm so excited for you."

"Thanks, my love," Adesuwa smiled. "I can't believe it either."

She had been sceptical about flying in her condition, but they had been planning this trip for so long, and she didn't want to miss the opportunity to bond with her girls. With everything that had been going on in her life lately, she needed the break.

"Don't worry, you all have about three hours to snooze before we go to Table Mountain," Ladun said. "Please, can I have everyone's passports? Let's check in."

"Good morning, madam," The lady at the check-in desk said, as she smiled at Ladun taking the passports from her.

"Good flight?" She asked as she searched the computer for their booking. "Yes, thank you," Ladun replied.

"Which one of you is Ladun Ashoni?" the lady asked.

"I am," Ladun responded. "Is everything okay?"

"Everything is perfect!" she smiled. "I just have a note here that says our guest relations manager would like to greet you personally when you arrive. One moment, please."

Ladun smiled as the lady picked up the phone to make her arrival known to the manager. She was already feeling the VIP treatment they were getting, and it was just day one.

"Hello, Mrs Ashoni," A voice said from behind her. "My name is Didier Bayeye. I am the acting general manager for Africa sales for Sun International."

"Oh, nice!" Ladun said as she shook his hand. "It's so nice to finally meet you in person, after speaking on the phone for so long. I actually wasn't expecting to see you. The lady said the guest relations manager wanted to greet us personally."

"Ah, yes!" Didier smiled. "I wasn't sure your flight would land before I had to go back to Johannesburg, so I had asked that the guest relations manager come to meet you when you arrived. But when I heard you were here, I decided to come myself."

"That is so nice of you," Ladun smiled. "These are my friends, Zuri, Lara, Tami and Adesuwa."

"Pleased to meet you, sir," Zuri said as the rest of the girls shook his hand. "Your hotel is beautiful."

"Thank you," Didier replied. "It's the best address in Cape Town. You'll enjoy the views of the V and A Waterfront as well as Table Mountain. The mall is also next to the hotel, so you can actually access it directly through those escalators on your right."

"Wonderful," Lara said as Ladun handed them their key cards.

"You'll also be happy to know that we have upgraded you from the junior suites to the executive suites," Didier informed the ladies. "The porter will bring your bags up to your room."

The girls barely contained their excitement.

"I wish you a wonderful stay," Didier said, "but unfortunately, I have to leave you now, as I have a flight to catch. Please enjoy our wonderful facilities."

"Thank you so much," Ladun said. "Have a safe flight, and I'll be in touch to give you details of the campaign we hope to plan for Sun International."

****

Tsola

Tsola looked at the time on his Rolex watch. It was two in the afternoon. He had hoped this meeting wouldn't take more than an hour so he could make it to the airport to catch a flight to Cape Town. He and Zuri had been working really hard to rebuild the trust in their relationship in the last few months. After coming so close to losing her, it was important to him that he made an effort to make sure they were whole.

He had back-to-back meetings, but he had planned to surprise Zuri in Cape Town and at least get to spend the day with her before he flew back to Lagos. They had been speaking every day since she left on holiday, but he had given her the impression that he was in Ghana, not Johannesburg. He couldn't wait to see the look on her face when he surprised her that evening. Lara and Tami had already given him the heads up that they were having dinner at Botanik social house that evening.

"We should go big or go home," Ebuka said. "The land we are looking at can certainly take it. I say we push for a thirty-thousand-person capacity instead of ten thousand. That way, we are prepared for growth, and it'll be set up in a way that we can partition it for smaller events. Tsola what do you think?"

"I agree!" Tsola said, trying his best to stay focused on the conversation. "The financing we've secured can support it. We should certainly be planning for long term growth."

They had decided to invest in an indoor entertainment arena similar to the O2 in London that could potentially be the largest on the continent. The plan was to become the destination for both pan-African music acts as well as international ones. It would have an exhibition centre, restaurants, bars, clubs. There was nothing like it in Nigeria at the moment, so they had come to South Africa to meet with technical partners in the hospitality industry to ensure that the project was world-class.

"We fly into Nigeria next month to survey the build site," Sven informed the group. "You Nigerians certainly are bold, but I like it. I think this is going to be a history-defining project."

"Good stuff, gentlemen!" Tsola said as he rose from his seat. "I have to leave you now to catch a flight. I'm sure you and Ebuka will be able to finalise the details. I'd love to see a work plan by close of business today."

"Cape Town?" Ebuka said with a knowing smile.

Tsola looked positively gleeful as he replied, "Yes, Ebuka. Cape Town!"

"Does she know you are coming?" Ebuka asked as they walked towards the entrance.

"Not a clue!" He answered, pushing through the door and out on to the street.

****

Lara

"It's magnificent!" Lara said as she moved across the room, gliding through the space that comprised of a dining table that sat twelve, an all-white living room with sliding doors that opened up to a pool and jacuzzi area that overlooked the ocean.

It was their fifth day in Cape Town. They had arrived at a beautiful villa to meet Tosin Durotoye, the founder of The Bloom Africa. It was a platform for ambitious African women to gather, speak and grow as it relates to their career, business, and self. Lara had met Tosin at an event and loved the work she was doing. They called her the dream executor.

Bloom Africa had planned a retreat for pan-African women in Cape Town. Women had flown in from all over Africa to create vision boards for the coming year, articulate and set their goals over champagne and good food. Lara had managed to convince Tosin to host a private two-hour session for her and the girls. This way they were on holiday, but they could also get something productive out of it.

"Hello, hello, hello!" Tosin said as she walked towards them carrying a tray with glasses of Bellini's. She was a beautiful, dark-skinned, slender, and tall woman. She was what you would describe as a Nubian beauty.

"How are you all doing?" She greeted in an American accent. Tosin was one of those Nigerian women who had spent most of her life in America getting an education and working before she moved back but could also break out the Yoruba at any given time. It was endearing.

"Thank you so much for having us," Zuri said. "This place is amazing!"

"It is, isn't it?" Tosin said with a smile. I've rented it for two days to accommodate the women who are flying in for the retreat, starting this evening. We have two to three hours to get some work done before I send you on your way."

"Fabulous!" Tami said. "I'm actually so excited about this. Can't wait to put my goals on paper for the coming year."
"Me too," Ladun chimed in.

"We have you set up at the breakfast table," Tosin said as she led them to a room that seemed to be all glass tables and windows, with the most amazing light coming in. "The chef is making us brunch, so I hope you are hungry. Please settle in, we'll start in ten minutes."

They settled into their seats as they waited for Tosin to come back into the room to facilitate the session. There were magazines stacked on the table, paper, pens, glue. Everything you could imagine would be present at a vision board party.

Lara smiled to herself. She had often disregarded the idea of visioning as one of those new-age, airy-fairy things that had little to do with success. However, one of her colleagues swore by it, and she had tried it a while ago and was surprised by how powerful just putting your goals down in writing and having a visual depiction of what you wanted for your life to be, to look at every single day could be.

"Ladies, we are going to start with something called the lemon squeeze," Tosin said as she sat at the head of the table. "It's an exercise where each person picks a woman in the circle and tells them what they think their strengths and weaknesses are."

They looked at each other in bemusement.

Tosin took in their wary expressions and expounded on the process. "It sounds a little scary, I know, but trust me when I say this is a handy tool in helping teams be more productive and profitable. I find it's also very effective in friendship circles, as well. I usually ask the women to write it down but this is a smaller group, and we are in a safe space, so I encourage you to just say it out loud. The idea is not to tear each other down or be destructive, it is designed to help us see ourselves through the lens of our friends or team members."

"I'll start." Lara volunteered, taking a deep breath. "Adesuwa, I love you, but for a long time, I resented the fact that you were weak in your marriage. It amazed me how you could be a killer in the boardroom, one of the sharpest lawyers in Nigeria and an amazing mother. You just seemed to be strong everywhere else, but when it came to Soji, you let that man walk all over you. You allowed him to mentally and financially abuse you over and over again. You cared more about appearances when it comes to marriage as opposed to actually being happy."

Adesuwa stared at her blankly.

The rest of the girls looked nervous.

Lara felt like she had hit a nerve, but she continued, "But I love and respect you because you are also the bravest person I know, and you've overcome obstacles that could break a lesser woman. The way you've handled the devastation of your marriage with grace, looked after SJ like nothing happened, and taken on this new pregnancy has been super inspiring to watch, and I just want to say that I love you and I'm rooting for you."

Tears began to roll down Adesuwa's cheeks as she reached out to squeeze Lara's hand. It was painful to hear, but she knew it came from a pure place. She was used to Lara's brazenness, and this had touched a raw nerve, which might have caused them to fight a year ago. Right now, all she felt was gratitude. She was grateful that she had friends that could be honest with her about her weaknesses but were also kind and were there for her no matter what.

"It's okay to cry," Tosin said softly. "I suspect there'll be a lot of tears here today. Let it out! Who wants to go next?"

"I'll go!" Ladun said, smiling as she took a deep breath. "Lara, it irks me that you never really talk about your issues, you internalise your problems, and sometimes it makes you lash out in other ways. You take on everyone else's problems, but you never really share the burden of yours, and while that can be very admirable, you must realise that we are your sisters. We love you, we can handle it. You must trust us."

The rest of the girls were nodding their heads in agreement as Lara rolled her eyes playfully.

"I love you because you are a warrior!" Ladun continued. "I've watched you take on job loss, financial woes, the death of your mum like a champion and frankly there's no one I'd rather have in my corner when I'm going into battle. I may not tell you enough, but it meant so much to me that you loaned me the money to invest in our property when I was too ashamed to ask. I'll never forget it."

Lara was silent for a few seconds then she smiled.

"Thank you, Ladun," she mouthed from across the table.

"I'll go next!" Zuri said. "Ladun, I hate that you don't trust how brilliant you are and that you are always second-guessing your abilities and trying to talk yourself out of opportunities. Our entire friendship you have most certainly been a baby girl, too fancy to work, too busy living a fabulous life to bother with purpose, and that was kind of fab, too. Now that you are a working girl, I hope that you'll have more confidence in your abilities."

She paused to consider her next words.

"I love you because even when life dealt you some mean cards and the Ashonis lost all their money, Bode's inheritance along with it, you took it like a champ and carved a new path for yourself. It's been such a blessing watching you bloom in your career and side hustle this past year. I'm so proud of you. We are all so proud of you."

Ladun smiled. "Thank you, Zuri. I love you too."

Tami volunteered next. "It's my turn. Zuri, you scare me because you are constantly living on the edge when it comes to your money and I say this from the sincerest place, being a spendaholic myself. It's sometimes difficult to watch you go back to the brink of broke when you've just gotten out. You need to watch it. I love you because anytime we each have a problem, you actively seek out solutions for us. I want to thank you for making my problems your problems, especially when it comes to my business. I can't remember a time when I've had a crisis that you haven't been by my side putting out fires. Recently, I'm especially thankful for your role in helping me scale and raise financing for my business by asking Tsola to help me out. Thank you, boo."

"For the record, you are a bigger shopaholic than me, *sha*," Zuri laughed as she reached over to give her a hug. "I love you."

"I guess I'll go next," Adesuwa volunteered. "Tami! You are the flightiest person I have ever met in my life! You've never really been able to commit to anything seriously for more than five minutes, and while that makes you such a fun person to be around because once you are bored of one thing you find another exciting thing to do, I always thought it wasn't a great attitude to have in business. I was always worried that you would have to marry a rich, generous man because I didn't trust that you could commit to working hard enough to support yourself financially. I love you because, in the last year, you've surprised all of us with your commitment to Irawo. Raising capital, restructuring your business, and building a fashion brand that I'm sure will be a global household name very soon. It's been inspiring to watch. I'm incredibly proud of you."

"I think I'm going to cry! I love you too, boo-boo." Tami blew kisses to Adesuwa.

"That was great!" Tosin said. "I love how open and honest you all were. There was a lot of talk about finances. I wish you were going to be here for the session we are having later on today with Samke Mhlongho, a South African wealth coach flying in from Johannesburg. You would have enjoyed her. Her energy is very Real-Housewives-of-Atlanta-meets-money. She's super smart and eccentric but makes personal finance so much fun."

Zuri looked intrigued, as did the other girls. "Sounds amazing. Send us her details maybe we can connect another time. After this, it is back to our regularly scheduled holiday."

The rest of the girls laughed.

"Will do," Tosin said. "Now let's start to have a conversation about our goals and the action steps we need to achieve them. Think about who you want to be in this world. How do you want to show up? How do you plan to manifest it? And what kind of legacy do you want to leave?"

****

Tsola

Tsola tried to contain his excitement to see Zuri. She and her friends were dining at Botanik, a Carribean cuisine restaurant tucked away on Queen Victoria Street in Cape Town. The turn-of-the-century exterior hid a lush botanical interior that instantly transported you to another world.

As he walked through the doors and scanned the room to see where the girls were seated, he was greeted by Mala Bryan, who he recognised as a model-turned-restaurateur and creator of the Malaville dolls. The restaurant had a relaxed vibe, everything about this spot was stylish, from the bespoke staff uniforms to the sophisticated crowd.

Mala pointed him in the direction of where the girls were seated a split second before he heard and recognised Zuri's laugh. She had her back to him, but he would recognise that laugh anywhere. He walked up to the table as he made eye contact with Tami, placing his forefinger on his lips as he snuck up to the group. As he reached their table, he put his hands over her eyes and didn't say a word.

"Oh my God!" Zuri laughed as she felt his hands trying to figure out who it was. She finally peeled his hands away turned and saw him standing behind her.
"Stop it!" She screamed as she got up to give him a hug.

"Babe! I thought you were in Ghana," she shrieked in delight.

"Nah! I had meetings in Johannesburg, and I wasn't sure I'd be able to make it to surprise you in Cape Town," Tsola said as he glanced at his watch. "In fact, I literally have thirty-six hours before I have to turn around again and head to the airport. Meetings in Lagos."

"I don't care, I'm just so happy you are here. Even if it's only for one hour," Zuri replied before Tsola grabbed her by the waist and kissed her on the lips.

"*I go love, oh!*" Lara smiled. "You two love birds need to get a room."

"We will!" Tsola winked as he sat down next to Zuri.

"You guys don't mind, right?" Zuri asked, smiling shyly. "That Tsola crashed?"

"Of course not!" Tami laughed. "How exactly do you think he found us? Telepathic powers? Madam, we knew he was coming,"

They chatted animatedly as they made room for Tsola, before settling into conversation. The topics ranged from Tsola's business meeting in Johannesburg, to where Tami had gotten with her investors, Zuri's triumph at work selling multiple units of the Yaba property, Lara's bonus, and all the joys that came with Adesuwa's pregnancy.

"Speaking of," Tsola said. "You'll never believe who just showed up at my office the other day,"

"Who?" Zuri asked. "One of your ex-girlfriends?" She joked as she ran her fingers through his beard.

"Not this time," Tsola teased. "Actually, it was Soji! I was stunned when my assistant said he was at the reception."

"What did he want?" Adesuwa and Lara asked in unison.

"Apparently, money!" Tsola said, shaking his head. "He said he had this oil and gas project he needed to raise capital for and was hoping I could assist, but to be honest, the transaction made no damn sense. Not that I would have worked with him anyway."

"It's always one shady deal or the other," Adesuwa said. "I got a phone call a few weeks ago from one of the guys he was doing his last transaction with threatening me because they were looking for Soji and he owed them money. I didn't even want to hear the details. I promptly told him never to call my number again because Soji and I were no longer married, so it was not my business."

"That guy is so shady," Tami said. "I'm just glad you are finally rid of him."
"It's only a matter of time before he ends up in a cell," Lara said. "And honestly, Adesuwa, if you had continued with that façade of a marriage I wouldn't have been surprised if you ended up in the cell right next to him because your finances were so entangled."

"Larraaaaa!" Zuri said. "This your mouth, *ehn*."

"I'm just saying," Lara laughed.

"She actually has a point," Adesuwa agreed. "That's something I will definitely not miss. The phone calls from people saying Soji owed them money or he had screwed them in a deal."

"You guys!" Tami said, sheepishly. "I didn't want to say anything before, but a little bird told me that Sonia's child isn't even his!"

"Stop it!" Zuri shrieked. "It serves him right, *sha*! I can't say I feel sorry for him. He's only getting what he deserves."

"That's his own personal problem," Adesuwa said, unbothered. "I wish him well. I'm just happy to have moved on from his shenanigans, and I'm looking forward to building an amazing life for my children and me."

"Cheers to that," Lara said, as they clinked their champagne glasses.

As the conversation moved on to other things, Zuri looked around the table, and a wave of gratitude washed over her. Her life was far from perfect, but she felt lucky to be surrounded by the people she loved, who loved her deeply. They had all been through significant ups and downs this year but in one way or the other, they had been there for each other, and that was a blessing in itself.

****
Zuri

Zuri blinked awake and took a few seconds to get familiar with her surroundings. Then she remembered that after dinner last night, Tsola had taken her back to his hotel room at The One and Only. She turned around to find that his side of the bed was empty. There was a note resting at the top of the pillow beside her that was marked Zuri. She smiled as she recognised Tsola's handwriting.

What is this man up to? Her face threatened to split from her ear-to-ear grin as she opened the piece of paper.

Meet me on the balcony, the note read.
Zuri flung the five-hundred-thread-count sheets away from her body and got out of bed with the abandoned enthusiasm of a six-year-old child on Christmas morning.

She grabbed a white robe and wore it as she made her way to the balcony. A table covered with at least five kinds of breakfast options was in the middle of the balcony, with two chairs, a fancy tablecloth, and a bucket with a bottle of champagne on the side and the most gorgeous view of Table Mountain. It was like something out of a movie. It was picture perfect.

"You like?" Tsola whispered in her ear as he wrapped his arms around her waist from behind.

"I love it!" She tilted her head up to kiss him. "I'm just wondering how you got this in here without waking me up."

"I told them to be very, very quiet," Tsola replied with a grin as he pulled out a chair and gestured for her to sit down.

As Zuri buttered her croissant and watched Tsola make them mimosas. She couldn't help thinking about how romantic this all was. This was the stuff her dreams were made of. She loved, and she was loved. She smiled to herself. "I could get used to this, you know?" She said, her mouth half full, her butter knife in one hand, waving her hand up and down as she pointed at the length of his frame to make her point. "You in your boxers half-naked, serving me," she laughed.

"You could?" He smiled, walking towards her with a champagne glass to feed her a sip of the mimosa. He put the glass down, then lowered himself to kiss her on the lips.

"I hope so," Tsola said.

Then he lowered himself even further, taking both her hands in his before he got on one knee.

Zuri's heart began to beat fast. A thousand thoughts crossed her mind at the same time. *Was he doing what she thought he was doing? Could this really be happening?*

"Tsola Preware, are you really proposing to me in your boxers?" Zuri laughed and cried at the same time. She had never been happier in her life, but she was a little nervous and couldn't resist ribbing him a little.
"Yes, I am, but shut up and listen," Tsola joked, smiling like a little boy that just won a prize.

"Zuri Guobadia," Tsola said. He paused, squeezing both her hands a little tighter and looking her straight in the eye. "You are the most amazing woman I have ever met. You are beautiful, brilliant, and so damn sexy. You are stubborn, strong-willed, funny, and you make me so much better. My life is so much better with you in it, and I can't imagine living the rest of this life without you. Will you do me the honour of being my wife?"

"Yes!" She squealed.

A Letter to the Smart Money Tribe

It has been such an incredible journey building the Smart Money brand. Creating these characters, their stories, the lessons and seeing it touch so many women across Africa in such profound ways has truly been humbling. I can never describe the feeling of being at a supermarket, the airport, or a country I have never previously been to, only for strangers to walk up to me and say, "Are you Smart Money Arese? I've read your book, and I love it!", "It changed my financial life!", "I bought land because of you!" and "I started a stock portfolio after I read the book."

It's been three years since I wrote the first book and this feeling doesn't get old. It is still overwhelming. I still can't believe that Arese, small Bini girl of yesterday could have such an impact across Africa.

This journey began for me when I was 27 years old. My marriage had fallen apart, I had a one-year-old child and I had to start again. In Lagos, that meant paying two years rent upfront, service charge and buying new furniture. I couldn't believe how expensive it all was. The expenses threatened to wipe out my entire savings, but I had to put on my big girl pants and deal. That was the first time I realised that I wasn't saving and investing enough, especially in comparison to the income I earned.

I started to ask who was creating financial content for women like me who worked in finance, oil and gas, fashion etc., but didn't have the excuse of being low-income earners to blame for being in a financially precarious position. These would be women who had decent-paying jobs but spent more on lifestyle expenses than they were saving and investing causing them to live from paycheque to paycheque with no assets to protect them in the future.

In Africa, even when we hear multiple stories of women who have gone through financial misfortune, sometimes because of divorce, death, or job loss, we subconsciously think that's something that happens to other people until it happens to us. I wanted to create financial content for African women that broke down the financial jargon and helped them understand how to earn, keep, and grow their money through relatable stories and practical lessons I have had to learn myself.

Smart Money began with an article on BellaNaija 'A Chanel Bag versus A Stock Portfolio'. I honestly wasn't sure anyone would care because at the time millennials were mostly concerned with entertainment content, but I was pleasantly surprised by the response, and I was even more surprised when a friend of mine suggested I write a book. You see, I was always an avid reader, but "author" was never on my list of goals. I won't lie; when I started, I was not sure I could finish because it was hard. Writing is a skill I have discovered I am good at but it is still an incredibly difficult process for me. I can honestly say, though, it is one of the most rewarding things I've been able to accomplish. The book tour was one of my most fulfilling experiences. I got to travel across Africa to countries like Tanzania, Kenya, Uganda, South Africa, and Mozambique, meeting women face to face and having heartfelt conversations about money.

However, I wanted to address a few things that came up during the last book tour. There are people who read the first book and did not feel represented. There will probably also be people who will read this book and not see themselves in the characters, and that's okay. As a writer, I've realised for me to write authentically I have to write from a perspective I understand. People have suggested that maybe I should have written about girls from a rural area who were poor, but I'll never be able to do justice to that story.

With the first book, I got lots of questions that said, "But I'm a low-income earner, the characters in your book earn a lot more than I do." My answer is this: the lessons apply whether you earn ten naira or whether you earn ten million because the way you spend ten naira is the way you will spend ten million and its more important to understand the lessons and know how to use the tools. Sometimes a character, a story, a passage is aspirational, it might not reflect your situation now, but there will be lessons to be learnt.

Listen! Life is hard, the economy is hard, making money is hard. Life has knocked me down at least twice in my life and put me in situations where I've made a lot of money and I've lost a lot of money. Aside from my reliance on God, two things have always been instrumental in helping me bounce back, and these are the main takeaways from reading this book.

First, your mind is your most powerful asset, if you harness it, it will be your most useful tool even in the worst of times. No matter how hard it gets, try to keep your head in the game and maintain a champion's mindset because once you give in to a negative mindset, you've already lost.

Secondly, build your tribe. Invest in your circle of friends because the sort of people and relationships you surround yourself with have an impact on your ability to make, keep, and grow money.

Wishing you and your money tribe lots love, joy and success.
Arese

Made in the USA
Monee, IL
08 September 2021